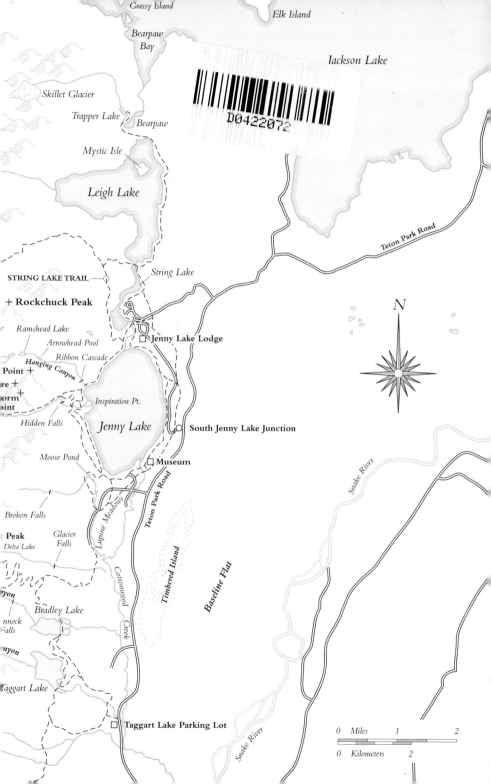

# TEEWINOT

ALSO BY JACK TURNER

*The Abstract Wild*

JACK TURNER

# TEEWINOT

*A Year in the Teton Range*

Thomas Dunne Books

ST. MARTIN'S PRESS ✖ NEW YORK

THOMAS DUNNE BOOKS.
An imprint of St. Martin's Press.

TEEWINOT. Copyright © 2000 by Jack Turner. All rights reserved.
Printed in the United States of America.
No part of this book may be used or reproduced in any manner
whatsoever without written permission except in the case of
brief quotations embodied in critical articles or reviews.
For information, address St. Martin's Press,
175 Fifth Avenue, New York, N.Y. 10010.

*Book design by Kate Nichols*
*Endpaper maps by Jeff Ward*
Photograph used on the title page and on chapter openers courtesy of
Picture Quest

www.stmartins.com

Library of Congress Cataloging-in-Publication Data

Turner, Jack.
Teewinot : a year in the Teton Range / Jack Turner.
p. cm.
Includes bibliographical references (p. ).
ISBN 0-312-25197-1
1. Natural history—Wyoming—Grand Teton National Park.
2. Mountaineering—Wyoming—Grand Teton National Park.
I. Title.
QH105.W8 T87 2000
508.787'55—dc21                                    00-024802

First Edition: June 2000
10   9   8   7   6   5   4   3   2   1

For

Glenn Exum

Harry Frishman

Gary Hemming

John Hudson

Alex Lowe

Max Lyon

Leigh Ortenburger

Bold men

who loved the mountains

# Contents

# Acknowledgments

I thank the following people for assistance in producing this book: Al Read, Rod Newcomb, Kim Schmitz, Tom Kimbrough, Mark Newcomb, Steve Koch, Dick Dorworth, Jim Kanzler, Susan Stone, Nelson Foster, Casey Walker, Renny Jackson, Linda Olsen, Rich Perch, Mark Magnuson, Jim Woodmency, Jeff Foott, Tom Mangelsen, and Weston Walker.

Hannah Hinchman encouraged me to use watercolors to illustrate my journals. The improvement was immediate, and I remain forever grateful.

Emily Stevens allowed me to live at her remote ranch on the Mexican border for several winters. I wrote most of the book in the old bunkhouse, aided by silence and solitude.

Renee Askins and Tom Rush provided me with a writing studio during a time of great need.

Susan Read read the final manuscript and saved me from numerous errors.

Mattie Sheafor, Chuck Schaap, Keith Briggs, Mike Keating,

and the staff of Teton Mountaineering provided many years of advice and assistance.

The Teton County Library, the Jackson Hole Historical Society, and the Grand Teton Natural History Association offered various forms of assistance and information.

Dan Burgette, my companion on many of the trips described in the book, deserves a special note of gratitude. I have pirated his ideas and drawn upon his vast knowledge of both the park and its natural history.

Three bows to Bob Dattila, Jim Harrison, and Bob Schuster. Without their affection and support, this book would not have been written.

# Introduction

When I was ten years old, I moved from Virginia to California. After boarding the Union Pacific Domeliner City of Los Angeles in Chicago, my mother purchased a deck of cards so I could play solitaire. The face of the cards featured the Union Pacific Railroad logo, the slogan "Be specific, say Union Pacific," and a photograph, rimmed in silver, of mountains and aspen trees. The caption read: "Jackson Lake and the Teton Range, Wyoming."

When we entered Wyoming, I took up residence in the dome car, waiting to see the Teton Range, but all I saw was a sea of sagebrush. As night approached, I grew disappointed, especially when it was announced we were crossing the Continental Divide, another sagebrush plain. Finally it was dark and I was alone in the dome car. My mother arrived to take me back to my seat, but I wouldn't go. She argued. I fussed. The conductor was summoned. He told me the Teton Range was hundreds of miles north of the railroad, so I would not be able to see it, even in daylight. Angry at Union Pacific for deceiving me with their playing cards, I clung petulantly to my seat, staring out the window into a vast and empty darkness. Eventually I fell asleep and the kindly conductor took me back to my berth. The next morning we crossed the Utah desert, and my intense desire to see the mountains faded with the novelty of red cliffs. But a trace remained in my memory, a prospect of great snowy mountains somewhere far to the north, in darkness. Before I reached California, I fell in love with Wyoming.

In the years that followed, I played with those cards until some were worn, others missing. Like most boys my age during the fifties, I was obsessed with cowboys, outlaws, and Indians. The Wild West still dominated weekly television shows and movies— *The Roy Rogers Show, The Cisco Kid, Zorro,* and, of course, *Shane,* the classic Western filmed in Jackson Hole. The myth of the Wild West was not yet buried under layers of irony, or declared finished, as Sam Peckinpah's *The Wild Bunch* would later declare it so. And if cowboys were the human incarnation of the Wild West, then mountains were its physical incarnation. I lived beside the ocean, I surfed, I worked on fishing boats, I was a lifeguard, but the mountains gripped my imagination in ways the sea could not, a collusion of memory and desire.

I read every book about mountains in our local library, some several times. I climbed mountains in Southern California—San Jacinto and San Gorgonio—but they only enhanced the stature of the Teton Range in my imagination. Compared with the Tetons, other mountains looked like they had been worn down. The Tetons became for me archetypal mountains—real mountains—and, of course, more than mountains.

When I was seventeen years old, I left California for college in Colorado. Then, in the spring of 1960, I dropped out of school and went to Wyoming with my friend Dennis Fisher to look for work. Fisher was a ranch kid and a ski racer from Steamboat

Springs, Colorado, who was destined, like me, to study philosophy. I was one ignorant surfer: Fisher had to explain to me why the barbed-wire fences didn't trap the pronghorn, deer, and elk. We found jobs in Pinedale, Wyoming, working for a geophysical exploration company.

At that time, Pinedale was a place where a young man felt odd wearing tennis shoes and only children wore shorts. We lived in a room at the Camp o' the Pines Motel with a kid from the mining town of Reliance, near Rock Springs. There was one double bed and a bathroom. Two of us slept in sleeping bags on the bed; the third slept on the floor. Each night we rotated positions. We ate breakfast and dinner at a local café and lunched on candy bars we carried in our pockets. Pay was a dollar and a quarter an hour, but we didn't care.

We worked on the plains south of Pinedale—between Farson and Big Piney. The land was that same sagebrush sea I had found so uninspiring from the dome car, a rolling plain with bare ridges, occasional furrowed cliffs, a few grasses, and miles and miles of sage. But by working on it instead of riding though it, I discovered other things as well: pronghorn, wild horses, many tiny flowers, the vast blue sky.

Mountain ranges surrounded us, though they were far away: the Wind River, the Gros Ventre, the Wyoming ranges. Sometimes in the heat they hung on the horizon like a mirage. Through the sagebrush plain flowed clear rivers filled with trout and white-fish. Cottonwoods and willows fringed the rivers; there were blue herons and beaver dams, monuments to the mountain men and the Oregon Trail.

I watched the thunderstorms coming for hours, trying to predict if they would hit me or pass benignly to the side. I never learned to predict them, and I still can't. I learned to fear lightning, to love emptiness and silence. I tried to guess where I would find wild horses but never succeeded—they were always a surprise. The coyotes and pronghorn were surprises too, as was the bull moose I watched one day, far from water, making his way, all too casually, it seemed to me, from one mountain range to another. I discovered that the wildness I liked was not to be found in cowboys or mountain scenery, but within larger forces, forces that were dynamic, random, nuanced, unknown, forces that gave daily life the risk and solemnity of myth.

For a while, Fisher and I drove a four-wheel-drive Dodge Power Wagon, looking for topographic survey markers. Then I worked with dynamite. But most of the time, I spent my days picking up seismic jugs and rolling up a quarter mile of wire onto a chest harness. When storms arrived, I put on the Levi's jacket I carried tied around my waist and hid behind sagebrush to cut the force of hailstones. I began to look forward to violent weather, and as I wandered under this great sky, a certain scale of being became requisite for my sense of well-being. The farther I could see, the happier I felt.

One week, on our day off, Fisher and I drove eighty miles northwest, crossing the Green River at Warren Bridge, then up over the Rim, down the Hoback River to the Snake River, and north along the Snake into Jackson Hole. I wanted to see the mountains on those playing cards. When we approached the town of Jackson from the south, on U.S. 89, there was a moment when the highest peaks of the Tetons were framed between two buttes. It was June, the buttes were vivid green, the sky the clearest blue, the Tetons gleaming under a mantle of fresh snow. I was not disappointed: They were more magnificent than that photograph of them.

During that road trip, we stopped at a turnout on the east side of Jenny Lake. On a bluff overlooking the lake was a pair of binoculars mounted on a pillar; for a nickel, you could view the mountains for five minutes. After scanning the mountains for a while, I pointed the glasses across the lake at the cliffs and forests where Cascade Canyon joins Jenny Lake. People in brightly colored clothing were climbing on the cliffs, and I spent several nickels watching them. Then we drove on. At the end of the lake we stopped at the Jenny Lake Ranger Station, where a ranger on duty told us we had been watching the Exum climbing schools. Minutes later, we crossed Cottonwood Creek to the Exum office and signed up for our first class.

The following weekend we were back. There were two guides for our beginning climbing class. One was only a few years older than I was; his name was Al Read. Of medium height, with a thick crop of hair and a pleasant though reticent manner, he had a compact toughness I would soon associate with climbers. The other guide was a middle-aged gentleman of the old school, elegant and handsome—Glenn Exum, the owner of the school and a local legend. Fisher and I were impressed.

After crossing Jenny Lake, the class walked up the trail toward Hidden Falls. Exum led, we students followed, and Al brought up the rear. I was directly behind Exum. He moved so slowly, and I was so eager, I wanted to pass. At the moment I was about to say, "Excuse me, sir, but . . ." Exum turned and smiled. "This is your first lesson of the day. It's called the guide's pace."

Forty years later, I walk the same path to the same rocks. Sometimes I feel a kid's eagerness boring into my back, goading me to move along. I step aside and ask if they would like to walk in front. Most decline, but occasionally one will walk right out in front of me. I still give the little talk about pace, but I always take their frustration as a good sign. I remember Glenn Exum, his smile, his gentle instruction. I don't recall anything else about my first day of climbing school.

The following weekend we were back to do intermediate

school. I remember only three things about intermediate school: The instructor was Bill Bird; the 120-foot over hanging rappel was the most terrifying thing I'd ever done; and at the end of the day, Bird climbed an impossible-looking rock face on the last few feet of the Tree Route with style and grace.

For the next two years I climbed continuously in Colorado. In the spring of 1962, I went to Yosemite to climb some of the harder routes in the country. It was the golden age of American climbing and I was fortunate to climb with some of the finest climbers of my generation. If there is still a considerable élan associated with the period, it is also true that the age gauged well its ranks. I learned that I was a climber of the second rank, good enough to climb with the great, but not their peer.

When I returned to the Tetons that summer, I continued to climb at a high standard, and I loved it. Nonetheless, my soul was divided. I also wanted to return to school, to study philosophy. Thus began a split that lasted much of my adult life—traversing back and forth between a life in the mountains and a life of the mind.

In 1968, Pete Sinclair left his position as Grand Teton National Park's chief climbing ranger to run a fledging guide service called Jackson Hole Mountain Guides. Peter Koedt and I were his first guides. I guided for JHMG for three years. I lived in a tent cabin at the foot of the Jackson Hole Ski Area, rode the tram up to the climbing schools, and guided throughout the range, often casually climbing routes that today I can no longer climb at all. We were freer spirits then. When another JHMG guide, Jim Greig, and I put in the Jackson Hole Mountain Guides high camp at the edge of Teepe Glacier on July 4, 1969, we shot fireworks all over the glacier.

Later I so immersed myself in teaching philosophy that when I returned to the Tetons, I did not climb. I had traversed too far. Eventually I realized I had to return to a previous path. In 1975, I went to the Himalayas and discovered, *felt,* the truth of the old

Vedic texts: "In a thousand ages of the gods I could not tell you of the glory of the Himalayas." I worked in the Himalayas for years, mostly in Pakistan and Nepal. This brought me back into contact with Al Read, who in the late seventies was the managing director of Mountain Travel, Nepal in the winter and the president of the Exum Guide Service during the summer. In 1978, he hired Kim Schmitz and me as junior guides. I have guided for Exum ever since, working and living in the Tetons until they became home.

When my mother died and I went east to settle her estate, I found among her possessions a pine chest filled with my childhood toys. At the bottom was a single playing card—the jack of spades. I turned it over, and there was the picture that had so informed my life. Now framed, it rests in my cabin beneath the peaks of a child's desire. Freud says we are never so happy as when we attain the dreams of our youth.

This is not a book about Wyoming. Most of Wyoming is steppe, not mountains. Furthermore, the Teton Range is part of a national park, a federal entity devoted to preservation but surrounded by people who despise the government, its powers and possessions, its obligations. If there are fewer freedoms in a national park, there is also something more: the privilege of wandering among wild animals and wild places—an adventure that pretty much disappears when you leave federal lands.

This book is not a climber's guide to the range. Everything a climber wants to know is covered in Leigh Ortenburger and Reynold Jackson's *A Climber's Guide to the Teton Range*, 3rd ed., a labor of love every climber in the Tetons should own.

It is not a book about all of Grand Teton National Park, because the mountains occupy only a third of the park. And I have little to say about Jackson Hole, part of the wealthiest county in the United States and representative only of itself. I offer no insights into polo horses, the worship of cows, dude ranches, Gothic log palaces, or that most quintessential of New West towns, Jackson.

Nor is the book restricted to the Teton Range. Some stories lead out to other ranges, for occasionally I must refer to events in China and the Himalayas to understand the fears and the camaraderie of life in my home mountains.

Most important, this book does not describe a single year in my life here. Instead, it portrays a representative year. It is more like a painting than a photograph—a temporal collage of events drawn from nearly forty years. My imagination has arranged them, not the race of time. Dropping the linear, I emphasize certain events and ignore others, selecting with the hope that, like the painter, I will capture something essential. In short, it is not a memoir, but a series of recollections. And much is missing, especially the vicissitudes of heart and society that bring joy and anguish to mountain guides as to anyone: lovers found and lost, marital relations, children, fame won, fame sacrificed to greater gods.

No, this book is about a mountain range, its austere temper, its seasons, its flora and fauna, a few of its climbs, its weather—the coming forth, here and now, of the freedom and the glory of the wild. It is also about a small group of climbers, nomads, who partially inhabit the Teton Range each summer, who know it as intimately as it will ever be known, and whose souls feed, sometimes voraciously, upon its many charms. I wish to praise the mountains and the climbers—for lightening my heart, for making rich my days.

*Old now, I feel it more than ever—so good*

*to be here in the mountains!*

*Die at the foot of the cliff and even your bones are clean.*

—ZEN MONK JAKUSHITSU GENKO

# TEEWINOT

# 1. Return

S now. Each year it seems winter will never end. Today is May 1, according to the Gregorian calendar, six weeks into spring, but snow lies two feet deep along the road where I am parked and it is snowing lightly, the wet flakes as big as dimes. A snow-filled clearing courses through the forest, all that is left of Cottonwood Creek this time of year. The trees beside the creek are naked—the aspen a study of silver, soft greens, and grays, the cottonwoods a dark charcoal where the trunks are wet. Pale gray alder branches are tinged with pink, and from those branches dangle small russet tassels. Willows add a smear of dull yellow beside the creek bed. To the west, lines of conifers stand cloaked in white at the base of the Teton Range; above them, miles of timbered ridges fade into clouds. East of the creek, tips of sagebrush dot a white plain beneath ghostly patches of forest, the dark green trees bleached by falling snow. Everything is subtle and austere—the lightly adorned landscape of a Wyoming winter.

I've been walking around for half an hour, waiting. A few minutes before eight o'clock a ranger arrives in a Ford Bronco and stops in front of the steel gate that has barred vehicles from the interior of Grand Teton National Park since November 1. He turns off the engine and sits, also waiting. I nod and he nods back, both of us content with silence. At exactly eight o'clock he unlocks the gate and swings it off the road. I drive across Cottonwood Creek and head north, toward the cabin I call home.

Snowplows have sliced walls on both side of the road. In front of me, cloud-capped ridges slope into the valley at the same angle—what geographers call the versant of a range. The ridges are stacked one behind another in many shades of gray—slate, graphite, pearl—until they merge with the snowy sky. Deprived of the sky and their summits, the mountains are magnified, mysterious. Static, Buck, Shadow, Nez Percé, Cloudveil Dome, the South, Middle, and Grand Tetons, Disappointment, Owen, Teewinot, St. John, Rockchuck, Moran, Rolling Thunder, Eagles Rest, Ranger—the heart of the range, rising south to north for eighteen miles. When I am away, I see them in my mind's eye like a sailor sees the reefs of his home waters.

After several miles, I turn off the highway and head toward the mountains. When I first turned this corner forty years ago, a marvelous log building stood on this corner with a grocery store and an old-fashioned soda fountain run by two old women, one of whom was named Kimball. The park bought them out the following year and razed the building, but the cabins they rented still stand, scattered along Cottonwood Creek.

I cross Cottonwood Creek again, now a trickle among quartzite cobbles. The bridge is old, wooden. Beyond it lies Lupine Meadows, just south of Jenny Lake. The meadows are roughly rectangular: a mile long, north to south, and half a mile wide. Their northern edge is a moraine, a mound of debris deposited by the glacier that gouged out Jenny Lake. To the east, they are defined by the course of Cottonwood Creek; to the west, they abut the lower slopes of Teewinot Mountain, a 12,325-foot peak that commands the meadows. A mile south of the bridge, the creek turns west and flows to the base of another moraine at the bottom of Glacier Gulch and Garnet Canyon; this dogleg in the creek marks the south edge of the meadow.

Old glaciers ground these meadows flat, leaving cobbles, gravel, and sand. More recently, a shallow layer of loess—a rich mixture of windblown silt—provides habitat for a hundred species of grasses and flowers. Lupine covers the meadow in late June, and when the last slants of light fall through the peaks, the meadow glows with lavender light against the dark conifers along the mountain's base. Thus its name. Now an undulating plain of snow covers everything. No tips of sagebrush break the surface. Siberian.

After the bridge, the road is dirt, and muddy from the melting snowbanks on either side. For the next couple hundred yards, it skirts scattered lodgepole pine along the meadow's edge. Bowl-shaped depressions in the snow surround the pines. Occasionally a tree has absorbed enough heat to melt a circle of bare ground around its trunk. At the edges of these circles, just beyond where the limbs cast shadows, are clumps of sagebrush buttercups, the first harbingers of spring.

On both sides of the creek are log cabins—the old Kimball cabins—that will soon house the Jenny Lake climbing rangers. Once the cabins were dark brown, but now the paint has blistered with age, exposing bare wood silvered by long winters. The roofs are metal, another dull brown. Some trees stand so close to the cabin walls, they bend outward around the eaves of the roof. One cabin—Mrs. Kimball's home—has a fireplace made of river stone, petrified tree trunks, and cobbles. A small Buddha and an incense holder sit in a niche between the rocks. During the summer, a handful of guides and rangers gather here each morning to meditate in front of this fireplace. Snow blown across the meadows is deeper here at the edge of the trees. It lies level with the windowsills, and the cabins seem to have settled like old folks into deep chairs.

Beyond the ranger cabins are eleven plywood shacks and a new log cabin belonging to the Exum Guide Service, a park concession and the oldest, most prestigious mountain guide service in the United States. Though the guide service is based in Wyoming, our guides work throughout the world: They guide Aconcagua, Denali, and several Himalayan peaks, including Mount Everest. One of our guides has summited Everest with clients six times.

This cluster of shacks is called Guides Hill, though it is not on a hill at all. I have guided for Exum for twenty-two years and lived in one of the shacks for eighteen summers. I built it myself, and even though I live here only four or five months each year, it is home.

The dirt road ends at a snowbank four feet high. I get out of my truck and look around with binoculars. Two mountain bluebirds dart about the meadow, little streaks of cerulean blue. They have probably been in the meadow since early April, feeding on midges and snow flies. Robins search for worms in the mud along the road. In a white landscape, these common thrushes are miraculous—the robin's golden breast, glamorous; the bluebird's cool blue, shocking.

Flocks of dark-eyed juncos, common sparrow-sized birds, peck nervously on the bare ground, muttering little *snit, snit, snit* sounds, then flee into the trees with a loud group flutter as I approach. Black-capped and mountain chickadees flit about the tops of lodgepole pine. A male red-shafted flicker drums his mating call on the top of a stovepipe—a sound that lifts you out of your chair if you happen to be inside. There are Brewer's blackbirds with their piercing yellow eyes, three killdeer, and two ruby-crowned kinglets fluttering from perch to perch so fast, I can't get a good view of them. No matter. Their song is loud, clear, and musical—for me, the sound of spring.

Uinta ground squirrels have tunneled up through the snow, leaving piles of dirt and a network of shallow trails leading to the new grasses along the plowed road. Their journey is perilous. A good part of the food chain is concentrated around the plowed road, and being there can be an advantage or a disadvantage, depending as much on fate as on one's status in the food chain. Detritus, grasses, and roots feed flies, worms, beetles, ants, aphids, mites, spiders, deer, and elk, which in turn feed birds and mice, shrews, voles, coyotes, hawks, owls, martens, weasels, badgers, cougars, and bears. Life in the meadows is a harmony based on feeding, a harmony of feaster and feast. The presence of one implies the presence of others: If the migratory passerines (perching birds) are here, it means goshawks are about, for like all predators, they move in strict counterpoint to their prey.

I walk a hundred yards over crusted snow to my cabin. I call this crusted snow "coyote snow," good snow for chasing critters, snow so hard that it will support a thousand-pound bull moose. The thermometer near the window reads 29 degrees. Rolling swells of snow stand two to three feet deep on open ground; the drifts in the trees along the creek are five feet deep. I've heard the snow level is 36 percent above normal for this time of year, and I believe it.

I shovel a bit off the front porch, unscrew a sheet of plywood from the front window, and take a deep breath of the cold, slightly metallic air before opening the door. Inside, the air is stale, fetid from dead things in the walls—and not in the walls. The head of a chipmunk lies perfectly preserved on the rug, its delicate cinnamon face and striped head quite at odds with the absence of a body. I take the head outside and place it on the woodpile for our resident pine marten, a member of the weasel family about the size of a house cat, though much more agile, clever, and bold. I light incense—for the cabin and for the chipmunk—open the window, turn on the fan, put water on to boil. The Ashley woodstove is filled with twisted paper and split lodgepole pine. I squirt charcoal lighter on it and toss in a match from a wooden box on top of the stove. It roars. Not quite what the *Boy Scout Manual* suggests, but it works well at forty below and becomes a habit after a while. While the water heats, I shovel the rest of the snow off the porch and dig a chair out of the drift on the east side of the cabin. Then I sit on my porch and drink tea and celebrate a new year.

This *is* the beginning of the new year, regardless of what the rest of the world thinks. All ways of marking time are arbitrary. January 1 is simply the time Roman consuls entered office, and despite my best efforts, I can find no reason why I should emulate Romans. In contrast, the annual cycles of flowering, melting, and migrating are not at all arbitrary, and their repetition furnishes a precision well suited for people living in the natural world, a repetition that is both reassuring and comforting—reassuring in that the cycles are still there, comforting in that we are, too. Why not begin the year with sagebrush buttercups, the arrival of kinglets, coyote snow—cycles the old naturalists refer to as phenology? If one's life is tied to the manifest hand of nature, rather than to the hands of markets and clocks, there isn't much choice, for like the kinglet, our presence here, our business—climbing mountains—is indexed to natural cycles.

After tea, I fetch a mountaineering sled out of the loft. For two hours I haul boxes from my truck to the cabin, boxes of books, climbing gear, a computer, paints, more boxes of books. By mid-morning the crust has softened as the temperature climbs into the high thirties and the sun breaks through the clouds. Even on a cold night, there is only time for the top five or six inches to freeze.

The snow below remains wet and mushy, old winter snow with big crystals and a structure as hollow as a honeycomb. The state between spring snow, or "corn snow," as the skiers call it, and summer snow—firn—has no name, but cycles of melting and freezing cause the large granules and air pockets. I call it "junk snow."

When post-holing up to my crotch in this junk drives me nuts, I retreat to the cabin. It is warm but not cozy. A cabin requires time to become cozy after being frozen for months, just as a body takes time to become comfortable after being chilled. The wood must reabsorb heat; the stale air reabsorb the smells of food, incense, and sweat; the space reabsorb a human presence. This takes several days at least. I cook and unpack and shove books back into their summer slots, filled with a happiness known only when I am here. Wherever else I live, I feel like an alien, an exile.

The cabin is a two-by-four frame sided with plywood and painted the usual Park Service brown. It is twelve feet wide and twenty feet long, slightly smaller than Henry Beston's "outermost" house on Cape Cod—sixteen by twenty feet; slightly larger than Henry Thoreau's cabin at Walden—ten by fifteen feet; and more than twice as large as the traditional Asian hermit's hut—ten by ten feet. All my heroes lived in small dwellings.

The cabin is insulated with fiberglass; the interior walls are Sheetrock, most of it unpainted. There is a countertop with a three-burner propane stove and above it three shelves for food and supplies. An old door serves as a desk, a built-in platform supports a mattress. There is a small closet, two floor-to-ceiling bookcases four feet wide, and a waist-high table with shelves underneath. The Ashley stove is on the south wall, next to the door. Two small lofts at each end of the roof provide storage. There are four windows, two next to the bed, a double window over the desk, and one up front near the stove. One window above the bed faces dense conifers; the other offers views of the mountains: Teewinot, Symmetry Spire, St. John, and Moran. At present there is nothing outside the double window but a dark wall of snow.

Next to the bed hangs a watercolor of the Ohio River by my mother; a water lily on a black ground, in pastel, by my father; and a charcoal study of a juniper by Russell Chatham. The other pictures are prints, mostly pages of old calendars: a sketch of Lower Yellowstone Falls by Thomas Moran; a fly fisherman resting on a log beneath a waterfall by Winslow Homer; two Karl Bodmer portraits of the Sioux; one of Cézanne's studies of Mont Sainte-Victoire; a Wolf Kahn landscape.

The porch is small, eight by twelve feet. It faces south toward the round, barren summit of Sleeping Indian, a peak in the Gros Ventre Range east of Jackson Hole that is named more formally on the maps as Sheep Mountain. Outside is a picnic table rescued from a Park Service dump, several chairs, and a hammock. Otherwise, the cabin is rather plain. The Park Service frowns, correctly, on domestic flowers (alien species), gardens (more alien species), and bird feeders (unnatural), especially hummingbird feeders. The sugary liquid attracts bears, and a bear who has feasted on sugary liquid is a dead bear, for it will visit human habitations again and again until it is shot—even in a national park.

We have lived at this Guides Hill in Lupine Meadows since 1981. Before that, Guides Hill was on the moraine at the south end of Jenny Lake, about half a mile upstream. In November of 1974 heavy rains loosened the meager soil covering the glacial till; then strong west winds tore over the mountains and slammed down, flattening the mature trees. Such windstorms are not common, but occasionally they do visit. In 1987 a similar windstorm flattened fifteen thousand acres of trees in the Mink Creek drainage of Teton Wilderness twenty-four miles northwest of here.

With the trees gone, the old Guides Hill was exposed to public view from the Jenny Lake parking lot, so the park moved us to our present location. We built the new Guides Hill in another area of blow-down trees, working for a week with chain saws to clear the debris. Now grown trees separate the cabins. The pine next to the porch was a foot high then; now it rises eighteen feet.

In the evening, after the sun has dropped behind Teewinot, I eat clam chowder on the porch in falling snow. A great gray owl hoots from the cottonwoods along the creek—another welcoming sound. Great grays, fairly rare in the Tetons, sport absurd faces, with two sets of concentric circles around enormous yellow eyes, and a booming voice out of all proportion to their tiny skeleton. I search the trees along the creek with my binoculars, but cannot find it. I leave it to its hunt, probably for mice and voles.

For the next two weeks, I will have the cabins and the meadows more or less to myself. A few skiers will come skating through in the morning when the snow is crusted, but the trails into the mountains are still closed, the snow in the mountains is too weak for climbing, and the weather is nasty. If you want solitude, few places are better than Lupine Meadows in early May.

The solitude is brief, however. Soon it will vanish like the snow. Starting in mid-May, guides and rangers move into the cabins and visitors begin to arrive. Over 4 million people visit the park each year, the majority of them during summer. But for now, the mountains are empty. I sit on the porch and watch the snow fall among the trees. Time passes slowly. Snow falls slowly. The evening is filled with the silence peculiar to snowy evenings. Like many children in the forties, I had a small globe with a snowman in it. When I shook it, snowflakes slowly drifted down around the snowman. Its magic was the same as this evening's magic: so much motion, so little sound.

# 2. The Teton Range

I awake to Teewinot, a great triangle of snow that fills the western sky. The base of the mountain lies west across Lupine Meadows amid a jumble of old avalanche debris and alluvial fans stretching nearly two and half miles north to south. Devoid of foothills or terraces, this side of the mountain, the east face, rises for more than a mile in a single sweep. The first three thousand feet consist of broken forests, cliffs, and open meadows divided by two huge gullies; the final two-thousand-foot pyramid is a labyrinth of snowfields, ice, and rock walls now covered with a layer of brilliant new snow from the recent storm. The snowfields are pink in the early-morning light, the twin summits a pale gold. To live in Lupine Meadows is to live with Teewinot and its many moods. This morning it stands aloof, regal in its white mantle, our own guardian spirit.

*Teewinot* is a Shoshone word meaning "many pinnacles" and was probably their name for the whole range. Indian names are rare in the park. In addition to Teewinot, I know of only two:

Shoshoko Falls and Taminah Lake. French names are common—
Gros Ventre, Nez Percé, Tetons—because so many French trap-
pers roamed this country. The names of explorers, mappers,
geologists, climbers, and early settlers constitute an unfortunately
large category: Bannon, Bradley, Colter, Doane, Jackson, Jenny,
Leigh, Moran, Owen, Phelps, Raynolds, Spalding, Webb, Woodr-
ing—the list is long. Some are deceiving. Buck Mountain has nothing to do with deer; it is named for George A. Buck, a member of
a mapping expedition in 1898. Berry Creek has nothing to do with
the berries that are so abundant there; it is named for A. J. Berry,
an early homesteader. Teepe Pillar has nothing to do with Indian
dwellings; it is named for Theodore Teepe, a climber who fell to
his death in 1925.

Naming suggests ownership, and early visitors were obsessed
with demonstrating ownership. When President Chester Arthur
visited the region in 1883, every camp along his route was named
for forgettable public figures—for example, Camp Isham, named
for the Hon. Edward S. Isham, and Camp Hampton, named for
Senator Wade Hampton. Again the list is long, and it includes, of
course, Camp Arthur. But then, naming is the privilege of con-
querors, and I doubt many American Indians sat on the United
States Board of Geographic Names.

What a pity Thoreau didn't visit the range. What a feast we
would have if, in addition to *The Maine Woods*, we had his *The
Teton Range*. To consider the wonderful Indian appellations in the
appendix to *The Maine Woods*—Chesuncook, Mettawamkeag, All-
gash, and Umbazookscus—is to realize our poverty. If we had had
a compiler of Indian life in the Tetons, we would, to my mind,
have a richer heritage, one suggesting how earlier visitors related
to plants and animals and place. I would like to know, for example,
the "Ridge-where-the-huckleberries-are thickest."

From my bed I can see only Teewinot's summit pyramid.

When I built my cabin, I placed a window next to the bed, high enough so that when I lie down I see only the mountain and a lone lodgepole pine—its scraggly branches and barren crown. Birds often sit on these branches and the movement of its few needles tells me about the wind. I keep the binoculars on the windowsill to watch the birds and to study the mountain. This morning there are no birds and the wind is still.

The temperature in the cabin is 18 degrees. I get out of my sleeping bag and make an offering to the fire gods, put the water on the stove, and then get back under my sleeping bag. Since I can no longer sleep under sheets and blankets, a single sheet covers the mattress. As the Ashley roars, I study the mountain with the binoculars.

The spring storm has plastered the mountains with snow. The mile-high mass of faces, ridges, ledges, forests, and meadows is completely covered, as though sprayed with coats of white paint: a bone-white mountain against a cobalt blue. The geometry is elegant, simple, barely lit by the rising sun. I drink coffee and watch robins perched on the lodgepole snag.

When the sun reaches the cabin, I walk out into one of those brilliant days that define the American West. Not a cloud, air you want to gulp, a sense of unlimited space, of freedom to wander, and everywhere the light of diamonds. The snow glitters with a million scintillations; the bare trees that yesterday looked so dark and menacing are now a friendly gray, the conifers a mellow green. The air is filled with the sound of robins and kinglets. Teewinot soars above it all, so high you must crane your neck to see its summit.

The Teton Range rises sheer from the valley, precipitous and bold. It is sometimes said to be fifty-five miles long—roughly from Teton Pass, west of the town of Wilson, to the Grassy Lake Road just south of Yellowstone National Park; or, more technically, forty miles long—the length of the fault that created the range. But the major peaks occupy a considerably smaller area. Since timberline averages from 10,000 to 10,500 feet, and in a few locations goes even higher, only peaks above 11,000 feet high are, well, *real* mountains. These high mountains stretch for only twenty miles—from Prospectors Mountain (11,241) in the south to Ranger Peak (11,355) in the north. Farther south, the peaks are lower and composed mostly of sedimentary rock; father north, more sedimentary peaks diminish in altitude until they finally disappear under the lava flows of the Yellowstone plateau.

Although the area is small, it is complex: a maze of peaks, serried ridges, spires, pinnacles, crags, glaciers, snowfields, ice gullies, and steep canyons. It is also quite narrow. From Lupine Meadows west to country of the same elevation is about ten miles. Numerous canyons bisect the range, bypassing the high peaks and cutting into sedimentary strata several miles west.

There are advantages to this small size: It is accessible and offers the possibility of intimacy. The summit of the Grand Teton is only three miles from the main park road and all the major peaks have been climbed in a day from the valley. Indeed, the Grand was run— from the valley floor to the summit and back to the valley—in three hours, six minutes, and twenty-five seconds by Boyce Thatcher in 1983. His record still stands. One of our guides, Alex Lowe, climbing solo, traversed the dominant circle of peaks— Teewinot, Mount Owen, the Grand, Middle, and South Tetons, Cloudveil Dome, Nez Percé—in eight hours and forty minutes. Nonetheless, few have climbed all the peaks, traversed the canyons, and visited the lakes. Fewer still have traveled the range in all seasons. For some of us, such intimacy stands as one of life's worthy goals.

Four forces created the Tetons: faulting, earthquakes, glaciation, and erosion. The geology is fiendishly complicated and a number of bright people have devoted their careers to understanding it. A geological map of the Tetons, an object of considerable beauty, was not published until 1992. On it, 120 colored and coded map units represent different kinds of formations ranging in age from 8,800 years old to 3.5 billion years old—give or take a few hundred million years, depending on your expert.

For reasons only recently understood, reasons inferred from the volcanic and tectonic histories of the region, the earth's crust fractured along a line running from north to south about 9 million years ago. Technically, this fracture is known as a block fault. The fault line runs forty miles along the eastern side of the range. Just west of the cabins, it runs along the base of Teewinot and the western edge of Jenny Lake.

The two halves of the fault split. The eastern block tilted downward to the west, becoming Jackson Hole. The western block also tilted down to the west, and its eastern edge rose—like the bow of a sinking ship. This rising bow became the Tetons; the western end of the western block—its stern, as it were—remained buried in sedimentary strata. The vertical displacement between the tops of the peaks and the base of the eastern fault is nearly six miles. Both blocks are still moving. The Tetons grow about an inch in a hundred years, while the eastern block sinks four inches over the same period. Jackson Hole is relatively flat because the maw where the eastern block once abutted the western block is filled with thousands of feet of sediment and rubble topped by glacial cobbles.

The forces creating the fault were seismic, and our cabins stand merely half a mile from one of the more active points in the fault. We could have, at any time, a 7.5-magnitude earthquake, with surface slippage up to twenty feet. Earthquakes occur constantly along this fault—the seismograph at the park headquarters registers small quakes every day—and ten years ago, the Jackson Lake Dam was rebuilt to withstand a 7.5-magnitude earthquake. Like many people, we are waiting for the big one.

Ice created much of the landscape here, glacier ice, ice with no connection between its air pockets, ice that technically is mineralized water. And like everything else in Lupine Meadows, the glaciers return and their cycle is somewhat predictable. Over the past million years, glaciers covered Jackson Hole approximately every 100,000 years, just as they covered much of Europe and North America. Each scoured the land, erasing most of the evidence of its predecessors. But the last two periods of glaciation have been studied carefully, and we now understand the major events that carved the Teton landscape.

The Bull Lake glaciation began 140,000 years ago and lasted for 10,000 years. Gathering ice from the Yellowstone plateau and the vast mountain uplands east of the valley—the Absaroka and the Gros Ventre—a glacier 3,000 feet thick plowed down Jackson Hole, covering all the buttes in the valley and burying the land where the town of Jackson now stands under 1,200 feet of ice.

The Pinedale glaciation, starting 80,000 thousand years ago and lasting 70,000 years, did not move as far south—it ended about fourteen miles north of town—but created many of the terraces and moraines that are prominent features of the present landscape. At the height of this glacial period, an ice cap extended 120 miles from the Snake River Overlook in Grand Teton National Park north to Chico Hot Springs, twenty miles north of the northern border of Yellowstone National Park. This ice cap covered the highest mountains in Yellowstone but did not reach the continental ice fields still farther north.

Sometimes the glaciers flowing out of the Teton Range joined these huge glacial systems, sometimes not. However, these mountain glaciers did not greatly influence the structure of the valley, for the simple reason that they were too small. The size of a glacier is a function of the area that can collect snow to make the glacier. Again, the Tetons are a small mountain range. Surprisingly, the present glaciers in the range are not remnants of the Bull Lake or Pinedale glaciations; they are only 4,500 years old. But they helped carve the steep mountain faces, canyons, and piedmont lakes along the base of the range, thus providing the grandeur and beauty we associate with the peaks.

Unfortunately, glaciers in the park are shrinking. The Teton Glacier, on the north side of the Grand Teton, has shrunk significantly since 1929. Indeed, mid-latitude glaciers are shrinking everywhere from global warming. The largest glacier on Mount Kenya, in Africa, lost 92 percent of its mass over the last century. Half of the glacier mass is gone from the 1,500-mile Tian Shan Range along the borders of China, Russia, and Mongolia. In fifty to seventy years, Montana's Glacier National Park will have no glaciers.

In our minds, or from a distance, a glacier is a lovely thing, but up close it is rather ugly. Glacial ice, often black, is filled with shattered rock ranging in size from sand to house-sized boulders. The surface of a glacier is often a sea of this rubble. Between the piles of rubble, melting surface water cuts moulins and the pressures of gravity split the ice into cavities called crevasses. Occasionally, shafts lead down to dark silted rivers flowing in the glacier through "caverns measureless to man"—I cannot look at them without thinking of Coleridge.

Indeed, most glaciers are skidding on a thin sheet of water. Rubble is sliding down the moulins, the front of the glacier is calving chunks of ice into the rivers, and the whole glacier's grinding up the landscape like a million-ton piece of sandpaper 3,000 feet thick. The result is a mess, and deglaciation—a melting glacier—is even messier, a barren landscape of rubble, spotted with small lakes, piles of mud, silt, and sand, and braided rivers.

Vegetation returned slowly to Jackson Hole after the last deglaciation—first sagebrush and grasses, then juniper in the drier ground and willow and birch along the rivers. Then came the Engelmann spruce, the pines and firs. The mammals returned, too. Because of the successive periods of glaciation, the paleontological record inside the park is scant, but evidence from the surrounding country, and from archaeological sites, suggest there were not only the elk, bison, deer, mountain sheep, pronghorn, coyote, and black bear that we still see today but also lions, cheetahs, musk oxen, mammoths, ground sloths, horses, dire wolves, and camels—including one with the charming name of Yesterday's camel.

There were no moose or grizzly bears. Like the first humans in the Americas, the grizzly and the moose crossed Beringia, the now-sunken landmass that once connected Asia and Alaska. Some say the grizzly followed the humans, but more likely the humans followed the bear. The grizzly was wiser, tougher, a better hunter; no doubt it followed its nose to a new land that teemed with millions of large mammals and lacked its only natural enemy—*Homo sapiens.*

Those intimate with the range often notice several anomalies resulting from faulting and glaciation. First, because of the block fault, there are no foothills, a feature that makes the range seem especially precipitous. It is the steepest range in the Rockies and the impression of steepness is heightened because the valley— Jackson Hole, the sunken eastern half of the fault—slopes down *into* the mountains.

Second, although the Tetons are the youngest range in the

Rockies, they contain some of the oldest rock on the surface of the earth. Those who love the Grand Canyon often make much of the age of the rocks at the bottom, Precambrian schist and gneisses from 500 million to a billion years old. However, rock in the Tetons is much older—at least 3.5 billion years old. Most of it is hard, dense, solid, eroded into lovely handholds, and virtually impervious to water. As the climbers say, nice gneiss.

Third, the structure of the watershed is peculiar. Since the range is asymmetrical—the steep eastern prow, the gradual western stern—streams and glaciers on the east eroded rock more rapidly, thereby extending their valleys westward through the range. Today the watershed is well west of the highest peaks—two and a half miles west of the Grand Teton, five miles west of Mount Moran. Thus the skyline you see from the valley is not the watershed.

More oddities follow from this peculiarity. For instance, all the water draining off the Grand Teton eventually drains into Cottonwood Creek. Indeed, most of the water from the heart of the range—from the north face of Buck Mountain and Static Peak to the south face of Mount Moran eleven miles north—flows into Cottonwood Creek, a creek so shallow you can walk across it in the spring or fall wearing a pair of irrigation boots. Glaciers, each like a fist, punched natural reservoirs—Leigh, String, Jenny, Bradley, and Taggart lakes—along the way that slow and store water, but still, Cottonwood Creek is a *creek*.

Since Cottonwood Creek runs north to south next to the base of the range, none of the large canyons empty directly into the Snake River. Early travelers marveled at this anomaly. Owen Wister's party was hungry and thirsty as they approached the Tetons from the northwest on August 13, 1888. He described in his diary a jesting argument over why they couldn't find water. "But where, I thought, in creation is a big mountain range twenty miles long and 13,000 feet high with snow in giant patches and green valleys and no water at all at the bottom?" Just then, when the situation was "strained," they struck a stream. Soon Wister killed an elk. Two days later, they caught two hundred trout, probably in Cottonwood Creek.

But these facts about the range and Cottonwood Creek—I think of it as my creek—interesting, even amusing, as they are, do not account for why we love the place. Like a sense of place, love is a function of time, and time is but of sequence of nows.

I wander across the snow to my creek. The main channel runs a hundred yards to the east of the cabin, but when the water comes up during spring runoff, it fills a slough only fifty feet away. In summer it vies with Teewinot for my attention, perhaps even devotion, for the channels and the islands between them attract many birds and game. Now, with junk snow preventing me from moving around most of the day, the creek is the main place to watch birds. I have a place next to the slough where I meditate almost every day. There is a bird's nest a foot from my head. Sometimes the birds land on me.

I brush the freshly fallen pine needles off the cushion and sit down. After a while, a pair of mallards float slowly by, feeding. A pair of Canada geese rise with their hysterical honking. For fifteen minutes I watch a great blue heron fishing in the shallows, his neck coiled like a viper. The heron sees me but pays no attention. Suddenly, nonchalantly, he floats out of the water like a balloon released from a child's hand and glides silently down the creek.

Soon the snow will melt and I too will travel the creek.

# 3. The Vicissitudes of Spring

T he weather continues fair. Nights in the teens and daytime temperatures in the forties bring corn snow to the high country and diminish the frequency of avalanches, at least until midday. This is the best time of the year for traversing the range on skis or skiing extreme routes on the peaks.

One morning I notice a battered red Toyota truck in our parking lot and a single set of ski tracks heading off toward Teewinot. The truck belongs to Mark Newcomb, one of our young guides and among the finest extreme skiers in the country. Extreme skiing is not what you do at ski areas; it involves skiing down what are usually climbing routes on big mountains. The definition of extreme skiing is simple and concise: If you fall, you die.

Exum guides have a history, indeed a tradition, of first descents of extreme routes on the Grand Teton and throughout the range. Bill Briggs first skied the Grand Teton on June 16, 1971. In 1982, Rick Wyatt skied it with three-pin, touring bindings. Stephen

Koch snowboarded the Grand in 1989—when he was nineteen years old. Since 1990 a small group of skiers have been working on other descents at the cutting edge of extreme skiing and snowboarding. Now Exum offers ski and snowboard mountaineering camps. No doubt skiing descents of the peaks will one day become as common as climbing ascents.

In some ways, this is unfortunate. Winter in the mountains was once a time of solitude; now ski tracks are everywhere and some animal populations—particularly mountain sheep—are feeling the pressure. Deprived of their wintering grounds in the valley by real estate development, mountain sheep in the Tetons survive winter in the mountains by occupying windswept ridges and eating alpine tundra plants—when they can find them. The presence of skiers forces them to move, expending valuable calories when they can't afford to. Since there are fewer and fewer sheep and more and more skiers, the problem isn't going to go away. Fortunately, there are no sheep on Teewinot.

Since I imagine Mark will ski the east face of Teewinot, I get my binoculars, put on a parka, and sit in a chair on my porch to watch the fun. There is cloud cover, but it is high—a mackerel sky. I cannot see him with the naked eye, even though he is a dot of red against the snow. With the glasses, I find his tracks just above the Apex, the triangular crown of conifers that divide the two big avalanche gullies coming off the face. Then I spot him higher still, kicking steps in the steep snow, ski poles in each hand, his skis strapped to the sides of his pack. He advances with metronomic regularity; his tracks look like the tracks of a machine. When he reaches the col near the serrated summit, he does calisthenics. Watching him, I am amused because he thinks he is alone. Then he puts on his skis and stretches his arms a few more times. He's set. I'm set, too. I've never seen anyone ski the east face, and I'm delighted to watch him do it. Then, suddenly, Mark drops off the other side of the mountain into a snow gully.

Later, he told me he had already skied the east face. The cloud cover kept the temperatures down and the north side of the mountain offered perfect snow conditions. Mark had seen the snow gully many times from the climbs we guide in Cascade Canyon, but he had not studied the route in detail and he did not climb Teewinot with the intention of skiing it. It was unknown. This couloir averages 50 degrees for several thousand feet. Worse (from my point of view), he was on telemark skis. Nonetheless, he let go and went for it. Near the top he had to sideslip around a boulder stuck in a crack; lower down, he had to take off his skis and down-climb a thirty-foot rock slab in his ski boots. But he made it: the first descent of Teewinot's Northwest Couloir, a route so difficult no one has skied it again.

Few people have skied 50-degree snow. Mark has skied even steeper routes, most famously two couloirs on the north face of Buck Mountain, both of which have sections of 60-degree snow. As a rule, 60 degrees means you can touch the snow slope with your elbow when you are standing straight up. At 65 degrees, your hips get in the way when you edge your skis into the slope. At present, this is the limit for extreme skiing. As for the limit for routes, the descent made by Mark Newcomb and Hans Johnstone of the Hossack-MacGowan on the Grand Teton, a 2,500-foot rocky, icy couloir that averages 52 degrees, takes the prize. I don't like climbing *up* 52-degree snow.

Many of the guides are as comfortable skiing the mountains during the winter as they are climbing during the summer. Mark's father, Rod Newcomb, one of the owners of the Erum Guide Service and president of the American Avalanche Institute, is also in the mountains on one of his favorite trips. He leaves at midnight, alone, traveling with skis equipped with climbing skins, and climbs eight miles and five thousand feet to the saddle between the Middle and South Tetons. He arrives at eight o'clock, just in time for breakfast and, not accidentally, the best time of day for skiing corn snow. Then he makes one long run back to his truck. Few sixty-five-year-olds enjoy such freedom of the hills.

We also have our crashes. One afternoon as I was walking near Jenny Lake, I saw Ken Johnson's Long Ranger helicopter flying up the valley next to the mountains. It turned into Cascade Canyon and disappeared toward Mount Owen. He was looking for another young Exum guide, Stephen Koch.

Koch's passion is extreme snowboarding. In the ten years since he first snowboarded the Grand Teton, he's descended what were once considered significant climbing routes in the Tetons: the Skillet Glacier on Mount Moran, the twin couloirs on the north face of Buck Mountain, and, with Mark, the first descent of the Black Ice Couloir between the Enclosure and the Grand Teton. When I first climbed the Black Ice Couloir in the sixties, it was considered the definitive ice climb in North America. And this is just in the Tetons: Stephen has also snowboarded the highest peaks on five continents: Denali (Mount McKinley), 20,320 feet, in Alaska; Aconcagua, 22,834 feet, in Argentina; El'brus, 18,481 feet, in Russia; and Mount Vinson, 16,864 feet, in Antarctica.

Now Stephen had crashed in an exemplary accident: an accident where you are on the edge, an objective hazard (not a mistake, or at least not your own mistake) clobbers you, and you are tough enough to survive the consequences.

Climbing alone to make the first snowboard descent of the northeast snowfields of Mount Owen, Steve was hit by an avalanche at 11,000 feet and was swept 2,000 feet down the mountain. He sailed over bumps, jumps, and cliffs, rolling like a rag doll, fighting to stay on the surface. When he stopped, he had snow in his mouth and down his throat. He destroyed all the ligaments in his right knee and two in his left, but was otherwise unharmed. After hobbling and sliding down the mountain to get out of the avalanche zone, he spent a night in the open with little clothing, food, or water.

The helicopter I saw carried two climbing rangers, Renny Jackson and Mark Magnuson. When they reached Stephen, he was hypothermic, dehydrated, and in great pain. The accident didn't slow him down. Within a year he went back and did the first snowboard descent of Owen. When I last talked to him, he was planing to snowboard a new route on Mount Mc-Kinley.

This capacity to return to the edge, again and again, is perhaps what we admire most. It is, of course, a version of the heroic myth. Everyone at Exum has at some time in their lives lived out this myth, although it is increasing difficult to do so when the myths are buried under layers of cynicism and irony.

The weather clears, but not for long. I crank up the computer and get the weather forecast for Jackson, Wyoming, trying yet again to make my unpredictable world more certain.

> TONIGHT . . . OCCASIONAL SNOW SHOWERS. SNOW SHOWERS DECREASING AFTER MIDNIGHT WITH AD-DITIONAL SNOWFALL OF AN INCH OR LESS. MOSTLY CLOUDY. SOUTHWEST WINDS 10 TO 15 MPH IN THE EVENING. LOWS IN THE MID TO UPPER 20s.
>
> FRIDAY . . . MOSTLY CLOUDY WITH A 70 PERCENT CHANCE OF SNOW SHOWERS AND A FEW AFTER-NOON THUNDERSTORMS. SOUTHWEST WINDS 15 TO 25 MPH. HIGHS IN THE MID TO UPPER 40s.

FRIDAY NIGHT . . . 70 PERCENT CHANCE OF SNOW
SHOWERS. MOSTLY CLOUDY WITH BRISK WINDS.
LOWS FROM 20 TO 25.

SATURDAY . . . 40 PERCENT CHANCE OF SNOW
SHOWERS. BECOMING PARTLY CLOUDY IN THE AF-
TERNOON. COOL. HIGHS IN THE UPPER 40s.

Typical weather for this time of year. A milky sky, snow, mist, rain, and sleet can last for weeks. One year it rained or snowed twenty-eight days in May. And this is the weather report for Jackson. Moose, the village at the southern entrance to the park, averages two degrees colder than Jackson, and the village of Moran, near the northern entrance, averages three degrees colder. Since the cabins are five hundred feet higher than Jackson, and closer to the mountains than Moose and Moran, the temperature probably averages five degrees colder. This, and the fact that we are closer to the mountains, means more snow. There hasn't been snow on the ground in Jackson for six weeks, but there is still three feet in Lupine Meadows.

R aining now. All day yesterday. The snow level dropped eight to ten inches yesterday. The snow is pure mush. Wet snow avalanches slithered down Teewinot. At dusk there were acres of fresh avalanche debris.

I step off the porch to test the snow and go all the way through to the ground, flailing with my ski poles. After a couple of steps I return to the porch and go back inside the cabin. Even with skis or snowshoes, it's hard to travel in these conditions. Square yards of rotten snow collapse beneath you, often landing you in the bushes below. Getting out of these holes is wearying; then you go in again, struggle out.

Junky snow is hard on critters, too. Having burned their fat supplies all winter, they're weak, and now they face difficult environmental conditions. When the snow isn't crusted, elk and pronghorn can plunge through, injuring their legs. Or they posthole around, exhausting themselves as I did.

The melting snowpack also creates difficulties for smaller creatures. The thick winter snowpack provides insulation and protection, but a melting snowpack floods the homes and tunnels of shrews, mice, and voles, and they are often wet and cold. As more snow melts and the runoff begins, flooding increases; and when it freezes again, the ice sometimes cuts them off from their food supplies. Predators also have trouble running in junky snow, so they must feed on winter kills. When rain and warmer temperatures weaken the ice on the streams and lakes, moose and migrating elk break through and die of hypothermia. In the Tetons, May is the cruelest month. Smart humans tend to read or travel.

Morning. It is snowing again, and colder. The crust is back, frozen hard enough to walk on with tennis shoes, at least for a few hours. For the first time in a week, I venture around the cabin.

Uinta ground squirrels are still trying to eat grass along the dirt road without being killed while traveling to and from their dens. Locally known as "chiselers," a derogatory name that underestimates their importance in the food chain, the squirrels are pathetically conspicuous—dark gray dots against a white backdrop. At a distance, they appear undistinguished, but up close they are lovely, their bodies gray and finely spotted, their delicate faces ending in cinnamon noses. Their primary reason for existence, it seems, is to feed predators when there is little else to eat. Great gray owls watch them from the cottonwoods along the creek and red-tail hawks circle the sky. Coyotes lie flat as rugs at the bottom of shallow depressions in the surrounding snow and rush to make their kills. Badgers, long-tailed weasels, and pine martens also take their toll. Eighty percent of the six to eight squirrels in each litter will die before their first birthday. A two-year-old Uinta ground squirrel is a tribal elder.

They should be called "underground squirrels," because (here at least) they spend eight months a year in hibernation. When I arrive, they are up and about, having emerged in April. In August they go underground again.

Southeast of the cabins is a mound of dirt five feet in diameter, piled two feet above the snow. The hole is sufficiently large for a small dog to enter, but they don't. Even coyotes won't tangle with a badger. In Wyoming, a twenty-five-pound badger is a big badger. In Europe and Russia, they are bigger, fifty- and sixty-pound badgers being common; one killed in Russia weighted seventy pounds. I do not want to live next door to a seventy-pound badger. Nor do the marmots that live under some of our buildings. Occasionally a badger moves into a marmot den and exterminates the residents.

Two mallards and a blue-wing teal are on the creek. Chickadees, flocks of robins. A dipper in a riffle. For as long as I can remember, a dipper has cruised this riffle. Four piles of moose droppings lie on top of the snow. Their dark color has absorbed heat, sinking them into gently rounded cavities. They look like nuts in porcelain bowls.

In the winter, moose sleep around the cabins to avoid the wind. In the spring, they hang around the cabins because the dark stain on the wood absorbs heat and melts off the snow sooner than in surrounding areas. On several occasions I have found moose sleeping on my porch. Once I got up in the night to pee off my porch. As I walked out the door stark naked, a figure rose up, snorting. I ran—straight into the doorjamb. Bleeding from the nose, I stumbled into the cabin, found my headlamp, and shined it into the night. A cow moose stood a dozen yards away, her eyes glowing, her head down, vapors purling from her nose—formidable and every bit as upset as I was. I defiantly peed off the porch in her direction and went back to bed. She slept somewhere else.

I head back to the cabin. One has to get home on time, like Cinderella, before the snow softens. In the evening, clouds pour over the mountains like waves, waterfalls, rapids, swirls of lava—the domains of complex dynamics. Again it snows, but then in the night the temperatures warm, and by morning it is raining and the snowpack turns to slush.

With the snow in such bad shape, I travel to other parts of the park—and beyond—visiting the same places every year, like seeing old friends. I drive down to the Snake to watch the herons at their rookery, their nests scattered through a stand of blue spruce. Nearby, a pair of ospreys occupy the top of a broken cottonwood. The female is on the nest; the male circles, calling. Herds of elk and pronghorn swim the river. An eagle steals a fish from an osprey. Once I found a beaver a mile from the river in a stretch of sagebrush. He tore off toward water faster than I thought possible, with a look of one who had been caught doing something stupid.

I look for porcupines along the river and I usually find them. Today I surprise one at the top of a terrace. He waddles off down the hill with slow sideways glances at me. He eats some buds off a toppled aspen, then climbs down through the limbs at the top and confronts the bare trunk. He turns and goes down butt-first, mewing and muttering, as though to himself. His large, long, soft nose contrasts with everything else about him.

Porcupines are my choice for the most maligned critter in North America. Lumber interests hate them because they eat bark off trees, sometimes killing them; home owners hate them because plywood is produced using sodium chloride, and porcupines love salt; motorists hate them because salt used in the winter on highways sticks underneath cars and trucks, seasoning, for instance, the radiator hose.

In *A Summer on the Rockies*, Major Sir Rose Lambert Price's account of his 1898 hunting expedition to the mountains around Jackson Hole, the author remarked the number of trees barked by porcupines. His Indian guide, Tigee, killed porcupines whenever he could because his wife used the quills for embroidery and ornaments. Since the average porcupine has thirty thousand quills, one would like to assume the Shoshone's need for porcupines was limited. But no. Quills were used as money or traded to Plains tribes which had no porcupines to kill. While returning from a hunt, Price watched Tigee kill a porcupine with a stick. It was not easy. When attacked, a porcupine sticks its head under a log and lets its quills do the rest. Knowing this, Tigee first hit the porcupine on the head. Price reported, "I don't think I ever saw an animal take so much pounding or show such tenacity of life." Obviously a manly, English sort of porcupine.

Price also noted, en passant, that "there were very few porcupines left on the Shoshone Reservation." Then, untroubled by contradiction, he went on to say the porcupine's liver is a "positive delicacy, ever so much better than chickens" and "if the gourmets in New York only knew what an excellent thing his liver is, *en brochette* with bacon, there would be many less trees barked and ruined in the Rocky Mountains." Fortunately, porcupine liver hadn't caught on in New York.

Porcupines remain unappreciated. Unlike the wolf or grizzly, not a single state offers the porcupine protection. In Wyoming, they are varmints; you can shoot or trap one any day of the year you wish. Although porcupines play an important role in forest ecology, anyone who points this out or suggests we might not salt roads or could take the sodium out of plywood is judged a bit precious, perhaps whimsical.

Cacti dot the terraces along the western side of the river. Most people don't believe there are cacti in Jackson Hole, but they are fairly common here and on the southern ridges of Blacktail Butte and on the National Elk Refuge in sunny, exposed places where winter winds scour the snow. The plants are small, low, and fragile—hence their name, *Opuntia fragilis*. Perhaps a thousand elk dot the sagebrush flats above the river terraces, returning north to their summer homes in the mountains. There are flickers, a mourning cloak butterfly.

I drive up to the Oxbow, a well-named bend in the Snake River a mile below the Jackson Lake Dam. It is one of the best places in the valley to watch birds. I walk to a favorite place in the willows and start glassing. Muskrats are feeding at the edge of the river. Willow flycatchers just up from South America are cruising the willows. There are geese, mergansers, mallards, loons, golden-eyes, two eagles, fifty or so cormorants, and, most important to me, nineteen white pelicans sleeping on a gravel bar, their heads tucked between their wings, their long yellow beaks pointing straight down their backs.

While I am sketching their sleeping positions, twenty-three more arrive and preen. Then six more arrive, flying low upriver. Switching to my spotting scope, I study the complex yellows and oranges of their faces and beaks—more complex than is usually represented. For a while I am consumed with my watercolors, but gradually I become aware of a vague stench—something dead. I glass the river. Two large, dark masses are bobbing in the shallows above me. Moose carcasses. They probably went through the ice when it softened this past week. The smell and the bloated bodies are so grim, I leave. Bad vibes.

I drive north to visit Dan Burgette, the Colter Bay subdistrict ranger who is responsible for roughly the northern half of Grand Teton National Park. He happens to be in his office at Colter Bay, a ten-foot-square cubicle with a metal desk, two chairs, file cabinets, some charts, a computer, and a phone. On the walls are pictures of his bird carvings, his family, pins showing attendance at various wilderness-management meetings, and photographs of various climbing and skiing exploits. Through his only window, I can see Jackson Lake and Mount Moran. Like most of these mountains, it looks magnificent from this northeast aspect. Dan is answering a complaint from a visitor.

Dan is fifty years old and built like a tackle on a high school football team. He's still blond, and his eyes still shine. As usual, he's wearing green Levi's and a gray shirt with a gold badge that says NATIONAL PARK RANGER, U.S. DEPARTMENT OF INTERIOR, MARCH 3, 1849. His hiking boots are polished. Around his waist is a heavy belt holding a .40 Sig semiautomatic pistol, two extra magazines of Hydra-Shok ammunition, a pair of handcuffs, a can of pepper spray, a radio, a Mini Maglite, a large ring of keys, and an Asp—an expandable baton that reminds me of the swords in *Star Wars*.

Dan is required to wear all this even when answering letters. In 1976, Congress passed a law allowing rangers to wear defensive gear. Before that, there was a revolver for each subdistrict—usually locked in a safe—and rangers in patrol cars each had a revolver locked in the glove compartment. Now they drive Ford Expeditions and carry Sigs, 12-gauge shotguns, scope-sighted rifles, and AR-15 assault rifles. They are indeed well armed, even at their desks.

Happy to be freed from letter writing, Dan talks pelicans and migrating eagles; we make bets on when the ice will go off the lakes—all subjects that interest him. Indeed, there is little about the park that does not interest him. The Teton Range has never had a more avid defender of what he calls "the resource," not only the flora and fauna but every stick, stone, drop of water, process, and relationship within the park's boundaries.

I tell him about the moose. "Yeah," he says, "we call them all Bob Moose. Every year a couple go through the ice, usually out on the lakes. Eventually they sink."

"Any good gossip?" I ask.

"Two mountain lion kills. Both sheep, both radio-collared. One near the Mount Hunt Divide, the other up north some-where."

I'm delighted to hear about the mountain lions, peeved about the radio-collared mountain sheep.

"Has anyone studied the mortality rate of radio-collared ani-mals?" I ask. "Seems to me a suspiciously high percentage of the collared mountain sheep in the park are dead."

Dan smiles. Neither of us like radio collars much: Collaring a sheep by trapping them in a net dropped from a helicopter is too great an intrusion into their wild lives. Airplanes track them. Some-times they are trapped again, and poked, and studied. Once they are collared, mountain sheep lose their privacy. Of course, there are those who think that mountain sheep don't have a right to privacy.

I leave Dan to his letter. Having driven this far, I decide to drive north to see if there are white pelicans on Yellowstone Lake. The snow level in Yellowstone amazes me. Along the road above the Lewis River Canyon, rotary snowplows have sheared ten-foot snowbanks that block the views. It looks like mid-February.

The northern end of Yellowstone Lake is frozen solid—no clear water, even at the edges. I drive on until I can look down the southeast arm of the lake; then I climb a hill with my spotting scope.

Far to the south, where the Yellowstone River enters the lake, I see a line of clear water. That's where the Molly Islands are, the only pelican rookery in Wyoming.

On the way home, I stop to see Dan again. He's still working on letters, so he's glad to talk more about pelicans and the state of ice on Yellowstone Lake. As I leave, he mentions that a boar grizzly walked out of the willows where I was painting at the Oxbow, swam to one of the moose carcasses, and hauled it out of the river in front of a flock of startled tourists. Not a mean feat with a waterlogged thousand-pound moose.

I head back to the Oxbow, trying to stay somewhere near the speed limit. The people are gone. With my field glasses, I see bear prints in the mud along the shore. I carefully examine the willow thickets. Nothing. I descend to measure the prints. They are five inches wide and nine inches long. Their resemblance to a human footprint is remarkable. I shiver. When you measure grizzly prints, you know, incorrigibly, corporeally, your status in the food chain.

# 4. The Meadow

Still cold—21 degrees this morning in late May. The mountains are hidden, the cloud layer down to 8,000 feet. Storms are stacked up all the way across the Pacific. It's cold and blowing a bitter rain. The snow is still melting. Where the snow is gone, the colors of the vegetation are worthy of Utrillo—tan, gray, rust, pink, sienna, umber. In the gullies along the lower slopes of Teewinot are new willows, their branches a faded purple. The conifers are nearly black. Everything seems somber, muted, neutral—again.

This is the best time of year for watching animals. Deciduous leaves are gone and winter snow has pressed last year's herbage flat. The animals are in clear view. Also, the animals' bold colors contrast with the somber neutrals: The bears and moose are black dots; the elk are pale dots. And with few people in the park, the animals are relaxed, unafraid.

The first pronghorn appear in the meadow in mid-May. Having wintered on the sagebrush steppes around the Green River, they've crossed the low passes between the Gros Ventre and Wind River ranges, walking on frozen snow, to descend the Gros Ventre River Valley, swim the Snake, and begin their long summer in Lupine Meadows.

Many of the first large mammals that arrive in Lupine Meadows go to the same place every year, a slope at the bottom of Teewinot where spring avalanches from cliffs above reduce snow cover for several hundred feet—one of the many benefits of avalanches. Because of its angle, this area also receives more direct sunlight; hence, it is the first place free of snow. Fresh tubers are everywhere.

Like the dirt road, the bare slope highlights the interactions of the food chain. From our parking lot, with my binoculars, I count ten elk, two moose, and a black bear sow with two cubs occupying an area two hundred yards wide and fifty yards high. Several cow elk are bedded down. When the sow approaches too closely, a cow jumps up and charges the bear, barking loudly. The sow backs off but continues feeding.

A peregrine is soaring above the meadow. Strange to see it so low, though there is probably not much to eat up high—the meadows are the only places free of snow. Juncos are no longer in flocks. Sandhill cranes are trumpeting at the Moose Ponds' three small lakes formed by Broken Falls Creek pouring off Teewinot. Lots of Cassin's finches, a few yellow-headed blackbirds, and a lone pine grosbeak.

As the snow melts, the park begins to teem with life, but the date snow melts to bare ground varies enormously. Every spring when the snow leaves, I climb as far as I can go up a favorite ridge on Teewinot. It has become a benchmark of sorts, a way for me to mark where things are in the natural cycle. Several years ago I climbed up to the Apex, halfway up Teewinot, in late April. At 9,000 feet, steershead and spring beauties were blooming. This mid-May, Lupine Meadows is mostly covered with snow, and at

9,000 feet on Teewinot, there is probably six to eight feet. I will not go that high until June.

To live in a place, truly live *in* it, is to project a private geography of such favored spots onto the landscape. The spots vary from inhabitant to inhabitant—everyone has his own geography—even the bluebird and the chipmunk. These spots never appear on maps as something special. A favorite view of Teewinot through the mint-green leaves of a cottonwood; the best spot for picking huckleberries; the riffle that always has a dipper; our osprey's nest; our badger's burrow; the lowest whitebark pine on the trail to the Apex—all exist in a mixture of memory and imagination. Visiting them each year for the first time is a ritual.

So, like a monk, as soon as the snow melts I go down Cottonwood Creek and circle the meadows to greet my Thoreauvian neighbors. I go clockwise, like Tibetan monks going around Mount Kailas: Just as they circle what they believe to be the center of the universe, so do I.

The first thing I visit are the dippers. South of the cabins, Cottonwood Creek turns west over shallow riffles for several hundred yards, then turns south over another riffle into a long run of shallow water. Dippers have always inhabited this stretch, though how many there are is hard to say since it is difficult to distinguish individual dippers. But because a dipper requires a half mile of stream in our part of the world, and since it will chase off other dippers that invade its territory, I've probably been watching a single pair all these years. The only time I saw three, they were fighting.

The American dipper is a slate-colored bird with a slightly brownish head, somewhat smaller than a robin, with a stubby tail, short wings, and eyelids covered with tiny white feathers. It is the only bird with feathered eyelids. It has nasal flaps, also feathered, to keep water out of its nostrils. When it is underwater, a thin nictitating membrane slides over its eyes. This membrane (from the word *nictitate,* meaning "to wink") is an inner eyelid, like a solid windshield wiper that protects the eye against grit and water.

The dipper's legs are long and strong. Its large feet help it cling to rocks and walk on the bottom of creeks in swift currents. Dippers are oblivious to cold water, primarily because their feathers are unusually dense, but also because they never get wet. An unusually large preening gland near the base of the dipper's tail provides a generous supply of oil for its feathers. A dipper dips constantly, lowering its entire body, not just flicking its tail. Once seen, a dipper will never be mistaken for another bird.

Although a dipper is a passerine, related to thrushes and wrens, no bird is more intimately associated with water. The pelagic wanderers spend most of their time in the air; ducks, geese, cormorants, and pelicans spend much time on land; shorebirds live at the edges of water. The dipper spends half of its day foraging in the water. When it flies, it flies fast and direct—like a kingfisher—above water. It builds its nest beside or above water.

Dippers are among my favorite birds. I enjoy spending time with them; I seek them out. I love them for much the same reasons John Muir loved them: They are a bird of the mountains, they love cold, clear mountain streams (like trout, dippers are a good indicator of water quality), and they are invariably upbeat and cheerful. It is impossible to be depressed around dippers. Then too, it seems they have traveled with me in my wanderings around the world, and a wanderer loves meeting a familiar friend. On a melancholy note, Muir said, "Among all the mountain birds, none has cheered me so much in my lonely wanderings—none so unfailingly." I can only agree. I have seen dippers in most of the places I treasure : in the valleys of the Hindu Kush, in Hunza, in Ladhak, in Nepal, in the obscure ranges of Tibet and western China, in the cordilleras of Peru, in western Canada, in England, and once in the White Mountains of Crete. Although not all of these dippers dip like the

American species (there are five species worldwide) and their coloration varies, they inhabit mountain streams everywhere and always display the same pleasure in swimming and diving.

Muir's description of dippers in *The Mountains of California* remains one of the best essays about American wildlife. He called them "water ouzels." Now, *ouzel* is a pretty word, and for a long time I preferred it. Then I looked it up in *The Oxford Dictionary of English Etymology* and found that it means "blackbird." Since I think the dipper deserves a more distinctive appellation, I have returned to *dipper,* though this still seems too plain. Other countries have been more imaginative. In Finland, it is *koskikara,* meaning "pickax of the rapids." In Polish it is *pluczsz,* meaning, simply, "splash."

> *Cold mountain steam*
> *bird jumps in*
> *pluczsz.*

Today I walk down the meadow before cutting over to the creek. I get out the field glasses, look upstream, and there she is, or he is—the sexes have identical coloration, though the female is slightly smaller—standing on a stone near the edge of the stream. She (let us assume) dips, blinks—showing her white eyelids—and pounds what looks like a little stick on the rock between her feet. On closer examination, it turns out to be a caddis larva in its case. She pounds it until the caddis begins to emerge—then gobble, it's gone. She dives into the water again.

She faces into the current, her head down, swimming with her wings in asymmetrical strokes as the current tosses her left and right. Kayakers do the same thing to paddle upstream: The blades of their paddles strike the water the same way a dipper's wings strike the water—a blur of motion, energy, attention.

She moves several feet up the river and continues to dive in the riffle. Although dippers can dive as deep as six feet, they rarely do so because it is an inefficient use of time and energy. They need shallow water. One study estimated a pair of dippers need 4,000 square yards of it.

Cottonwood Creek contains a smorgasbord of flies for dippers to eat—adult flies, larvae, and nymphs. They are particularly fond of caddis larvae, mayfly nymphs, and, to a lesser degree, stone fly nymphs and small fish.

My dipper keeps her head underwater, winkling out larvae from between rocks. When she eats flies on the surface, she eats in place—she can devour three per second. Soon she is back on a rock, smashing another caddis. On those rare occasions when I have seen a dipper catch a fish, it also take the fish to a rock and pounds it for a while—to kill it, or to soften it up?—then swallows it headfirst.

She looks downstream, bobbing constantly, then takes off with a high-pitched, almost shrill, call. It is surprisingly loud for a small bird, and continuous, with many repetitions of the same note. She lands in another riffle 150 feet upstream and immediately dives underwater.

Spring beauties are plentiful beneath the pines at the end of the meadows, so much so that when backlighted, the ground appears pink. In one square foot of meadow I count twenty-seven plants with a total of sixty-three blossoms. Indians boiled their corms—the fleshy bulb at the bottom of the stem—like potatoes.

Fritillaries are up. The flowers go nicely in salads, and their corms are also edible. I eat a fritillary every spring—for good luck. More rare are steershead, a pale, drooping flower that looks just like a steer's head, though upside down. Much more rare, here, is orogenia, or Indian potato, with its umbel of minute white flowers. Even eaten raw, the corm tastes like a potato.

Living at the edge of these meadows one touches, however slightly, an older world, a named world, a world where everything was known, ingested, used. This world is forgotten now, the knowledge that remains being the province of specialists. Yet to touch this world brings pleasure—to know what could be done, the possibilities of this place. No doubt the Indians who camped here each summer enjoyed many things we still consider delicacies. Whitefish and trout were plentiful, and there were slews of morels and chanterelles if you knew where to go—and they did. But the Indians could not limit themselves to delicacies.

Indians boiled alder bark for a dye the color of burnt sienna. They used the needles of the alpine fir as a tea, a tonic, and a medicinal. Serviceberry was dried and pounded into powder, then formed into loaves. Its branches provided arrow shafts. The branches of the red osier, a common dogwood, became arrow shafts too, or held together tepees, or were braided into fishnets. Oregon grape roots supplied a yellow dye. Pipsissewa provided an astringent, a tea, and a tobacco. Chokecherries brewed as a tea killed intestinal worms, and the wood was burned when traveling through enemy territory because it made no smoke. When times were hard, the Indians ate the inner bark, or cambium, of the lodgepole pine—just like bears do. Sage became an incense, a tea for colds, and a purifier. Cheyenne warriors passed their shields though sage smoke four times before riding into battle.

Two sandhill cranes fly over, silhouetted against the snowy face of Teewinot, calling loudly. Their croaking, bugling cries can be heard for miles, the loudest call of any bird species. They've come from the Moose Ponds, just north of here. For many years a pair nested just south of the meadows where the creeks braided, creating islands where the cranes were somewhat protected from predators. Then one year the creek flooded their nest area. They have not returned.

The crane's footprint, nearly four inches long, has graced the planet for 60 million years and entered human culture along many paths. The Taoists believed in the transmutation of cranes and pines. Thus Po Chü-i could say, with subtle allusion, "Clear cries, several voices—cranes under the pines." Crow and Cheyenne warriors carved flutes from the crane's hollow leg bones and played them as they rode into battle, brandishing their sage-smoked shields and waving lances fringed with eagle feathers.

A t the corner of the meadow is an osprey nest built directly above the trail leading up Garnet Canyon to the Grand Teton. Since ospreys migrate back to the park during April—from as far south as Argentina—the nest was built in ignorance of the trail below, unused then and covered with snow. A female is on the nest. She rises to take a better look at me but does not cry. She is probably still on eggs. Soon she calms down and lies lower in the nest, with only her head showing, her head feathers blending with the branches of the nest, the limbs of trees. I begin to sketch the nest but soon weary of the detail. A male osprey returns to the crying female, but he is empty-handed and does not land. She has turned her back to me now, ignores me.

While I am watching the ospreys, a coyote with a clown's face walks into the meadow from the forest and spots me. Slinking back and forth, she keeps watching me attentively. She remains spooked for perhaps five minutes: Every once in a while she will jump at the sound of trees creaking in the wind. Then she returns to the forest, walking on logs to avoid the melted snow, probably to her den. Soon she returns and sits on the snow, carefully watching me. Suddenly she bolts toward me, stops abruptly, then casually wanders off north into the trees again. The osprey is back up in alert position, watching the coyote.

I walk north along the western edge of the meadow toward the Moose Ponds: The ponds are free of ice, but snow still covers the edges. A spotted sandpiper wanders the shore of the upper pond. When I sit down to watch through my field glasses, I find two bears in a gully above the pond, and one moose. The bear is unusually colored, with a blond body, chocolate head, legs, and butt. She is ripping up roots with her jaws in a rocking motion. Above her on a grassy slope, her yearling cub does the same. After a few minutes the sow returns to the trees. Two more cow moose arrive. After thirty minutes the sow is still in the trees, and finally the cub joins her.

The temperature has dropped. Squalls of snow are blowing through, hanging in the sky like smears of graphite. It is now snowing above me. The tree line on Teewinot has paled; the rock ridges are barely discernible—I can see nothing above the Idol and Worshipper, two towers at 10,900 feet. I drink some tea from the thermos and wait for the sow to return. Elk feed in the meadow and on the lower slopes of Teewinot. A marmot, two pair of mergansers on the pond—but no more bears for the day.

I walk on down the trail to Jenny Lake to see if the water is free of ice. Some time during the middle of May, about the same time the meadow is free of snow, the lake ice melts. As early as May 10 or as late as May 23 the first small holes appear, then large fractures with channels of blue water. On overcast days the ice appears gray or green, soggy with slush and meltwater. In sunlight it seems a pale, milky blue. When the wind blows, the ice can break up in a single day; by evening the lake is a mix of dark water and white shelves of ice, though coves protected from the wind are still frozen solid. Along the east shore will be a residue of slush ice perhaps ten feet wide—like a ring around a bowl.

The lake is clear now. Feeding trout dimple the surface beneath a fishing osprey. On my way back to the cabin I see a kestrel carrying a limp mouse. It is dusk. Above my cabin a male snipe advertises for a mate. His courtship flight, called winnowing, is performed several hundred feet in the air. He flies in circles, then dives steeply, his wings partially tucked, his tail feathers spread so the outer ones are separated from the rest and interrupt the flow of air from the wings. The result is a tremolo of *hoo-hoo-hoo-hoos* — another sound of spring.

There are both residents and seasonal migrants in Lupine Meadows. Guides and rangers are seasonal migrants. Kim Schmitz is usually the first guide to arrive, moving his few things up from Jackson in spurts of activity. His cabin is at the edge of the meadow, facing Teewinot. Next to his bed is a large plate-glass window that allows him to look at the mountains. This is appropriate. During the winters in Jackson, he will drive up to the parking lot at Taggart Lake, sit in his truck, and appear to read, though this is a ruse. What he is really doing is looking at the mountains. Of the many guides and climbers I have known, none is more intimately allied with them. I have known him to be happy only when climbing or skiing. Like all great passions, the price has been high.

Kim is fifty-two, of medium height, and built like a young wrestler. He looks like Jack Palance—square jaw, widely set pale blue eyes, and a mop of thick hair. He works part-time and reads, but mainly he works out, climbs, skis, and practices Zen Buddhism.

Kim began climbing when he was twelve and has never stopped. By the age of fourteen he had climbed Mount Robson in the Canadian Rockies; when he was sixteen, he climbed Mount Waddington, a remote, difficult peak in British Columbia. In the sixties he and his friend Jim Madsen arrived in Yosemite and, through sheer courage, strength, speed, and talent, simply subdued what were then the hardest rock climbs in the world.

Al and Susan Read arrive next from San Francisco, cruising into Guides Hill in their silver BMW convertible with its EXUM license plate. Susan is Exum's office manager and Al is its president. The rest of the year, Al is vice-chairman of Geographic Expeditions, an adventure travel company, and Susan works for United Airlines.

Al is the only guide who manages to hold down an ordinary desk job—our only suit, as it were. He is a velvet hand in an iron glove, a leader of expeditions to Alaska, the Himalayas, Russia, and China, our chief, and the only resident of Guides Hill to catch deer mice using Havahart traps.

When the snow is definitely gone and the temperatures rise into the seventies, Chuck Pratt arrives. He drives straight to his cabin in his recent buy—a beautiful California-customized lime-green 1967 Volkswagen hatchback, filled with tools and climbing gear. His last VW, also a 1967 Volkswagen hatchback, had no passenger's seat. When you rode with Pratt, you sat on a toolbox on the floor. Once someone asked him if he was married. Pratt replied, "Married? I don't even have a passenger seat in my car."

When Pratt arrives, he doesn't immediately say hello; when he leaves, I often don't know he is leaving until he is gone, and there are no good-byes—even though we have known each other for forty years. One day he just appears at Guides Hill, like sagebrush buttercups pushing up in the spring; another day he drives out, like the aspen turning yellow in the autumn.

We may not speak for a day or so. When we run into each other at the washhouse or the Dumpster, we shake hands, ask how everything is and how the winter went. He has always been in Thailand. It was wonderful, he says. Perhaps he has just arrived from the Utah desert. It too was wonderful. The Tetons—well, it still might snow. . . . Pratt hates cold and bad weather. When I was a young climber—nineteen years old—he told me, "Death comes from clouds." And he was right. I had no idea how right he was.

Pratt is short and powerfully built. His knowledge of literature, music, and movies is legendary. Many people believe he was the finest rock climber of his generation.

Slowly the other resident guides move in. Dave Carman moves up from Jackson; Peter Lev, Rick Wyatt, and Evelyn Lees from Salt Lake City; Jane Gallie and David Shlim from Katmandu, Nepal. Jack Tackle arrives in a trendy new black VW with custom plates announcing JAVA—his nickname. He is just off some horrendous face in Alaska or Patagonia. Jim Williams arrives from guiding clients on Everest and Denali—with barely a break in between. Dick Dorworth returns from a winter of skiing in Sun Valley and a spring of guiding in Idaho and California. Rolando Garibotti—"Rolo"—is back from Patagonia, where he has often done some of the hardest routes in the world.

Some of us stay in touch over the winter, but most do not. Al, Kim, Dorworth, and I stay in touch with E-mail. Rolo writes me on the backs of paintings and photographs from Argentina, France, or Italy. He is at heart as much a metaphysician as a climber. His passion and intelligence remind me of Neruda. They are the kind of letters that end up pinned to walls or lying among art books.

With the rangers and their families and our assortment of spouses, lovers, and children, there are sixty people living at the edge of the meadows. Some of the other Exum guides are locals and live in town. Others live at the Climbers Ranch, a hostel-like arrangement run by the American Alpine Club.

Our lives are in some ways primitive, even brutal, but in most respects we are typical middle-class Americans. At the end of the season we go back to teaching jobs, ski patrols, management positions, year-round guiding here, in Alaska, South America, the Himalayas. We have not escaped civilization. We share a communal bathhouse with showers and a washing machine. We have telephones, fax machines, computers, and cellphones galore—all the accoutrements of modern life. In our parking lot, battered trucks vie for space with a BMW and a Mercedes. *The New Yorker* and *The New York Times* are read along with *Rock and Ice*. Several guides study *The Wall Street Journal* as assiduously as *Climbing*—and use their cell phones to call their commodity traders while they are climbing mountains.

We have little in common save our love of mountains and the private life of the guide service, a life neither the clients nor the Park Service can enter, a matrix of old friendships, alliances, feuds, arcane traditions, eccentric preferences, mutual understandings. The history of this secret life is oral, its soul a collection of methods, maxims, and stories—the mark of tribal culture. We are a guild, our labor a craft, our helm a never-stated but thoroughly integrated creed. Generations of guides have accumulated a wisdom that is rarely examined, rarely changes. And our sense of these mountains—as strong and singular as a life's great love—comes primarily from this private, almost secret, life.

Like the special days of other cultures—the days of plowing, planting, harvesting, or the religious holidays honoring saints— Exum has its own calendar: the opening of the Exum office, the digging out of the Exum hut on the Lower Saddle between the Middle and Grand Tetons, the first guided ascent of the Grand, the first Guides' Day Dinner, the weekly guides' meetings and potlucks around the fire pit at Guides Hill, the Exum end-of-summer dinner, the last guided ascent of the Grand, closing of the hut. By October, everyone is gone but Kim and me, and at the end of October we will leave. Like most things in the Tetons, the guide service migrates.

W e are not the first people to summer in Lupine Meadows. Archaeological sites in Jackson Hole suggest seasonal use by Indians beginning 12,000 years ago. The great rivers of the American West, the Missouri, the Columbia, and the Colorado, all have major tributaries—the Yellowstone, the Green, and the Snake—with headwaters in mountains around Jackson Hole. Fifty miles southeast of Lupine Meadows, Triple Divide Peak drains water into all three watersheds. In the West, water means life, and these mountains teem with life, especially during summer. Indians came to hunt, fish, gather plants, and chip obsidian on Hominy Peak and from a source at the southern end of the range, obsidian being favored for arrowheads and spear points. But no Indian spent the winter in Jackson Hole: It was too cold.

The most common visitors were the Shoshone, a tribe with linguistic ties to the Hopi and Aztec, who traveled to the Tetons from the Great Basin; the Blackfoot, a powerful warrior tribe from what is now Montana who spoke Algonquin; and the Crow, a tribe related to the Plains Sioux, who lived in nearby valleys to the north and east and must have known the region intimately. The Sheepeaters, a subtribe of the Shoshone, may have lived here year-round, though we lack evidence to decide the issue. Indeed, evidence of Indian presence in the Tetons is limited—a few temporary shelters, stone circles on the summits of the Enclosure and the Middle Teton, flakes left from the production of arrowheads, roasting pits. Not much, and a lot of it lies buried under Jackson Lake. There is no evidence Indians attempted to organize the landscape with fire, game management, or agriculture. They influenced the environment but did not attempt to control it, though not, I think, because of an ecologically pure vision, but because they lacked technology to do the job. As a result, parts of the Tetons are among the wildest areas of the American West.

Mountain men visited the Tetons during the first half of the nineteenth century, beginning with John Colter, a member of the Lewis and Clark expedition, who remained in Montana when the expedition returned to St. Louis. Colter probably traversed the valley alone during the winter of 1807–1808, looking for beaver. Most of the famous mountain men—Jedediah Smith, David Jackson, William Sublette, Kit Carson, and Jim Bridger—trapped here before the fur trade collapsed in the 1840s. Their tales piqued the curiosity of those in power and Washington sent more reasonable men to distinguish what was real and what was fantasy. Bridger guided the first government expedition to the area in 1860 led by Capt. William Raynolds. Others followed—the Hayden survey in 1872, and a smaller expedition, led by Lt. Gustavus Doane, in 1876. By 1878 the range was both known and relatively safe. Exploration was over. Agriculture, resource extraction, and entertainment became the primary forces of environmental change. Like everywhere in the American West, these forces remain—and the tensions caused by these individual interests remain.

In the closing decades of the century, gentleman hunters arrived, many of them British men of leisure for whom the sporting life was life itself. They appear silly now, with their long names, monocles, and fustian prose, but they had an eye for the curious and beautiful that scientists and later visitors lacked.

The first, and the most adventurous, was William A. Baillie-Grohman, a mountaineer and hunter whose travels in northwestern Wyoming resulted in a book, *Camps in the Rockies,* the most interesting early account of Jackson Hole. The range was, he said, "the most sublime scenery I have ever seen." He fished Cottonwood Creek along Lupine Meadows, near where our cabins are: "My favorite spot for the sport, was, as I have said, at the outlet of one of the lakes ('Jennie's' Lake it is called on the latest Government Survey map). . . ." He caught twenty-five pounds of fish in an hour—and this was only the beginning. "Three times a day did six big frying-pans appear on our primitive greensward dinner table, and never did fish taste nicer, and never did four men and two dogs eat more of them. Hardly credible as it sounds, thirty pounds a day was hardly sufficient to feed our six hungry mouths; and when, towards the end of my stay in the Basin, great economy in flour became imperative, forty pounds vanished in a similar wonderfully speedy manner." Now, Cottonwood Creek is closed to fishing most of the year and a good fisherman would be hard-pressed to catch forty pounds of trout a season.

The Tetons remained isolated until after the turn of the century. In 1880, when Baillie-Grohman left Fort Washakie, 107 miles to the southeast and the last outpost of what was thought to be civilization, he could not find "a single person there who knew the way to [Jackson Hole] or who had ever been there." During his visit he met only two white men from the end of July to the end of November and didn't see any Indians for three months. Thirty-one years later, in 1911, when Fanny Kemble Wister visited the valley with her father, Owen Wister, the author of *The Virginian,* a team hauled food for their dude ranch 104 miles team from St. Anthony, Idaho.

With farming and ranching came the first and only attempts at permanent habitation in Lupine Meadows. Old irrigation ditches scar the surface in several places, and just south of us, alongside the creek, stand the remains of a small cabin. Farther south are pieces of rusted farm equipment, barbed wire, and squares of exotic grass. With the creation of Grand Teton National Park in 1929, and its expansion in 1950, the ranches within the park closed, were bought out, or switched to entertaining dudes. Permanent settlement in Lupine Meadows failed, seasonal occupation prevailed. The guides and the rangers are only the most recent tribes in the area. Certainly we are not the last, and I predict our neighbors will remain when we are gone, our lovingly recorded histories a momentary blip in their greater cycles.

# 5. *Into the Mountains*

June. Twenty-four degrees at 6:00 A.M. The weather map in *USA Today* shows northwestern Wyoming has the same temperature as Alaska north of the Arctic Circle. The snow depth is 41 percent above normal in the mountains, but now it is consolidated snow, summer snow, firn.

Cottonwood Creek is flooding its banks; a rivulet from it courses among the cabins, leaving pools and swampy spots. The mountains are yellow with arrowleaf balsamroot, a gaudy flower reminiscent of sunflowers. Lupine are up. Alders are leafing out. The serviceberry is blooming, but willows are still in bud. The sagebrush buttercups are gone, the spring beauties going. The aspens are murmurous again, their leaves fluttering in the breeze— their so-called quaking. It is said that the Indians hung their babies in hammock-like pouches from the limbs of aspens because the motion and glitter of the leaves kept the babies happy. Degas, in a letter, says, in the same spirit, "If the leaves of the trees did not move, how sad the trees would be and we too!" I've always wanted to hang a hammock high in an aspen grove and live among the leaves.

Rod and Mark Newcomb have been up at the Saddle between the Grand Teton and Middle Teton to set up our hut for the season. Then Mark went back up with the first clients. They came down when it snowed a foot.

Above 10,000 feet it is still winter; below 10,000 it is raining. The snowy summits are hidden. When the mountains are buried in clouds and rain this time of year, they look dirty, unkempt, the snowfields ragged, dead as chalk, instead of the glistening alabaster of a sunny day. Snow must dominate a landscape in order to be beautiful.

Summer storms return, storms with cumulus and thunder, lightning and wind. In the afternoon, one pours out of Garnet and Cascade canyons, blotting out Teewinot, and advances across the meadow like a wall of ash. The cabin shudders under the first blasts. The trees bend thirty degrees off their axis. The rain is horizontal, big drops that sting the eyes, and when it hails, it hurts. When it clears, in the evening, the mountains are powdered with fresh snow. I go outside to lie in my hammock and smell the pungent aroma of wet conifers. Under the bushes, the ground is still white with hailstones.

A doe is near the porch, feeding. Evidently she doesn't mind humans in hammocks. The same deer return to Lupine Meadows each spring—they have their traditions, too. She hangs around for an hour, working the serviceberry and the grasses as I fiddle with dinner. A sharp sound or a fast movement makes her bound away. I talk to her as I grill a slab of salmon, and she returns, watching me. She curls her lips back and snips grass with the incisors in her lower jaw, pressing them against the pad on her upper jaw (it lacks incisors). I continue talking to her. She raises her head occasionally and licks her lips with a small, sensual tongue.

Children's voices cause her to bounce away with a loud snort. Then she begins to feed again on serviceberry leaves. She is pregnant, about to calve—mid-June is calving season for mule deer. She is not tame. The mule deer in Lupine Meadow migrate out of the park in the autumn, and both bucks and does are hunted. Yet she trusts us, as do most of the other large mammals. It is common to see pronghorn sleeping within twenty-five yards of the cabin even though they too are hunted in the fall. Once during a Guides Hill dinner I walked out of my cabin to find a little girl named Claire feeding a bull moose an ear of corn. He considered it with a detached air, then munched away, like a horse eating an apple.

I believe some birds build their nests close to the cabins for protection against predators. Robins' nests are particularly common. Once a robin built a nest on the windowsill of a cabin we were remodeling. She put up with chain saws, power saws, crowbars, hammers. She produced her brood of four chicks and continued to feed them despite the racket. Then one day I noticed a raven pluck the last squiggling chick from the nest while the mother sat forlornly on a nearby branch with a large grub in her beak.

A pine marten ate the chicks in the robin's nest just outside my east window. I went out and found the marten in a lodgepole surrounded by Brewer's blackbirds; he probably got their eggs, too. The house wrens are smarter. They nest inside the cabin, entering from a hole above the ridge beam where it extends over the porch. They are not bothered by predators and become quite tame over the summer, even though I do not have feeders. They live around the cabin, often perching several feet from me. Their song is joy itself.

M ost of Exum's guided climbs of the Grand Teton start from the Exum hut on a gently sloping saddle between the Middle Teton and Grand Teton known as the Saddle, or more accurately, as the Lower Saddle, there being an Upper Saddle between the Grand Teton and the Enclosure. Some guides take their gear up with them on their first climb of the Grand. The younger guides, working on their fitness, carry all their gear each climb. Some of the older guides, and that includes me, carry gear up to the hut before guiding season begins. The trip allows me to suffer alone with a heavy pack on snow—my prescription for a day in hell. For compensation, I can move at my own pace, paint, write in my journal, and wander alone in the mountains before the maw of summer guiding.

But the primary reason I like to go up to the Saddle early is to circumambulate the Cathedral group of peaks—the Grand Teton, Mount Owen, and Teewinot—the most beautiful mountains in the range. Unfortunately they have inspired prose with some rather Gothic images—for example, "Chartres multiplied by six, a choir of shimmering granite spires soaring high above the nave and transept of the valley below." Be that as it may, they *are* beautiful mountains—*just* beautiful mountains—and to walk around them at the beginning of the climbing year is another rite, though with age I'm becoming less devotional.

To begin the trip, I cross the meadows and hike four and a half miles up the Garnet Canyon Trail to where it ends at a place called the Platforms, at 9,000 feet. The next three and a half miles are snow, some of it steep snow, to the Lower Saddle. I spend the night in the hut, often alone. The next day I descend a snow gully into Dartmouth Basin, a remote cirque to the west of the Grand that drains into the South Fork of Cascade Creek. From the cirque down to the creek is a classic bushwhack of snow, boggy slopes, waterfalls, and the usual snare of willow and alder—a mess, really, but I've never met another human being on that descent. After reaching the trail in the South Fork, it's an easy eight miles down Cascade Canyon to Jenny Lake, and then two more miles around the lake to the cabin.

The trail up Garnet Canyon ascends the moraine between Garnet Creek and Glacier Gulch, then zigzags through open meadows until it is easy to cross into the upper reaches of Garnet Canyon. Most of the trail is clear now, with scattered drifts in the shade. Occasionally, I see Calypso orchids in deep shade, their swollen pink lips spotted with carmine. Their nickname is perfect—"fairy slipper." Around a small spring are violets, pure white with delicate purple lines on the largest petal that direct pollinators to the flowers' hearts, and bog orchids with stacks of small white flowers. A single Indian paintbrush is up, surrounded by acres of arrowleaf balsamroot.

When I turn the corner into Garnet Canyon, the air becomes cool and dry. There is always a breeze here. Above is the alpine world of rock and snow, with views of Shadow Peak, Nez Percé, Middle Teton, and the buttresses on the south side of Disappointment Peak.

At the Platforms, I change into mountaineering boots and gaiters, then put on sunblock and glacier glasses. I get out ski poles. There is a slight trail and the angle is low for the next mile to the Meadows, so I can walk along without having to kick steps in the snow.

It is traditional to stop in the Meadows—it is one of the loveliest places in the Tetons, with views of several major peaks—but now it is still buried under deep snow. Even the cottage-sized boulders are buried. A few willow tips stick up near where the creek will be and I find a thin slit with running water. I fill a liter bottle and put in a thick slice of lime. Then I move on; I have covered two-thirds of the distance to the Saddle but only half the elevation gain.

The sky is cloudless. Bowls of snow and thousand-foot rock walls surround me. The radiation is intense: There is no shade here and I am still in shorts and a T-shirt. Several thousand feet above me to the south I see two climbers approaching the east ridge of Cloudveil Dome. Nearly a mile above me to the northwest is the top of the Grand, with a stringy plume of snow blowing off the summit to the northeast. Footprints in the snow lead up to Nez Percé, the Jackson Hole Mountain Guides high camp, and to the Lower Saddle. Directly above me is the sharp triangle of Irene's Arete, one of the most elegant rock climbs in the park, perhaps my favorite.

The canyon forks at the end of the Meadows, the north fork leading to the Saddle between the Grand and Middle Tetons. As I approach the base of the Middle Teton, the angle of the snow steepens and I begin to kick steps. I do it carefully, methodically. Most falls on snow result from not kicking a good platform for your boot. If you take your time, climbing snow, even steep snow, is easy and quite safe. But when you tire, you get sloppy: Falls on snow account for over a third of the climbing accidents in the Tetons.

I take my time. The pack creaks; I breathe hard. Climbing snow is pleasant if you don't have a heavy pack. It is the essence of repetition and routine: kick, kick, step up, kick, kick, step up, kick, kick. An hour passes before I ascend the last steep section and walk up what in summer will be a huge boulder field at the bottom of the Middle Teton Glacier. Now it, too, is buried under snow.

The Glacier Route on Middle Teton rises directly above me in a thousand-foot sweep. To the right is 4,000 feet of rock—the south face of the Grand Teton. In front of me is a 600-foot face of snow known as the Headwall. I am in the bowl of a classic alpine cirque, a steep-walled basin carved by a glacier, in this case the Middle Teton Glacier. In Wales, or in those parts of the Himalayas

British climbers got to first, it would be called a *cwm*. Whether bowl, cirque, or cwm, it is as quiet and still as a church.

To climb out of the cirque, I must go up the Headwall. In the summer a fixed rope on a short cliff to the north renders this easy, but it too is still buried. I hike up to a long diagonal set of steps in the snow. The sun has dropped behind the Headwall. I am in shadow; the snow is freezing again. I know of no place where the soul more immediately registers the difference between sunlight and shade than in the mountains. Snow and rock in sunlight are inviting, but ominous in shade. There is the cold, the exposure, the failing light, and then the rock, solemn and gray.

I put on more clothes—stretchy ski pants, a ski hat, and a thick fuzzy (my nickname for polypropylene fleece). I collapse my ski poles, put them in the pack, and get out my ice ax. Then I climb the big steps up the Headwall. It is early in the season, I have a heavy pack, and I am approaching 11,600 feet. I am tired, hence careful. When climbing, you must attend to climbing, nothing else. This takes practice. I stop several times, drive in my ax, and enjoy the emptiness and the silence of steep cliffs.

Chinese mountain paintings and nature poetry drew many of us to the study of Buddhism. This is not an accident. The sky, the mountains, and mountain climbing are central tropes of Buddhist practice. Monasteries were associated with a mountain, most hermits were mountain hermits, and great teachers were named after their mountain abodes. And the sky? The sky is *sunyata*—emptiness. Like ours, the path of a Buddhist is steep, with few holds, and leads nowhere. Eventually everyone returns.

A tongue of snow extends from the top of the Headwall nearly to our hut. I unlock the door and turn the stove on for tea—we try to leave one pot filled with water. Then I go back outside to indulge in the exquisite pleasure of looking over hundreds of miles of mountains. The sky to the west is clear, though there is a dark band of clouds in the southwest. I can see far into the ranges of Idaho—the Lemhi, Lost River, White Knob, Pioneer, Beaverhead, and Pahsimeroi mountains are silhouetted in a hot sky, purple and pink. Especially prominent is Borah Peak, 150 miles away, and, at 12,662 feet, the highest peak in the state. Behind me, the shadows of the Tetons stretch across the floor of Jackson Hole. Seventy miles southeast, Gannett Peak basks in alpenglow. Gannett is 34 feet higher than the Grand Teton, and, at 13,804 feet, the highest mountain in Wyoming. The summit of the Grand Teton slowly turns yellow, then orange. The air is still; the tea water boils.

The Exum hut is twelve feet by eighteen feet and constructed of a fiberglass-reinforced vinyl tarp stretched over a series of arching steel poles and a plywood floor. Steel guylines are attached at various points to the tarp and bolted to the surrounding rocks. The hut holds a total of twenty-two people, guides and clients, arranged like sardines in a tin. Now it is empty save for piles of sleeping bags and foam pads. Since I think the cloud cover to the southwest might bring rain, I decide to sleep inside. Besides, my favorite cave is still stuffed with snow and ice.

Although the park has designated the Lower Saddle as wilderness, and manages it as such, there is, in fact, a community here during the summer that often exceeds the population of some Wyoming towns. In addition to the Exum hut, there is a hut for the climbing rangers—we call it Club Fed—two large steel boxes for equipment storage, and campsites marked by numbered steel stakes. Combine these with one of the world's great two-holer outhouses (featuring an unmatched view of the storms about to hit the Saddle), a cluster of meteorological instruments, and a landing pad for the helicopter that empties the outhouse every ten days or so—all in the space of little more than a hundred square yards—and the Saddle can seem downright urban. If you include the climbers coming up from camps on the Middle Teton moraine, the Caves, and even the Meadows, plus an increasing number of day hikers from the valley, it can get a bit crowded about midday.

Mark Magnuson, the Jenny Lake subdistrict ranger, whose area of responsibility includes the Saddle, has explained the issue to me many times, too many times, I fear, since I am rather dense on the subject. Since 1972, when the park recommended sections of Grand Teton that qualified as wilderness, two kinds of wilderness areas have existed in the park: recommended wilderness and potential wilderness. National Park Service policy requires these lands to be managed as if in fact they were designated wilderness, since such lands could in the future be classified as wilderness under the Wilderness Act.

The Saddle is not being managed in the spirit of the Wilderness Act, however, but Mark is not opposed to that. The old way of viewing wilderness stressed its physical characteristics; the new way stresses the authority and control park managers have by using a legislative category—wilderness—to reduce human abuse. And the Saddle needs all the help it can get.

If compared to other saddles at the same altitude between the South and Middle and between Teewinot and Mount Owen, there is no doubt the humans have abused the Saddle—myself not least: I've been tramping around on it for many years. But here is the anomaly. "Wilderness" in the national parks often turns out to be land that has been so abused that its present condition—as abused land—can be preserved only with the official designation of "wilderness." Wilderness becomes abused land that must be protected, even restored. This is definitely not what Muir, Leopold, and Marshall had in mind, although it is a perfectly noble project.

I have sympathies with both sides. I want big, wild wilderness. And I want protection for areas that are being destroyed. But I fear that in the process, the term *wilderness* will be drained of meaning and that future generations will accept this abused, managed wilderness as true wilderness, however devoid it is of the scale and the wildness of the old. I can mull this subject for hours, and do.

Later, I go out to check the sky. Cloud cover has arrived; the night is warm. A breeze skims over the Saddle now, westerly, mild. I sleep on piles of foam pads under one light sleeping bag. I leave the door of the hut open.

I sleep late—a treat on the Saddle, since I usually get up at three o'clock when I have clients. Banks of cirrus fill the sky above me, a dark mantle, but I can see they end slightly farther west. The summit of the Grand Teton is visible, somber and gray. No cumulus on the horizon—it will be a beautiful day.

Breakfast is tea, bagels, and cream cheese. I dump the gear I hauled up into our steel box, lock it, lock the door of the hut, and head northwest, angling up and across the boulders to bypass an intrusion of red rock that comes up out of Dartmouth Basin, another glacial cirque to the west of the Saddle. The intrusion is harder than the surrounding rock and forms cliffs I don't want to climb down. Instead, I work my way toward a snow gully stretching from the Upper Saddle, near the summit of the Grand all the way into the cirque below. The gully is wide at this point; below, it narrows, dropping about 1,500 feet before flattening out on a small glacier. People have died in this gully. Usually they fall higher up, in what is known as the Idaho Express, so named, with typical climbers' cynicism, because it provides a long, fast ride toward the Idaho border.

It is shady on the west side of the Saddle this time of morning. And lonely, quiet, and slightly dangerous. Not difficult, but a place where you can't be casual. I've brought crampons and an ice ax in case the snow is hard, but this morning it is still soft after the warm night—a bit too soft for crampons, a bit hard for kicking steps. It's another judgment call; they are inevitable in the mountains—and merciless in their consequences.

I leave the crampons on my pack and plunge-step down the couloir, driving down with my heels and using my ski poles for balance. After all, I keep telling myself, we have several guides who can ski and snowboard down this gully. And I do not wish to complain about the snow—it's bad karma. When we have a light snow year, this gully is a pile of talus and boulders, one of the finest foot-bashing, ankle-breaking, knee-twisting places in the range.

In some areas the snow has melted all the way across the gully, creating a bergschrund, or moat, with water running over steep rocks and disappearing into the next section of snow through an ominous hole, like the hole down a drain. The edges of the snow are thin; I must be careful not to break through. I kick steps and pound with the poles, break though a bit, slide, and finally reach the rock. Then I pick my way through the talus, trying to stay out of the water, and climb gingerly until I reach solid snow again. Impressed by that black hole, I keep to one side of the gully, since it is most likely thinnest in the center where the water is working at it from underneath.

Finally the gully broadens onto a fan that merges with the glacier, and I run and slide without worries to a point where the slope eases. Sunlight finally, day begins. A moraine north of the snowfield makes the going easy; the terrain is like tundra and studded with flowers growing among isolated clumps of dwarfed conifers. From the moraine, I plunge-step down another steep snowfield and walk into a fairy meadow with rocks the size of small houses and stands of whitebark pine. I lie next to the stream and glass the slopes under the west side of the Enclosure, the name of the west summit of the Grand Teton, before turning my attention north. One I saw sheep there, an unusual place for them to be, I think, because I've never seen them again. Nonetheless, I always look. And besides, there is always the possibility of seeing a bear.

From here, I can see my favorite part of the Tetons—the peaks north of Mount Moran. The great canyons of the range run west to east, parallel to one another. I study them both with binoculars, trying to absorb a bit more of their presence. Just to look at them from this unusual perspective pleases me. I stay in the meadow a long time, not wishing to leave. I will not return here until next year, at best. Sometimes years pass before I visit this fairy meadow again.

I also tarry because the next section of the descent is messy. The meadow ends abruptly in steep glacier-carved slabs of gneiss interspersed with equally steep bogs of moss and grass that lead down into nasty thickets of alder and willow. I zigzag back and forth, lower myself using tree limbs, make stupid jumps—the ski poles are worth their weight in gold. Soon my feet are soaked, the bogs become ludicrously steep, and the slabs are running with meltwater, so I am forced to the left, onto thin snowfields along the main course of the creek, snowfields that in places conceal waterfalls. With the sun up, the snow is soft. Suddenly I don't like it. Bad vibes again. Like most people who work with risks, I trust vibes, so I cross the creek and start down-climbing easy rock. Finally I reach old moraines, the descent goes more rapidly, and I enter the thick forest surrounding the South Fork of Cascade Creek. At the bottom I balance my way over a clutch of downed spruce that straddles the creek, then stop in a meadow just short of the trail leading down canyon to Jenny Lake. I've dropped 3,200 feet in less than three hours.

I remove the mountain gear—boots, gaiters, pants, fuzzy—and stuff them into the pack. After I change into shorts, tennis shoes, and a Hawaiian shirt, I lie in the warm sun with mosquitoes droning about, feeding on me. I eat my Snickers bar and prepare to reenter civilization—for me, the trail is civilization. I steadfastly ignore the high-tech gear that allowed me to travel the terrain above in comfort and safety—not to mention what I'm munching on. Denial is the first line of defense.

Soon I will meet people on the trail, and that always makes a difference in the mountains. Sartre said that people are hell. In the mountains, I tend to agree. It is one of the glories of knowing a place well that you know how to avoid people. But there is something else, too. To walk a trail after bushwhacking is to cross mental borders: the border between lost and found, not knowing and knowing, nonhuman and human, wild and tame, hard and easy, dangerous and safe, deciding and merely following. The mind goes limp, the body slackens. I will no longer need to watch each step or judge if a chunk of moss will hold my weight or if a stretch of snow is too thin. When you are walking a trail, it is too easy for the mind to separate from the body as the body goes on autopilot. You can daydream, ruminate in the manner of Rousseau and Wordsworth, but something is lost. To walk a trail after bushwhacking is to dumb down.

As I descend Cascade Canyon, I run into people who want to know where I've been with ice ax and crampons, how I got up there, how long it took. For a while I am civil; I explain. But explanations are wearying, and after a while I just smile, avoid eye contact, and keep moving. The time of many people is coming. By midsummer, there will be up to two thousand people a day walking Cascade Canyon, alas—another of the park's "wilderness" areas.

When I am directly north of the Grand Teton, I wander off the trail to get away from the people. I want to study in peace the north face of the Enclosure, the Black Ice Couloir, and the north face of the Grand Teton, mnemonic devices, parts of my private geography that return me to my past. I study the routes and remember a time when there were fewer people in the park and virtually no one on hard routes in the mountains. When I first climbed the Grand Teton in the summer of 1962, I climbed it via the North Face Route. We were the only team that climbed the route that summer, and we saw no one else going up or coming down. It seemed a vertical wilderness of rock and ice. Now there are days when a hundred people summit the Grand in a single day, days when multiple parties climb the North Face Route.

I walk on. Two moose feed along the creek and several pikas are hopping around the talus with tufts of grass in their mouths. The pika is a member of the family Ochotonidae, closely related to hares and rabbits. It is small—about the size of a pack rat—with short rounded ears, gray fur, and no tail. Its life is a study of simplicity: It spends half the year gathering grass and the other half the year eating it. Perhaps the most interesting thing about the pika is its name, which is the only word in the English language derived from Tunguse, a language native to Siberia.

Just above Hidden Falls, where the trail drops through the cliffs to Jenny Lake, I see a pine marten. Then, at Moose Pond, another moose. At last I cross the sagebrush flats of Lupine Meadows, the final lap in the circumambulation. The spring flowers are gone now, withered, replaced by the flowers of summer. A herd of elk roam the flats in shining new pelage and two baby pronghorn romp with their mothers. When I reach my cabin door, I bow.

# 6. *Symmetry Spire*

On June 10, the Exum office opens and we begin to teach courses in basic rock climbing, mountain safety, snow climbing, and other special courses. After a winter of heavy snowfall, there can still be snow at the climbing school near Hidden Falls, but the cliffs are clean. Snow schools are conducted up in Hanging Canyon, a lake-filled gash dropping into Jenny Lake, and at the Jackson Hole Ski Area. The mountain-safety courses, only for Park Service and park concession employees, are also taught up in Hanging Canyon. Exum guide Mattie Sheafor runs "Women That Rock," a day of rock-climbing instruction taught by women guides for women climbers. Some of the young guides work, Chuck Pratt always works, but most of the guides hold off until early July. Guiding for two months—July and August—is intense enough for most of us.

June is the wettest of the summer months in the Tetons. Major mountain storms still pass through, with heavy rain in the valley and snow in the mountains. Indeed, snow can fall any day of the year in the mountains; sometimes it falls in the valley during the summer. Nonetheless, we begin to guide the Grand Teton in late June, usually one-on-one, with strong clients equipped with winter mountaineering gear. We have guides who love to climb in these conditions, but some of us prefer to wander the mountains in June, getting in shape for the summer season. Business is lean until July 4, the lower crags are not overrun with newcomers dropping rocks on one another, and guides can enjoy the treat of climbing together.

On a pleasant day in late June, Kim and I pack our gear to climb the Southwest Ridge Route on Symmetry Spire, a pillar of rock that rises four thousand feet directly above Jenny Lake. We will approach its high-angle rock climbs on its south face via Symmetry Couloir, another snow gully. Some people call it "Cemetery Couloir" because a fair number of people have died there from falls on snow.

Teton Boating runs several boats across Jenny Lake from 8:00 A.M. to 6:00 P.M. An earlier boat crosses to collect garbage at the boat dock on the other side. We are on the garbage boat. It is empty except for the two of us and an elderly couple on an early start up Cascade Canyon. Since Exum uses the boats to reach the rocks near Hidden Falls where we conduct climbing classes, we know the boat folks well. Kim and I joke with Brent Miller, the current boss, trade gossip with the boatmen, and wait for other people to arrive. None do, so we enjoy an uncrowded ride.

The lake is mute, calm, and blue—cobalt blue, the blue of smalt, the blue of the Mediterranean off the Greek islands. We ride in the back of the boat, out from under the roof, and watch Teewinot pass. As Owen and the Grand come into view, we can watch the Cathedral group float by, seen here from its best aspect. It is all picture-postcard-perfect. It is like a film. After a while, the range begins to look like pictures of it, not vice versa, as the power of photography erodes the power of experience. The morning light renders the snowfields a glistening white. Even the north face of the Grand looks inviting. No one speaks. Like us, the couple prefers to watch the world pass.

The lake is spotted with feeding cutthroats. I put my hand in the water, hoping to catch some insects, but don't. I leave it there, enjoying the rush of cold water.

Kim and I hike up a trail to a point where Symmetry Couloir enters from the right, then turn onto a small climber's path and ascend a thousand feet until we hit snow. Then we go different ways, each kicking our own steps. Kim, as usual, is wearing running shoes; I'm wearing lightweight boots. Ice axes are out. The day is warm, the snow perfect for kicking steps—like kicking steps in a snow cone. Although the snow is only moderately steep, it is steep enough to be dangerous. If you take a fall and do not know how to use an ice ax, or arrest yourself with your hands, you can go for a long ride with a nasty ending: over the waterfall at the bottom of the snowfield and into a deep moat between the waterfall and the next snowfield. You are either dead or trapped and injured, with ice water pouring over you—soon to be dead.

There are no climbers above us and no clouds on the horizon. Soon we have climbed a thousand feet of snow and are scrambling among whitebark pines on the saddle between Symmetry Spire and Ice Point. Below us is Cascade Creek and Jenny Lake. Our route on the southwest ridge of Symmetry rises above us like the prow of a great ship.

We have one climbing rope, a light rack, fuzzies, rain gear, hats, gloves, snack food, water—not much. Like sailing and fly-fishing, climbing is a sport with lots of equipment and virtually every climber is a gearhead, but we are going light—on purpose. To travel light is to travel with speed and freedom.

Climbing ropes are usually 50 meters, or 165 feet, long. The outer, protective sheath, usually brightly colored, resists abrasion, and, if treated, water; long inner strands of nylon give the rope strength. All modern ropes are sufficiently strong; they are distinguished by their color and by their feel, especially by the latter. A good rope is soft and pliable, like a snake.

The primary use of a rope is to belay the leading climber, usually with a belay device. Belaying is what makes climbing relatively safe. *Belay* is a nautical term, meaning to coil a rope around a cleat or pin in order to secure it. A belay, then, has two parts: a solid anchor and sufficient friction to bear a load. In climbing, people are tied to each end of the climbing rope via a knot and a climbing harness. One person is designated to lead, the other to belay. The belayer ties into something secure and feeds the rope to the leader through a friction device—usually an aluminum belay device—attached to the harness. Now the belayer is *anchored* and commands sufficient *friction* to hold a fall. The leader climbs up to another secure anchor, roughly a rope length higher on the cliff.

A rack is a collection of climbing gear carried on a wide sling across the chest, like a bandolier. From it hang snap links called carabiners, nuts, and cams. Carabiners are carried in chains of two or three. Nuts and cams are devices that are placed in cracks in such a manner that they cannot pull out if the leader falls but can be removed by the second climber as he or she climbs up. All of this hangs in a particular order from the chest sling. The order varies with the climber and is as personal as a fingerprint. The smell of a rack is faintly metallic, like the grindings after you sharpen a knife.

Climbing is thus a combination of individual effort and mutual responsibility: No one can pull you up a climb; you must do it yourself. On the other hand, your safety is in the hands of your partner. If the climbers are roughly equal, they take turns leading and belaying; if not, and this is the case in guiding, one person belays and the other leads.

Our climb goes up the eight-hundred-foot prow of steep rock, six long, relatively easy leads. The last two hundred feet to the top of the spire are scrambling. We pay attention to good belay anchors but place little protection. We've climbed this route many times, but we do not care; it is enough to be here, on warm rock, in the sky, in the great silence. We switch leads, soak up sun, and, except for abbreviated signals, rarely speak. Kim takes all the hard variations; I take the easy ones now, the ones I know by heart. We smile, knowing well each other's foibles.

Slowly the ground recedes. At first I notice the surrounding spires, but soon we are above them and the world seems grander, the Cathedral Peaks thousands of feet above us and Cascade Creek thousands of feet below.

When Kim climbs, I find it hard to estimate the difficulty. There are always the same adroit moves, the same assurance. Many climbers, even very good ones, are tentative, and watching them reminds me of a person exploring a book in braille. Kim is never tentative: He climbs like a leopard stalks, like a dolphin surfs. Mind, body, and environment fuse into the elegance and refinement of grace. Rolo is the only other person I know who climbs the same way: effortless.

The day passes. We do not bother going to the summit, but cross the top of the summit ridge and wander down to a notch west of the spire. Here a snowfield drops north into Hanging Canyon, a classic U-shaped, glacier-carved canyon containing three lakes that are still frozen, even in late June. Walking on snow, we skirt the uppermost one, the Lake of the Crags, along its southern shore, then pass Ram's Head Lake on the north side. The ice at the east end of Ram's Head has melted out. The water is black. It seems bottomless, deeper than the sea, mildly sinister—a black hole in a world of white.

Below the lake we climb down rock to more snow, then

plunge-step and slide five hundred feet to the trail. We arrive at the boat dock at four o'clock. We've seen no one else all day, but the dock is crowded with sightseers from Hidden Falls, hikers, other climbers, families with toddlers. The sky is still calm, the lake still the color of smalt, but the light on the mountains has changed. The snowfields are in shade; the peaks stand dark and gray against a paler sky. We throw our gear on the roof of the boat and wait our turn in line. After everyone else has boarded, we sit on the step of the boat. As the boat plows slowly across the lake, a child asks his mother, "Who made the Tetons?" It is not clear he's asking a question about God.

Since we've climbed it many times with friends and clients, Kim and I have a history with Symmetry Spire. My first contact came early in my climbing career. When we stopped for lunch during intermediate school at Exum in the summer of 1960, our instructor, Bill Bird, took the class down to the banks of Cascade Creek. My friend Dennis Fisher and I asked Bird what we should do after intermediate school—an advanced school, a climb, the Grand Teton? He pointed up at Symmetry Spire.

"Why don't you try the Durrance Ridge on Symmetry?" he said.

Today if I suggested to clients that they try the Durrance Ridge after intermediate school, I would be summarily fired. Liability law has changed since 1960, essentially eliminating any recommendation of adventure.

But in those good old days, guides sent kids willy-nilly into the mountains to try their hand at something difficult. After all, that's how the guides had learned—a bit of instruction, if they were lucky, from an older climber or one of the few climbing clubs, and then into the mountains with a friend to attempt an easy route on the peaks. Glenn Exum did the first ascent of what is now named the Exum Ridge on the Grand Teton when he was eighteen years old, solo, in cleated football shoes, with no climbing equipment, and with virtually no climbing experience. I was eighteen years old, Fisher a year older. Why shouldn't we try an easy route up a little eight-hundred-foot cliff?

We stopped at the DD Camera Corral, one of the few places in Jackson that sold climbing equipment in 1960, and I bought my first climbing gear. Fisher, though he was more talented on the rock than I was, adopted a wait-and-see attitude. I bought a 120-foot ⅜-inch nylon rope, climbing shoes, a few pitons, a length of nylon cord, a piton hammer, and the first edition of *A Climber's Guide to the Teton Range*. It was a small, thin book—159 pages, compared with the current 418-page third edition. To put it as kindly as possible: The route descriptions were vague.

The following weekend Fisher and I obtained a climbing permit from the Jenny Lake Ranger Station and slept in the campground. Early the next morning, but not early enough, we rode the boat across Jenny Lake and started searching for the approach trail.

Fortunately for us, most of the snow was gone from Symmetry Couloir—because we didn't have ice axes and wouldn't have had a clue how to use them if we did. Although we thought we were in good shape from our work, we did not reach the beginning of the climb until late morning. The day was clear, not a cloud in the sky. We roped up and started up the ridge, using the book we'd bought as our guide—I carried it in my pocket. The route, though easy, is steep, the line obscure, the big face intimidating.

We climbed slowly, placed no protection, and belayed without anchors, bracing ourselves as best we could and running the rope around our waists—there were no climbing harnesses in those days, no belay devices. We thought for sure there would be little trees, old pitons, and flakes to anchor to with my pathetic nylon cord and shiny carabiners. After all, these were all present at the rocks we used during climbing school. But no, not here. Soon we stalled about four hundred feet up the climb, unsure of how to proceed and learning the meaning of commitment.

Since climbing back down looked even worse than advancing into a vertical desert that looked increasingly difficult, we pressed ahead, but our leads became increasingly shorter, our moves more provisional. Had we been better prepared, it wouldn't have been bad, but we had virtually no equipment. Then, on one of my leads, I traversed too far right, toward a huge gash called Templeton's Crack. Now I was climbing on an sharp ridge with exposure on both sides, sort of like climbing up the corner of a building. I was scared. Fisher's belay was worthless, since he wasn't tied to anything. We were afraid to use our few precious pitons because we thought we might need them to get down. The afternoon passed.

Late in the day two climbers descending from the Southwest Ridge yelled to us, asking if we were all right. We replied in mindless folly: "Fine!" They headed on down the couloir. Soon it was early evening and we were stuck with nothing to bivouac in, not even rain gear. We had to retreat, but the face below us was terrifying. What to do? It was to become a common situation in the mountains, a situation I think of as the reckoning.

We banged in the pitons and tied them off with cord I cut off the piton hammer. We passed the climbing rope through the tied end of the cord, doubled it, and lowered ourselves sixty feet with the ropes wrapped around our body for friction, a primitive form of what is called rappelling. This didn't help much, and we had used up our pitons and cord. We cut twenty feet off the climbing rope, tied it around a large flake of rock, and rappelled another forty feet. Again: Cut a length off the climbing rope, rappel a short distance. Before long, the law of diminishing returns set in with a vengeance.

Our predicament dismayed us, but determined not to be rescued off our first climb, we coiled our little piece of rope and down-climbed the last two hundred feet to the ground. Descending the gully in the dark was not fun; we hung off tree limbs like monkeys; we slid down mossy slopes into what seemed oblivion. We could not find the trail right away, and when we did, it was three more miles around the lake to the parking lot. By the time we arrived, it was closer to dawn than to dusk.

We left a note at the Jenny Lake Ranger Station, apologizing for our late return and declaring we'd had a wonderful climb. I feared that if I told the truth, I would be banned from the Tetons forever. We didn't attempt another climb that summer.

Kim's history with Symmetry is darker, more serious. On August 4, 1983, he left with a client to climb the Direct Jensen Ridge, another classic route that he had climbed and guided many times. At 9:30, after he and his client had climbed the difficult leads, Kim fell on easy terrain. He had placed no protection and was eighty feet above a ledge. As he fell, he thought, "Oh no, I blew it. This is it."

When you fall, you drop like a rock, like a bomb going out a bomb-bay door. The terminal velocity of a falling human body is 125 miles an hour. You reach that speed in twelve seconds. Kim dropped thirty feet and hit his head, ripping off a flap of scalp the size of his hand, then fell another fifty feet (a total of eight floors) and landed in a pile of talus and boulders on a ledge. He hit feetfirst, leaning slightly backward, then crashed onto his hands.

Both fibula and tibia exploded from the inside out in compound bilateral fractures. The remains of both legs—a surgeon described them as "gravel"—were driven up into his knee, the right one causing a plateau fracture. The left ankle suffered a compound fracture. He herniated two disks in his lower back. Since he had extended his arms backward, he broke both wrists. He injured his shoulder. He cut his tongue and the inside of his mouth. He does not remember how many teeth were broken. Indeed, he remembers very little. He lay on the ledge, a mass of blood and pain. Shards of bone lay about him in the dirt.

His client called to climbers on other routes and soon someone started down the couloir with a message to the climbing rangers. At 1:35 they learned of the accident, the description being that Kim had broken his leg. A broken leg may be a big deal if it is your leg, but in the larger scheme of things, it is not a big deal. Getting a person with a broken leg off a mountain is a relatively straightforward procedure for the climbing rangers. Unfortunately, Kim didn't have just a broken leg.

Eight rangers assembled at the rescue cache. At 2:15 a helicopter ferried two of them to a landing spot at Ram's Head Lake in Hanging Canyon.

Among the first rangers to go in was Tom Kimbrough, one of Kim's oldest friends. They had climbed together in Yosemite and ski-patrolled at Alpine and Squaw Valley. Later they joined an expedition to the Cordillera Blanca of Peru. Boyd Everet, who led the expedition, was considering them for a climb of Dhaulagiri, 26,810 feet high and the sixth-tallest mountain in the world. But Kim and Tom found Everet and his fellow climbers to be inexperienced, at least by their standards. Bad vibes again. One learns to pay attention to vibes.

The next year an avalanche killed Everet, five other climbers, and two Sherpas while they were climbing that most beautiful Himalayan peak. Al Read came down with both pulmonary and cerebral edema, was unconscious for thirty-six hours, clinically decorticated, and woke up blind in one eye. Had not several other climbers wrapped him in a tent and dragged him from 16,000 feet down to 12,000, Al too would have died. It was the worst Himalayan disaster in the history of American mountaineering. Fortunately, Kim and Tom weren't there.

Rescuing people is never easy, but retrieving injured or dead friends is one of the worst things a climber endures. The trauma to flesh and bone is invariably severe; the limbs are twisted, sometimes frozen. Worse, you must handle the victims, often in intimate ways, move them, cause them more pain, or stuff them into body bags or bury them under rock cairns. At my age, many climbers have thirty or more dead climbing friends and acquaintances roaming their memory. They never leave. After emotionally taxing rescues, the climbing rangers go through a therapy session.

After the helicopter dropped them off, Kimbrough and another ranger, Jim Dorward, climbed the gully leading up Symmetry from Hanging Canyon, traversed over the summit ridge, climbed down the upper Jensen route, and rappelled to the ledge where Kim lay stricken. It was now 4:25. Kim had been lying on the ledge for seven hours and had lost a lot of blood. His blood pressure was 68/0, yet he was conscious the entire time. When Tom saw the extent of Kim's injuries, he went into shock. All he could do was hold the IV bottle.

Even though Tom was eight years older than Kim, he revered him. "Kim was a demigod," says Tom. "He was so strong, he had the energy of six people, and he was very fast." When he and his friend Jim Madsen arrived in Yosemite in 1963, they simply overpowered the hardest climbs, sometimes knocking days off previous speed records. When Madsen died, falling three thousand feet down the west face of El Capitan, in Yosemite, it did not slow Kim down.

Now Kim lay folded like a crushed doll.

"Kim was hurting bad," Tom says. "I've never seen anyone in that much pain who was still conscious. His legs could be bent in any direction, like tubes of sand."

The climbing rangers did what they could: IVs, painkillers, and MAST trousers—MAST (military antishock trousers) trousers being inflatable pants used to control blood pressure; now they were used to control bleeding and as splints for Kim's crushed legs.

The thought of lowering Kim down the Jensen Route was harrowing, and the wall above the ledge was too close to allow a small chopper to do a short haul—a procedure whereby the victim is placed in a litter, then attached to a cable so a helicopter can yank him off a ledge in one rapid motion. The rangers decided a larger helicopter was needed. A Huey helicopter borrowed from Hill Air Force Base near Salt Lake City arrived above the ledge at 6:45. Kim was placed in a litter, winched up into the belly of the chopper, and flown to St. John's Hospital in Jackson, arriving at 7:25.

The rangers climbed back over Symmetry and descended the gully into Hanging Canyon. They reached the boat dock at midnight.

Waiting at the hospital were two orthopedic surgeons, Ray Cunningham and Ken Lambert, and the head of the emergency room, Jill Riegel. All three knew Kim and had climbed with him. Later, doctors at a Kaiser hospital in California would tell Kim they would have summarily amputated both legs. Fortunately, the Jackson doctors thought otherwise.

Each doctor took a different body part and went to work. They worked on Kim for nine hours. Jill put two hundred stitches in his head and mouth. Ken and Ray put his legs, ankle, and knee back together with internal and external fixators. His legs looked as if they were held together with a stainless-steel Erector set. They fused the left ankle and removed the fibula in his right leg, leaving a small stump beneath the knee. They worked on bone and skin grafts. Two days later, when I saw Kim in the hospital, I wept.

Kim recovered slowly. Several times, he nearly lost one or both legs from infections. The holes in the front of his legs were devoid of bone or marrow; the skin grafts covering them were fragile, thin, brutalized. Stitches pulled out; bacteria got in. There were setbacks.

Kim's feet were so weak from his time in bed he broke both of them while trying to exercise. Ken patched them up.

Years passed; Kim endured two dozen operations. They cut off the top of the clavicle and repaired his shoulder. Despite his injuries and ongoing operations, he continued to climb. He broke his heel in a minor fall. While they were fixing his heel, Lambert decided to straighten Kim's right leg. It took nine more operations. Kim again returned to climbing and skiing. His life revolved around intense pain. It hurt to sit, it hurt to walk on level ground, and it hurt to stand still. The mental and emotion struggle was even more difficult. Kim needed painkillers to function; in a sense, no amount of them could eliminate his anguish. Several times he abused the drugs and crashed. Each time he returned.

The Japanese have an interesting word—*nen*. It means the smallest unit of time a human being can experience. At each *nen*, one can return—to whatever: a discipline, koan, partner, breath, home, compassion, the path. The decision to return is essential to Zen practice, a decision that gets easier with time. Kim climbed and skied with a fused ankle, he mastered his abuse problems, and he practiced Zen.

All that was years ago. He still climbs at a high standard, and he still guides. He works as a drug and alcohol counselor. In the winter, he often skis deep in the mountains, alone.

> *Dead drunk, flat on the sand—hey, don't laugh.*
> *From ancient times—few return from battle.*
> —ZENRINKUSHU

B y the end of June the serviceberry is blooming. Cottonwood Creek is full, though no longer at flood level. Lupine fills the meadows. Yellow pollen from the conifers coats the cabin porch;

when the wind blows, clouds of pollen drift through the forest. There are mayflies on the dishes, against the windows, in your hair. A few mosquitoes are about, surprisingly few—they are not a major problem in the meadows. In the evening the caddis hatch and dance their erratic dances in the last shafts of sunlight. Swallows are everywhere. I lie in my hammock and watch them feed in the sky. At dusk, bats arrive and compete with the swallows. Occasionally, a bat enters the cabin, flies around, then stops and hangs from the rafters. I leave the door open at night so it can fly out.

Summer is upon us, though it can still snow in the mountains, and nights are still chilly. On the morning of June 26, it is 30 degrees at the cabin. And yet, at just the point when the valley is blooming and green, when the mountains open, at just this point the sun drifts north, as though such splendor required its utmost effort and it must rest.

We enjoy our last days before guiding full-time. People patch cabins, do things with their kids. There are fifteen children at Guides Hill and in the rangers' cabins. Generations have grown up here. Sometimes they return and walk around to see as adults the paradise of their childhood summers. And it is a child's paradise: the creek, the meadows, the flowers, the animals and birds, the scary storms, the looming presence of mountains, the conviviality of a community, of many potluck dinners, the sense of extended family. These are rare now—the children cherish them.

My friend Casey Walker arrives with her children—Brooke, Kristin, Weston—and their friend Seren. They are from Northern California and have never seen Wyoming. Though only twelve and fourteen, Weston and Saren are competitive climbers. Soon they are on the climbing wall at the back of the Rescue Cache and working with Kimbrough on the bouldering problems at Jenny Lake. Kimbrough, who is the best sixty-year-old climber in the Rocky Mountains, is so impressed with their ability, he takes them to Blacktail Butte to try some hard climbs. At sixty he retains an elfin manner, which places kids at ease, even though they have just met him. They all return grinning, with bloated forearms and dreams of greater glory.

The children are most taken with the animals. I've heard the main reason people visit Yellowstone and Grand Teton National Park is for the animals, not the scenery, and I believe it. Something deep in our brain makes us love seeing herds of animals on savanna-like plains. Acting like a foraging or hunting party, the four kids wander the meadows and climb the lower slopes of Teewinot. To see them brown, half naked, moving rapidly through the grasses, kindles old memories. Exploring, they climb to waterfalls and sun-bathe; they encounter five marmots; they worry about bears, al-though a party of four is quite safe: There have been no known attacks on a party of four by a bear—grizzly or black.

They write and paint pictures in their journals of pronghorn, Lupine Meadows, and the Tetons. Casey drives them to Yellow-stone to see more animals—two grizzly, one feeding on a carcass, numerous elk, and several hundred bison. The week passes swiftly. When they leave, I feel old; their absence diminishes my own delight in the animals.

Summer begins, work begins—a round of rock-climbing schools, snow schools, easy one-day climbs, and, of course, ascents of the Grand. We are here because of the Grand; it is the reason for Guides Hill, the whole of this precious life.

# 7. To the Lower Saddle

 y early July the guide service is in full swing and some forty guides are working all over the range. At the end of July, or early August at the latest, the approach to the Lower Saddle is free of snow and the mountains are filled with hikers and climbers—too many hikers and climbers.

In 1987 the parking lot at the Lupine Meadows Trailhead was doubled in size, without consideration for the carrying capacity of the mountains above it. Now, on nice days, 140 cars are parked in the parking lot and up to another 70 are parked illegally in the sagebrush. Since the park estimates that each car averages 2.8 people, between 500 and 600 people a day are roaming the Garnet Canyon watershed. This is not a big area—less than eight square miles—and the few trails concentrate the density. It may be managed as a wilderness, but it certainly doesn't feel like wilderness.

Exum, of course, is part of the problem—a small part. Typically, we have some thirty people in the area. However, most of the guides climb the Grand once or twice a week from the Lower Saddle, so it seems we spend much of our summer walking up and down Garnet Canyon.

Climbing the Grand Teton is what Exum is all about. Glenn Exum and Paul Petzoldt started the guide service sixty-five years ago to climb the Grand Teton, and it still constitutes the bulk of our business. We call it "the Grand," "the Hill," "the Mountain," "the Big One," "the Big T," "the Grunt." Except for our strongest guides, it is never easy. I climb it once or twice a week from early July to mid-September. It is easier in September, but never easy.

We usually climb the Exum (or South) Ridge or the Owen Route on the west face. For both, we spend the night at our hut. It is eight miles and 5,000 feet up to the Saddle. In the early season, a third of the trip will be over snow; by late July we are walking a trail through talus and boulder fields. From our hut to the summit is another 2,170 feet of scrambling and technical rock climbing.

We walk up to the hut the first day, then climb the mountain and descend to the valley the second day. Many people say it is the hardest thing they have ever done or ever hope to do. For everyone, it is a source of pride and accomplishment. For some, it becomes a tradition: In some families, three generations have climbed the Grand Teton with Exum.

Because we climb the two routes so much, the guides enjoy an intimacy with what is, after all, a small mountain. I have climbed the Grand roughly three hundred times; Rod Newcomb and Dean Moore are probably approaching four hundred ascents.

Like all people who know a place intimately, we have names, methods, and traditions particular to our tribe. Jackson Hole Mountain Guides is another tribe with its own nomenclature, traditions, and methods. The climbing rangers are another. The park resource staff and biologists are still another. Together, these tribes know the mountains better than any people ever have.

Our work is a mixture of sophisticated technology and hard labor in a natural environment, all mediated by a distinct tribal culture. There is virtually no crossover between one tribe and another, no Shoshone becoming Sioux.

When we guide the Grand we meet our clients at the Exum office to check equipment and outline a rough itinerary and talk about hydration, pace, rest stops. We usually have three or four clients. Sometimes we take another three or four along with us, they will join a guide who has remained on the Saddle after a climb—what we call "a stay-over."

My clients today are Lisa, Jim, and Martin. Lisa and Jim are a couple from Minnesota. She teaches school; he sells computers. Martin writes computer code in Atlanta. They look fit and eager. The sky is clear; the weather report posted in the office calls for scattered afternoon thunderstorms—normal. We do not ask for more. We drive to the Lupine Meadows Trailhead and head into the mountains.

We pick huckleberries on the moraine leading to Garnet Canyon, but they aren't quite ripe. We see a black bear within ten yards of the trail—also eating huckleberries. Martin takes pictures; then we move on. The bear is busy eating berries and ignores us.

Summer flowers cloak the open slopes on the way to Garnet Canyon with sheets of yellow—mostly arrowleaf balsamroot, showy goldenrod, some mule's ear, and, in deep shade, arnica. Clumps of pink spirea and square-stemmed horsemint mingle with the scent of snowbush ceanothus. Higher up are long stretches of pussytoes, Indian paintbrush, wild buckwheat, yarrow, and cinquefoil. We stop every forty-five minutes or so to drink water and nibble. The trail is steep, the air warm. We are down to shorts and T-shirts.

As we wind into Garnet Canyon, the high peaks appear—every time, it seems, like magic. The breeze freshens and cools—the skin responds before the mind. We stop for a drink. Martin asks about the big black stripe on the east buttress of the Middle Teton. I explain that the metamorphic rock of the range sustained so much pressure it would split occasionally and magma from the earth's interior would seep in. The resulting solidified rock is called diabase; the intrusion itself, a dike.

We reach the Meadows, at 9,200 feet, a pleasant spot now that the snow has melted, with several small streams, willows, large boulders, and many flowers. Other guides are here with their clients; as we eat, more arrive. The clients spread out on the rocks to soak up the scenery while the guides gossip and play Cassandra with the weather.

Jim Kanzler is an avalanche and mountain weather forecaster for the Bridger-Teton National Forest in the winter. When I first met him, we shook hands and he said, "I'm Jim Kanzler, I'm from Montana, and I have a black heart." He's another velvet hand in an iron glove, a character structure that is ubiquitous in the guide service.

Kanzler is one of the few people I listen to when the talk turns to weather. He is never—it is a matter of principle—optimistic about the weather and never pessimistic, either. For him, it is always an open-ended "We'll see"—an attitude I appreciate.

If I try to be optimistic, he answers with a "Yeah, well . . ." If I am pessimistic, he answers with a "Yeah, well . . ." But between one "yeah" and the other "yeah," I learn about weather. When Jim Williams was guiding Everest, he kept up a lively debate with Kanzler via E-mail and phone. Everyone wants to know what Kanzler thinks about the weather. So we talk weather; we sprawl in the sun, drink, nibble, and admire the extravagant Lewis monkey flower—named for Capt. Merriwether Lewis—a woody species of cinquefoil, paintbrush, and elephant head, a spike of purple trunks that one cannot confuse with any other flower. Voracious marmots stare at us while we eat; their corpulence and gray-whiskered faces suggest they've lived well here over the years.

I mention the usual factoid: At this point we have covered half our elevation gain and two-thirds of the distance. Martin, ever analytic, remarks that this means the afternoon will be steep, and he's right. After lunch, we zigzag up switchbacks past Spalding Falls to the Petzoldt Caves (named for Paul Petzoldt), another rest stop with water, and new flowers.

As we ascend, we pass through different ecological zones. Here at 10,100 feet we enter the alpine zone, with its cushions of pink moss campion, skunk-smelling sky pilot, and the lacy delicacy of Grass of Parnassus, a circumboreal species one assumes grows on the mountain sacred to Apollo.

Above Petzoldt Caves is the hardest section of the Grunt, a long series of switchbacks to some dwarfed whitebark pine, followed by a long traverse west to Teepe Creek. For the first time, we can see the Saddle and the final steep Headwall. We keep moving; it is midafternoon now, scattered thunderclouds are blowing through, the sun is gone, the air is brittle.

Between Teepe Creek and the Headwall is half a mile of moraine ground up by the Middle Teton Glacier—boulders, talus, scree, and shards of rock. My way of distinguishing them is this: Boulders, you can't move; talus, you can move but can't throw; scree, you can throw; a shard, you can put in your shirt pocket. Jackson Hole looked like this ten thousand years, at the end of the last ice age when the first humans entered the valley. Just as the ascent takes you up through different ecological zones, it also takes you back into geological history.

The Middle Teton Glacier is still covered with snow; in places it is red with watermelon algae. A flock of ravens silently saunters about, pecking at the snow, feeding on moths. Two climbers are descending the Glacier Route on Middle Teton, turning back, I assume, since descending the route is neither easy nor pleasant. At the bottom of the glacier, streams of meltwater have cut moulins in the ice. Depending on the light, thin sections are pale turquoise or malachite green, but always pale, glowing. We wander slowly up the moraine until we reach the Headwall.

No guide likes going up the Headwall on snow with clients. The only thing we dislike more is coming down the Headwall on snow with clients. As soon as the fixed rope is open, we use it, even if the bottom is a mess of disintegrating sugar snow with no bottom. Anything is better than the Headwall on snow.

Kanzler and I climb the fixed rope and belay our clients up. Another guide, Sean Sullivan, ties in the clients at the bottom to make things go faster. Eventually everyone is up except one of my clients, and Sean takes off to the hut with his group. Kanzler is still there when I accidentally knock my pack off the ledge. It rolls down the cliff, across the ledge, down the next cliff onto the snow, and on down the snow, bouncing merrily. I curse both the pack and the fact that Kanzler is watching. Kanzler gives me his best vulture smile. "Yeah, well, gravity never sleeps."

I sheepishly retrieve my pack while my client waits. No matter; except for a short walk, we are through for the day. We fill our water bottles at a spring and head for the hut and hot drinks.

On the Saddle, the trail passes through more talus and boulders until it reaches a more level stretch studded with flowers, grass, and moss. There are clumps of king's crown the color of merlot, more mats of moss campion, clusters of petite alpine forget-me-nots (the park's official flower) with their tiny blue petals and hearts of gleaming yellow, alpine phlox in shades varying from white to pale lavender, yellow alpine buttercups, and white tuffs of alpine smelowskia. A few of the rocks are furred with lichen.

A variety of critters live on and around the Saddle. The most obvious bird is the raven. Usually, they are just traveling through, using the low point of the Saddle to save time and energy. They sail past on extended wings, then suddenly tuck them back and drop like black stones down the steep cliffs.

Rosy finches are common. Some are so tame, they will hop around your feet, looking for crumbs and such. In the autumn, migrating birds—ospreys, bald eagles, white pelicans, tundra swans—pass, but there is no one on the Saddle to see them.

For the past few years, we've watched a pair of peregrine falcons that have nested lower in the canyon. Many peregrines migrate, but these birds are resident. From below, they appear buff-colored, with a falcon's narrow tail and pointed wings. Sometimes we see them hovering above the Saddle in a stationary position, motionless in a torrent of wind. Other times we watch them swooping at the finches.

There are pack rats, some kind of shrew, probably a dwarf shrew, and a surprising number of insects, many of which serve as pollinators of alpine flowers.

A pine marten spends its summer in the ablation valley north of the Middle Teton moraine. I've seen it twice between the Upper and Lower Saddles and I've seen footprints on the summit. Once Peter Lev actually saw a marten on the summit. In the sixty-five years Exum has been on the Saddle, only one bear has been sighted. There are many marmots. There are also, of course, lots of climbers and guides, and often rangers. It was not always so: One of the park's first rangers, Fritiof Fryxell, noted that as recently as 1922 a season passed without a single ascent in the Teton Range.

When they arrive, the clients pile into the hut. We urge them to put on more clothes so they won't chill, and we offer them cups of hot fluid. After dinner, each guide goes out with his or her group, studies the route for the next day, and explains the schedule.

From the hut, the Grand Teton rises to the north and slightly east. The Exum Ridge is obvious in the slanted evening light, a sharp profile articulated by wind and ice. The true summit, at 13,770 feet, is not visible; it is slightly higher and several hundred yards to the northeast of what appears from here to be the summit, the so-called false summit. To the west of the main mass of the mountain is a notch—in mountain lingo, a col—and minor summit. This lower summit is part of an irregular mass of rock named the Enclosure, the second-highest summit in the range. The col is the Upper Saddle, at an elevation of 13,160 feet.

The topography of this great mass of rock is complex, but its main features are fairly easy to identify. From the false summit a steep ridge, serrated along its upper section with prominent towers, drops nearly 2,000 feet. This is the Exum Ridge. To its right is a broad buttress, less distinct than the Exum, which blends into the Exum about two-thirds of the way up the mountain—the Petzoldt Ridge. Farther to the right, on the eastern skyline, is the Underhill Ridge. Two gullies descend from the Upper Saddle, divided by yet another fractured ridge of triangularly shaped towers. On the right is the Exum Gully; on the left, the Idaho Express.

We will climb the Exum Ridge to the summit, descend part of the Owen Route on the west face, and rappel into the Upper Saddle. Then we will scramble 1,500 feet down to the Lower Saddle—all before lunchtime. Because nasty storms are possible in the afternoon—even after a clear morning—we like to be off the upper mountain by midday. In order to do this, we will rise at 3:00 A.M. and leave at 4:00. We are in bed at nine o'clock, even though it is still light and a big dark thunderstorm is cruising through a pinkish sunset.

Kanzler spends the evening with his battery-driven two-inch

Casio television set in a shallow cave named the Rat Cave. He watches news, sport, or the weather with the TV balanced in front of him on his sleeping bag. In the morning he is often a fount of trivia about, say, the Olympics, and always an accurate predictor of the day's weather.

I sleep between two huge boulders forming a cave that is well protected against the wind and provides a good view southwest, the path of storms. It is quiet in the cave and I get a respite from the clients. Climbing out of it at 3:00 A.M. is tricky and the resident wood rat a nuisance, but the silence and solitude repay the effort in spades. At this altitude, sleep is precious.

# 8. An Ascent of the Grand Teton

The summer night is short at this latitude. The sun rises and sets in the north. We watch it come up over mountains a hundred miles away; we watch it set over mountains a hundred miles away. Nonetheless, at 3:00 A.M. it is dark, especially in a cave. In the darkness I study the sky to the west and southwest, looking for lightning. I search for the faint glow of the rotating light at the Idaho Falls airport, seventy miles away. This light is one of my weather indicators. If I can see the airport light I know I usually will have time to get up and off the mountain.

The wind, the wind, the miserable wind. I carry my sleeping bag and sleeping pad back to the hut, but they threaten to disappear toward the Middle Teton Glacier, and several times I must refold them and reposition the bulk under my arms.

Our old hut—the so-called Smith hut—was a Quonset structure of steel poles and sheet metal. In late September 1981, a severe windstorm struck the Tetons. It was so bad that several climbing parties roped up and crawled down the trail off the Saddle. Two other climbers hid behind a boulder just to the west of the hut. Suddenly a gust broke several of the guy wires and the whole structure began to vibrate wildly, flopping and smashing on the ground until it trashed itself to pieces. Then it disappeared. We found parts of it in the Meadows.

The clients, somnolent, barely greet me when I enter the hut. They are unaccustomed to getting up at three o'clock in the morning, they have not slept well because of the altitude, and they are invariably dehydrated. The guides make tea for everyone and provide hot water for the client's instant gruels. Java addicts go to elaborate pains to make coffee. Most of the guides munch bagels. After an hour of eating and preparation, we leave for the summit.

Among the many pleasures of mountaineering is intimacy with the sky. Even among those who work outside, mountaineers are especially privileged because of their early alpine starts. We are up and about at night and experience dawn more often than most. Some of the best moments in mountaineering literature describe alpine starts from high huts. If you are not in shape, this is the worst part of the day; but if you are, the uphill grind with its rest stops allows ample time to enjoy the night sky. Not many moderns know Homer's rosy-fingered dawn.

If the weather is good, the Wyoming sky is dense with stars, the constellations vivid, present; not the vague, barely perceivable glimmer you see (if lucky) in suburbs and cities. These stars are intense, distinct, like crystal rivets in a sea of indigo. We are lucky.

From our hut, a good trail leads up to the southern ridge of the mountain. The ascent is gradual, beginning in dirt and mats of alpine plants, then zigzagging through talus and boulders. At sea level, you would think nothing of it, but we are climbing at 12,000 feet, it is dark, the clients' stomachs are leaden with a hard ball of instant oatmeal, the wind is howling, and you wish you were still asleep. If your IQ is greater than your height in inches, your mind whispers softly, "Maui, Maui, Maui. Why didn't I go to Maui?"

Most people do not believe they can walk outdoors at night, but starlight is quite adequate, especially at this altitude. Some of the guides don't use headlamps—not because they are cruel but because the multiple beams from five headlamps create weird shadows among the rocks and makes footing more hazardous than if there is only one light—the guide's—or none at all. I used to ascend without a headlamp, but as I've grown older, my night vision has diminished. Now I use a headlamp. This creates a problem if I turn in the direction of a lampless guide, as I face abuse for ruining their night vision—one of the many issues guides fuss about.

The walk is never quiet. Sometimes the wind is mild and warm; often it roars over the Saddle, hard and cold. Parkas flap violently, breathing is heavy, and boots scuffle on the rough trail.

I stop every ten minutes or so to let people catch their breath and to see if anyone sits down. I turn off my headlamp. Above us are muted voices and an occasional flash of light from Jim Williams's party. Below, the beams of other headlamps dance in the darkness like fireflies—some are from Exum parties, some from private parties. There are headlamps on the Saddle, on the Headwall, and far below on the moraine beside the Middle Teton Glacier.

In a calm between gusts I smell sky pilot and remember it prefers sites that have been disturbed—in this case, no doubt, by our path. It smells like a skunk, hence its more prosaic appellation: skunkweed. No matter; at this altitude, blue flowers are welcome. The smell is faint. I think they smell more when the sun is on them. It is said they smell more at lower altitudes because the scent is produced to repel ants and there are more ants lower down. I reach for it in the dark and rub my fingers over the leaves and enjoy the reek of this dark place.

We are on the southwest side of the mountain, opposite where the sun will rise—the darkest side—but on the side where we can study the sky for storms. I search again for the light at the Idaho Falls airport. I watch for lightning. I don't know how far you can see lightning from here, but pilots tell me it is probably 200 miles at least.

After twenty minutes to a half hour, we reach the Black Dike, another intrusion of diabase approximately thirty feet wide that cuts all the way through the southern end of the Grand Teton. We rest, drink water, adjust clothing, get our breath back. I check clients' health and attitude. We can send a client back down from the Black Dike without a guide, but not higher on the mountain.

Everyone is fine, quiet, breathing, enjoying a brief protection from the wind. Lights from the valley glitter like Christmas decorations. Even in the dark, I can make out Lisa's smile, Martin's ongoing calculations, Jim's anxiety. We rest longer than usual. I do not want to leave. I want to snatch a few minutes of peace, to lull about like a mariner or shepherd, simply watching and studying the night and the stars. One sadness of guiding is that we are always in a hurry. We will not reach the parking lot until dinnertime, and much can happen between now and then, so we must keep moving. I do not want to hurry. So much seems possible up near the empyrean stage of Greek mythology.

On the horizon is Eos, the Greek goddess of Dawn, who loved Orion, now prominent in the eastern sky—the great hunter with sword, shield, and club. The blur of the Great Orion nebula glows near the tip of his sword. Orion wished to rid the world of all wild animals, but fortunately, Artemis, the Lady of Wild Things, for whom all wild animals were sacred, and who was, furthermore, jealous of Eos's love for Orion, killed him with a silver arrow. Since he had been chasing the Pleiades, the daughters of Atlas and the nymph Pleione, they were all set into the sky as constellations. The Pleiades are overhead. They mark one horn of the constellation Taurus, the bull. His neck is another collection of Atlas's daughters—the Hyades. Atlas slept around before offending Perseus, who used the head of Medusa to turn him into a mountain—not a bad end, all things considered.

We scramble on in darkness. The path is steeper now; occasionally we must use handholds to make a move. After another twenty minutes we reach a series of seeps, where one can get water, if it is not frozen, but we keep moving. A few minutes later, we reach a pitch we call Briggs Slab, named after Bill Briggs, a former Exum guide who first skied the Grand Teton. We rope up and belay, climbing in the dark up an easy but exposed slab. Then we recoil the rope and decide whether we will go for the Exum Ridge or proceed to the Upper Saddle and do the Owen Route.

Everyone wants to do the Exum, and they are a strong team, so we climb up over a ridge of triangular towers that loom like foreboding gargoyles. Suddenly Williams yells back to me: "Look up." A few minutes ago the summit was clear; now it's hidden in a pall of cloud that drifts down the walls toward us. Another new cloud caps the summit of the Middle Teton. Below us to the west, wisps of cloud are blowing up the canyon at startling speed, growing as they come. The wind is up.

I yell back at Williams: "I don't like it."

"Me either," he yells. Nonetheless, we keep moving down into the Exum Gully. We don't have to make a decision yet, so we won't. In a few moments, we may get information that will allow us to make a better decision. Wait.

Before us is a sheer wall a thousand feet high rising from a large ledge ascending upward to the right: Wall Street. Because you look straight at it, Wall Street appears steep, but you could ride around it on a mountain bike. Reaching Wall Street requires crossing the Exum Couloir, a wide, broken gully filled with boulders and talus. Until early July an ice field here requires time and attention, but now the half hour to the end of Wall Street is walking and scrambling. At its end, Wall Street narrows, then fractures into several ledges beginning at a small alcove that is both cloistered and exposed.

Williams is there, roping his two clients. Clouds are everywhere now; the peaks are steaming with them, forming summit caps as they catch the wind. Everyone is breathing hard, slurping water. They try to remember what to do with the ropes—uncoiling, stacking, finding the middle, tying in with appropriate knots, recoiling—the stuff they thought they had mastered in intermediate school. But under pressure and given the uncertainty of the weather and the terrifying exposure just beyond the alcove, they simply forget. We expect this and do much of the work for them, knowing well that they are dealing as best they can with their minds, their lungs, their fluttering bellies. I check knots and go through the signals again.

Williams and I continue muttering about the clouds. When we see Kanzler and his clients below us in the Exum Gully, we decide to wait for our weather oracle to catch up. In uncertain conditions like this, we like our decisions to be unanimous, and if we do decide to climb on, we stick together. So we wait and I talk about the climb to keep the clients' attention off the exposure.

The Exum Ridge is one of the classic climbs of North America. This narrow ledge on Wall Street ends in a bottomless chimney just short of the actual ridge. Glenn Exum jumped across this slot in his leather football shoes on July 15, 1931. He was unroped on his way up the first ascent—and the first solo ascent—of the Exum Ridge. The route is not difficult in good conditions; bad conditions are another matter. All of the guides have done the ridge in bad conditions—despite good judgment and a clear view of approaching weather. Sometimes we climb because we have strong clients and simply want the adventure; sometimes we say we will take a look, then go on because we hate the idea of retreating; sometimes the unpredictability of mountain weather simply jinxes what we do.

In any case, when things get grim, it's because of ice. Climbing in the rain is not pleasant, but it is straightforward—in Wales, they climb in the rain every day. Snow is not too bad either, since it is usually a squall and the rock is cold, so nothing sticks. Ice is a different matter.

Rime ice forms when the mountain is shrouded in cloud or fog, the water droplets are colder than 32 degrees and the wind is blowing. Feathers of rime ice grow into the wind: The stronger the wind, the longer the feathers. Rime ice is greasy, lubricating everything it touches. Climbing on it is like climbing on lard. Rime is also very beautiful. Few sights in the mountains are more grand than a steep ridge of good granite rimed with a filigree of ice crystals gleaming against the sky. Climbing on rime is always dicey, even if you are with another experienced climber; climbing on rime ice with three people who have only two days of climbing experience is mental torture.

Then there is verglas. Verglas forms when water flows over a cold surface and freezes. It is nearly always a shiny blackness darker than anything around it, so it can be avoided, if you can see it. In the dark it's hard to see it. If there is a lot of it, you can use crampons. All things considered, verglas is nicer than rime.

Since the village of Moose averages only thirty frost-free days a year and the mountain is a mile and a half higher, I imagine there are only several weeks a year when the upper mountain doesn't freeze. So if we have rain or cloud cover when it's cold, we have ice.

Williams and I continue to wait at the alcove. It does not look good: clouds swirling everywhere, lenticular clouds over the peaks. Directly to the south of us the Middle Teton glows in the muted light of dawn. Clouds sail over the Saddle, then beneath us, making the exposure even more noticeable, about a thousand-foot sheer drop-off—like standing on the top of the Empire State Building and peeking over the edge. Lisa and Martin are fine. Jim is tense and scared. You can always tell when someone is scared. Fear is the mind killer. They lose the finer mental abilities first: a sense of beauty, a sense of proportion, and, especially, a sense of humor.

Like, say, fighter pilots, surgeons, and hit men, climbers have a prizewinning talent for dissociating from emotion, a quality that is useful in the mountains. It is considerably less useful in relationships. As we say, when the going gets rough, the weird turn pro. That is, we dissociate. Most clients are not so blessed. As I watch the clouds build, I exercise my talent. When Kanzler arrives, I walk down Wall Street to where he's roping up.

"What do you think about the weather?" I ask.

"Spooky."

"Anything more helpful, James?"

"Yeah, well . . ." What follows is a technical discourse with big words I don't understand. I'm impressed.

"How in the hell do you know all that by looking around?"

"No big deal. I did a complete weather analysis yesterday for Doug Chabot [another Exum guide] so he wouldn't get fried on the north face. I think it's going to be weird this morning, then clear, then come back tonight. The main storm is north of us."

"Really. Well, I'm glad I'm not on the north face."

I yell back to Williams and he starts the lead off Wall Street. When his clients have gone, I place a large cam unit in a crack, clip it, and smile at my clients. "Civility pro. So if I fall, I won't rip you all off the ledge into the great void. Remember Civics 101?" Silence.

"Come on. I told you last night that it would look grim, and it does look grim, but it is easy. Without the exposure you wouldn't even need a rope." Silence. No one ever believes me.

And in my heart I don't blame them. I don't like the lead off Wall Street, even though it is indeed easy, even though I have climbed it many times, in high wind and no wind, in the dark and on still, sunny mornings, in the dark with a headlamp, in the dark with no headlamp, when dry, when wet with rain, when greasy with rime, when laced with verglas. I have climbed down it in snow with no belay, with and without gloves, climbed it in technical climbing shoes, running shoes, hiking boots, heavy mountaineering boots. No matter. Despite all that, the lead off Wall Street is still eerie.

I sidle across the ledge, loudly whimpering and complaining. Just before I disappear around the corner, I stop, look back, and smile. Lisa is the only one smiling back. After forty feet I reach a white triangular flake. I stand up on it with both feet, then reach up to the ledge above for several moderate handholds. I do a little pas de deux, stepping in front of my right foot with my left to smear it onto a sloping foothold. Then I stretch way off to the right with my right foot until I reach a small black foothold. I shift my weight onto the right leg, pull, grab a chock stone in the chimney, switch feet, stem up the chimney for several moves, and exit right behind a large boulder. The feeling is not so much one of difficulty as one of vulnerability. If you fell, it would be like falling down an elevator shaft. People rarely have trouble with the move; they do have trouble looking down.

Above are twelve leads to the summit. I bring Lisa over and check that she is set up to belay correctly. Most of the time we will be belaying with sitting-hip belays in good stances, with several people climbing, several belaying—a moving chain. In the mountains, the quality of a belay position must be weighed against the factor of speed, for in the mountains speed is safety.

The eastern sky is light, the shadows beneath us fainter. Suddenly the Middle Teton glows, severe and golden under the first rays of sunlight. With the sun up, the clouds begin to dissipate.

I climb the next lead, the Golden Staircase, up some of the most beautiful rock in the Teton Range, orange and yellow rock with cups and nubbins and chicken heads and a wavy, thin flake blasted by eons of blowing ice. It is still cold. My hat is over my ears, my hood up, my hands stiff. No gloves, though. I hate climbing in gloves and don them only as a last resort.

Far to the southwest the shadow of the Grand Teton separates from the earth's greater shadow into a purple sky, a lone shadow, dark and shaped like a tooth—the mountain's ghost, I think, its shade. As it approaches, it grows larger and diffuse until it is finally just another shadow among many.

We stop so Jim can take photographs. He points the camera here and there—*snap, snap.* Chris remarks that no camera can take it all in with anything approaching the appropriate scale, not even a panoramic camera. The best one can do, I say, is paste a series of pictures together, but then the sense of severe exposure is gone, not to mention the sky above, tinged with wisps of pink cirrus. The full expanse, the grandeur, cannot be represented, only experienced.

After another belay on easy rock, we coil the ropes and walk with the coils several hundred feet up and across the ridge to the Wind Tunnel, a slit in the ridge that sucks air off the big face above Wall Street and funnels it onto the eastern side of the mountain. We move slowly in the cold; the wind blasts, battering us. I am a bit grumpy over their confusion about walking with coils, something we start teaching in basic school. When they mutter defenses, I say, "Hey, when the going gets tough, the weird turn pro." This is sufficiently opaque to make everyone pay attention.

Above the Wind Tunnel, we enter a wide gully that goes straight up the mountain just to the east of the towers that are so prominent from the Lower Saddle. The mountain opens to us. The ridge above is sunlit; there is light instead of humbling darkness, a feeling of refuge instead of exposure. We climb five leads up the right side of the gully, easy leads with good belays. The sixth pitch, called the Double Cracks, takes us into the sun. We have traversed left out of the gully to the edge of the huge face above Wall Street, left the place of trolls and entered the place of elves. In the sun, climbing becomes friendly.

The next lead is the crux of the climb, the Friction Pitch. Since we are right at the edge of a ridge several thousand feet up in the air, there is a heightened sense of exposure. The lead goes up this airy face of cups and small nubbins to a series of platforms marvelously overhanging the void to the west. The climbers in the team can't see one another, and this makes things even more scary. The lead is long and hard to protect, since there are few cracks for nuts or cams. Most guides climb it without protection and anchor at the top. When I clip in, I always sigh with relief.

Looking down on a party climbing up to these platforms is the finest view on the Exum Ridge. The rock arches right over space, the climbers in bright Gore-Tex hues are in the sun on yellowish rock, while 2,500 feet below is the Middle Teton Glacier with its crevasses and bergschrunds.

If the wind is blowing hard—as it often is—the lead is a fine line between being careful on something one has climbed many times and sheer terror at the possibility of being blown off. One grips close to the rock in precisely the manner that we forbid beginners to do in basic class. Your body instinctively seeks a position with no air between you and the rock, because the wind is now more dangerous than gravity.

On one occasion the wind blew so hard on the Friction Pitch that I bit a nubbin of rock while I moved my right hand to the next hold. A young lady from Southern Methodist University was behind me on the rope that day. She was a fine athlete, but was inclined to comment on every difficulty. I belayed her up. About thirty feet beneath me, she froze. "I can't do this," she yelled.

I was silent.

"I can't do this!"

"Well," I yelled, "you have to do it, because we can't go down."

Eventually she would tire of being in that exposed position. The gusts would pound her. She would become desperate and try something, anything. I yanked on the rope.

Louder: "I can't do this."

"You must!"

"I do not. My daddy can come get me with a helicopter."

Spoken like a true southern lady, but false: no daddy, no helicopter.

I waited for her to accept the reality of her situation. There is a point at which one cannot turn back. As Rilke says in another context, this is the point that must be reached, the threshold where something real and important is at stake, the threshold that leads to magic. In climbing, the source of the magic is this: *You can't be bored and scared at the same time.* Even though you are standing on sloping holds over thousands of feet of air, eventually you will get bored and try something, *anything*. And then the magic: The mind lets go; the will leaps forward.

After a few more minutes she climbed up. The gusts were so grim, I didn't even tease her about the helicopter. We lay against the rock with our bodies bent away from the wind, entwined in an intimacy of necessity, the withering blasts humbling all sense of propriety. After she tied off to the anchor, I jerked on the rope attaching her to the next climber as hard as I could: no one could hear signals that day.

But today the wind is mild, the Friction Pitch is mellow, and everyone climbs rapidly. We stop to drink and snack and admire the airy spectacle. Like most clients these days, my gang is loaded down with high-tech goodies: PowerBars, Clif Bars, and various treats offering large amounts of protein. I refuse their offers. To bite into a PowerBar when it is cold is to chomp into a serious adhesive, like those that hold airplanes together. It affixes to your molars with alarming tenacity. Try to release its grip and you risk your crowns, your fillings, that funky old wisdom tooth. Tearing it off is like ripping a chunk out of Levi's with your teeth. Clif Bars are no better, but for different reasons: They are best left to heartier species of ungulates. And protein? By the time your body can use the protein, you will be back in your car; then, if you are smart, you will be powering Mexican beer, chips, and green salsa as you drive to the nearest pizza joint. I expound on these matters while I eat my Snickers bar—one of the great achievements of Western civilization.

We wander upward for several hundred yards, walking and scrambling in coils. We belay one lead up a smooth slab of rock named the Unsoeld Variation, then walk in coils again to a dark, wet chimney best climbed by jamming one's hands in cracks above one's head. Lisa and Martin do great; Jim is still a bit shaky. Now he's worrying about getting off the mountain, even though he still hasn't made it to the top. Chronic worriers love climbing mountains—so many things to worry about, most of them fatal.

Two more easy leads and we are on the summit ridge with glorious views all around. Then we scramble along in coils toward the summit, now only several hundred yards off to the northeast. The weather is clear, only puffy clouds on the horizon. We've been lucky.

Like everyone who works outdoors, climbers develop an exquisite sensitivity to weather, constantly guessing and predicting, shuffling variables, learning.

Fifteen years ago, I was less lucky on this ridge. A mean thunderhead approached us from the west that day; however, I could see sunlight beyond it, so I thought it was a narrow storm. But it was huge. An anvil-shaped mass probably 30,000 feet high stretched south for forty miles; the jet stream raked its cap, throwing shreds of false cirrus in its path. Lightning bounced around in it like pool balls.

The wind was from the west, but the cloud was moving north. I could not tell from the wind alone where the storm would go, because the mountains funnel and shift air currents and hence wind direction. I was a bit worried, but I guessed the storm would pass to the northwest. I was wrong. Suddenly the top of the mountain became charged with electricity and the rock buzzed like a million flies working a windowpane.

I cannot recall if we went to the summit or not; I think not. Somehow we scuttled off the ridge onto the descent route and managed to get down a section of slabs before the storm hit. We untied the wet ropes and coiled them; we put on all our clothes. I told everyone to crouch, feet together, allowing only one point of contact with the ropes or packs. We crouched on our exposed ledge at 13,500 feet and waited.

Normally we view clouds in two dimensions. This thunder-

Teewinot and Lupine Meadows in the winter. JACK TURNER

The cabin, May 1.
JACK TURNER

The north face of Buck Mountain. Mark Newcomb
skied down both of these snow couloirs. AL READ

Mark Newcomb skiing in the east couloir of the north face of Buck Mountain. MARK NEWCOMB

The Cathedral Peaks from the northeast: Teewinot,
the Grand Teton, and Mount Owen. JACK TURNER

A dipper. JEFF FOOTT

The Exum hut on the Lower Saddle. AL READ

Climbers on the Exum Ridge Route,
with the Middle Teton Glacier 2,000 feet below. AL READ

Climbers on the summit of the Grand Teton. JACK TURNER

Moose Basin Patrol Cabin. Weston Walker (left)
and Ranger Dan Burgette. WESTON WALKER

The Teton Range in winter. JEFF FOOTT

storm arrived as a layered three-dimensional mass six miles high. Seven thousand feet below us, bluish lines of squalls dumped rain across the valleys. The layer level with us was chaotic with disturbance, a maw of whirling vapors and faintly greenish light. Above us, mature cumulonimbus bulged like muscles; higher yet, ribbons of cirrostratus disintegrated like spiraled nebula. The world became lurid, apocalyptic—the mise-en-scène of opera. Visibility dropped to fifty feet. My climbing gear hummed in tune with minute halos of fuzzy sparks covering every metal surface. The rock buzzed in varying frequencies, like alarms.

Just before the cloud cover closed over us, a lightning bolt hit a glacier and turned it green. The world dimmed, the wind grew fierce, and graupel stung our faces and hands so hard that we shoved our hands into our armpits and put our heads to our knees. One of the men in my party asked if there was anything else we could do—the last clutch for control.

"You might try prayer," I replied. "We all have to die sometime. This is as good a place as any." All climbing humor is black humor, the joke of no control, the levity of fate.

Instantly—how else?—a light appeared in the cloud, looking and sounding like a big sparkler at a Fourth of July celebration. A bolt of lightning hit the ridge 200 feet above us. Several of us bounced in the air and landed on our elbows and knees in the talus. We scrambled back into our positions, wordless with terror. I noticed I was twitching, whether from fear or electricity, I do not know. The air stank of sulfur.

We waited. The wind dropped, then resumed, blowing hard from the south. I remembered the forty-mile-long train of cumulus. Ground currents from lightning strikes on the ridge hit us four times in twenty-five minutes. It snowed four inches. Still we waited.

Moving would be worse: The shocks could knock us off while

we were climbing; the cracks and chimneys below us were streaming with water, which provided a natural conductor for electricity; and being tied together with a wet rope in such conditions is plain stupid.

In Cascade Canyon, 7,000 feet below us, the storm was so severe it closed the Exum climbing schools for the day. For a while it stopped the boats from crossing Jenny Lake. Two climbing parties below us on the Exum Ridge suffered burns.

Finally the dull grayness of our cloud lightened and the edge of the storm arrived, ragged with billowing gauzy clouds. The sky changed so fast from sun to mist the effect was kaleidoscopic. Then we broke clear. The sky was pure lapis lazuli and filled with speeding columns of cumulus—facing them was like being blown through a temple in the sky.

Squalls filled the valleys to the west. To the south, another thunderhead moved slowly toward us. We climbed down toward the rappel anchor on the Owen Route that would put us on the Upper Saddle and off the top of the mountain. We tied into one wet rope, close together, and moved cautiously, belaying often. Where it was too steep to hold the snow, the wet rocks gleamed like quicksilver beneath the glare of the sun. The world seemed fresh, newly minted. The climbing was slick, scary. As always in such situations, I retreated into the climber's sanctuary—dissociation and method.

The black wall kept coming. It hit us as we reached the rappel point. More graupel, lightning, snow, blasts of wind. We turned away from it, bending into the stone wall as if, finally, in prayer. Again we waited. The second storm passed. I belayed the four men as they rappelled to the Upper Saddle. No one spoke. As Flannery O'Connor said, "Nothing produces silence like experience."

The fates had touched us lightly and withdrawn, leaving us with the freedom and glory of life. We were overjoyed but also too humbled to talk—it might anger the gods.

The summit of the Grand Teton is on the northeast corner of the summit block, amid shattered blocks of gneiss. We can see for 100 to 150 miles in every direction, each horizon rimmed by mountain ranges. To the east, the Absaroka, Gros Ventre, and Wind River; to the south, the Salt River, Snake, and Caribou; to the west, the Big Hole and the Lost River; and to the north, the Centennial, Madison, Gallatin, and Beartooth. Directly north is the blur of a geyser somewhere near Old Faithful, fifty-two miles away, in Yellowstone.

Everyone is happy. Lisa, Jim, and Martin are happy because they have achieved their goal. I'm happy because it is only 8:15—they have climbed rapidly and well—and the sky is clear.

Williams leaves for the rappel just as we arrive. Kanzler arrives on top a few minutes later. Everyone is taking photographs—of all of us in all possible combinations. I crawl down to a little ledge east of the summit, wanting a few minutes alone. In the parking lot 7,000 feet below, the windshields of our cars sparkle like tiny mirrors. Beside me are a few tufts of grass, fescue. I slice and eat an apple; I munch on cashews; I enjoy the clarity and count shades of blue as the sky pales into the distant mountains.

Despite the breadth of view, I always feel the summit is a place of great simplicity; but at 13,770 feet above sea level, one's perspective changes. Like the view from an airplane, one sees things that are invisible at ground level; but unlike the keyhole view from an airplane window, this view is expansive and whole, without artificial boundaries. Nor is one sealed in a machine, watching the scenery pass like a tracking shot in a movie and enduring the cacophony of roaring engines. The view from the Grand Teton is panoramic and embedded in silence, both of which invite reflection.

Here all the senses are clear, heightened, and vitally alive, for to reach this summit one uses the body, and in the face of perceived danger the senses grow keen, increasing one's chances of survival. One feels exulted, flushed with joy; the word *exult* is from the Latin *exultare*, "to spring out," and we have sprung free of the quotidian.

Like the perspective of earth that spacecraft provide from outer space, the view from the summit enhances some forms and diminishes others. The most obvious change is in boundaries. Most of the man-made boundaries—for example, the lines demarcating states, countries, city limits, private property, national forests, game refuges, and water districts—are diminished, though they do not disappear. Natural boundaries—for example, the patterns of vegetation and topology that emerge due to water, wind, rock, soil, and temperature—are emphasized. In a way that is never true at ground level, here one *sees* watersheds and bioregions.

Since what we see influences what we think, those who spend time on summits often disagree with those whose vision reflects more limited perspectives. I do not believe it is an accident that many leaders of modern conservation and bioregional movements—John Muir, David Brower, Arne Naess, George Sessions, Gary Snyder—have been mountaineers.

From this vantage point, one can also discern how the land has been affected by man. The land immediately east of the Grand Teton—peaks, canyons, and much of the plain surrounding the Snake River—is protected by the park. West of the Grand Teton is the Jedediah Smith Wilderness, part of Targhee National Forest. Farther west is the Teton Valley or Pierre's Hole, the place Jim Bridger thought was the finest valley in the American West.

Ranching, farming, and logging has chopped it into squares; now it looks like someone took a knife to the face of a beautiful woman. East and south sit the communities of Moran, Moose, Kelly, Jackson, and Wilson, with their junctures of highways and dense human populations. From this bird's-eye view, the explanatory principle is simple: What was protected by a handful of nature's patrons and the federal government remains beautiful; what was not protected has been forever despoiled for the benefit of a few.

Rosy finches arrive and wander about my feet. They are black, with a gray crown and patches of dusty rose about the belly, rump, and wings. Rosy finches are a true mountain resident, loving steep cliffs and snowfields, though in the winter they descend into the valley, often in large flocks.

What do they eat? What are they doing up here? The air up here is by no means empty. As naturalist David Lukas asks us to contemplate: "Consider that the atmosphere over a single square mile of the earth's surface contains twenty-five million airborne insects. Consider that the fraction of organic detritus that falls out of orbit can become thick enough to plow. Consider that within a very tall, imaginary top hat, fifty to one hundred million micro-organisms swirl above your head." The air is just another ecosystem, one that seems to favor spiders especially—flying spiders, spider legs, pieces of spiders. And there are indeed spiders on top of the Grand Teton.

I assume shrews are on the mountain, though I have seen one only once, and that was lower down—near the Upper Saddle. I assume it was a dwarf shrew, since they are the only shrew likely to be this high. Dwarf shrews are tiny, only three inches in length, and can weigh less than half an ounce. They are the smallest mammal in North America and they are rare. Between 1895 and 1960, only eighteen specimens were known from their entire range; as recently as 1989, only thirty-seven specimens had been trapped in the entire Greater Yellowstone ecosystem.

I look down the East Ridge for marmots, pikas, and pine martens. I've seen their tracks here, and over the years I have spotted two between the Upper and Lower Saddles; there is nothing today but the beautiful cornice at the top of the ridge.

No one knows what lives up here in winter, but when Jack Tackle and Alex Lowe reached the summit after completing the first winter ascent of the north ridge, they found it covered with tracks and an animal they believe was a fisher was wandering off down the west face toward the rappel!

When I'm on top of the Grand Teton, I always look and listen for white pelicans, though I've seen them only twice during the thirty-odd years I've climbed this mountain, and both times I've heard them before seeing them. The sounds are faint, so faint that they are sometimes lost—a trace of clacking in the sky. It is even harder to see them. Tiny glints, like slivers of ice, are occasionally visible, them invisible, then visible again as the sheen of their feathers strikes just the right angle to the sun. With binoculars you can see them clearly: Usually they are soaring in a tight circle far above the summit. Since this summit is 13,770 feet high, and in good light a flock of white pelicans is easily visible at a mile, the pelicans were at least a mile above us, or higher than 19,000 feet. This seems high for any bird, but geese have been photographed at 29,000 feet, and I have watched flocks of Brahminy ducks from Siberia cross the ridge between Everest and Cho Oyu, which is 19,500 feet at its low point. So although 19,000 feet is impressive, and no one knows how high pelicans can or do fly, the more interesting question is this: What are they *doing* up there? Soaring. Clacking. Yes, but why? I don't think anybody knows.

I have also seen them from the summit of Symmetry Spire and

from the long ridge on Rendezvous Mountain. But it is rare—in part, I think, because the conditions for hearing and seeing them are so rare. Perhaps they are often above us, but with the wind and clouds and the ever-present anxiety of climbing, we fail to notice them.

After half an hour on the summit, we leave. The weather holds for us and the descent is uneventful. We scramble several hundred feet down the Owen Route at the top of the west face, then belay three short leads in Sargent's Chimney before scrambling several more hundred feet down to the rappel.

The rappel off the Grand Teton is another spooky place. Technically, it is straightforward: The first half is on steep rock; the last half is in midair. The landing area is roomy, the distance only a hundred feet. However, the ledge approaching the rappel anchor is narrow and filled with rubble that funnels into overhanging cracks: Anything knocked off can hit people below. Further, you can't see the bottom of the rappel from the start, though it is obvious it will take you down to the safety of the Upper Saddle. Instinctively the eye wanders northwest to the icy chutes at the top of the Black Ice Couloir, a difficult climb that drops 3,000 feet into Valhalla Canyon. There is no sunlight on this side of the mountain yet, either; it's cold again, and the wind always blows here. Often a line of climbers are waiting to get off the mountain. The stress builds.

Today there is no line and Williams has left a rope hanging for me. I belay my group without a hitch. It is not always so. To face a storm here is always wild. We are on a ledge at the side of a notch near the summit of an isolated mountain. The notch accelerates the wind, the ledge is on the west-southwest side of the mountain, right in the path of storms.

I usually anchor, tie off the rappel rope, carefully lap it into several hanks, and throw it as hard as I can straight down the cliff.

Sometimes during a windy storm this doesn't work. Even though the rope is soaked with water, it drifts downward slowly; then it stops and uncoils into the air like an enormous snake before the next gust blows it back up the cliff, sometimes thirty feet past me into the rocks above. Sometimes another guide rappels first to get the rope down; other times, we just lower clients to the ground. In any case, the bottom of the rappel is another one of those places on the mountain that always bring a sigh of relief.

When we are all down, I coil the rope and take them down to the Upper Saddle proper for a good look down the Black Ice Couloir. Some people just can't believe Mark Newcomb and Stephen Koch have gone down there on skis and a snowboard. There are days when I don't believe it, either.

Just above us to the west is the summit of the Enclosure. The first ascent party found a ring of upturned black rocks on the summit, an obviously artificial arrangement that has led to speculations that it is everything from an American Indian vision-quest site to an entrance for little purple people who live under the mountain and have, let us say, a mysterious relationship to the Essences and certain Christian saints. I am inclined to the former interpretation. Lisa and Jim want to see it, so we dump our packs and scramble several hundred feet to the summit. The view of the Grand is great: You can see the Exum Ridge from the side and look straight at the Owen Route, our descent route, the route taken by the first ascent party, and the most popular route on the mountain.

Lisa, Jim, and Martin sit in the ring of black stones while I take their picture. Then I tell them a story about the huge face that drops off to the north so sharply you don't even notice it's there until you wander a few feet in that direction. Then you have the urge to sit down. The north face of the Enclosure is a great shield of rock that is home to the hardest routes in the Teton Range, routes that are cold, lonely, and rarely climbed. I've been on the north side of the Enclosure only six times in all these years, and it has always been an adventure.

On August 6, 1969, George Lowe, Leigh Ortenburger, and I bushwhacked up Valhalla Canyon, following a supposed trail that Ortenburger found, then lost, then found again. He knew, in his Ortenburgerish way, of a small, obscure shelf on the east side of Valhalla, snug against the big northwest face of Mount Owen, where there was space for three people to sleep—I call it Ortenburger's Ledge. It is, I swear, the only flat place in Valhalla Canyon. I doubt if anyone but Ortenburger even dreamed, much less knew, of its existence. Many climbers have climbed in the Tetons for twenty years without even entering Valhalla, much less spending the night. And for good reason—the upper sections are dark and ominous. Some never see sunlight.

Two ice routes—the Black Ice Couloir and the Enclosure Couloir—had been climbed by a few parties, including Exum guides Al Read, Peter Lev, and Herb Swedlund, but the big buttress between them remained untouched. Again, for good reason. It looked more like a buttress in Yosemite than anything in the Tetons: It was smooth and broken only by a system of chimneys and cracks that were wet, icy, and the wrong size—what we call off-widths. An off-width is too big to jam any part of your body into and too small to use the technique known as chimneying—back on one side, feet on the other—the way kids scamper up doorjambs in the kitchen.

Leigh knew every major route left to climb in these mountains—he was, after all, the author of the climbing guide to the range. He knew the north face of the Enclosure was one of the best unclimbed routes. He also knew it was going to be over his head—thus he badgered me and George to accompany him.

He had recruited us, but it was his vision, his will that led us to a bivouac on that ludicrous ledge, studying what was obviously a very serious piece of work. Leigh was, in his usual elfish manner, delighted to be there—he was delighted to be anywhere in the mountains. I squinted at the buttress and thought, What a mean-looking son of a bitch. We ate dinner and crashed. At least the weather looked good.

We left the next morning as soon as it was light enough to move, traversing up and right toward the junction of the Back Ice and Enclosure couloirs. For a while, we had scree and easy slab climbing, but eventually we hit sheets of ice. We stopped; out came the ice gear. At that point it was obvious we faced a generation gap.

George and I had 70cm Chouinard ice axes with hickory handles and drooped picks. Leigh carried something that might have been taken up the Matterhorn in 1865: It was long, the pick was straight, and it had a wrist loop, for God's sake. Yvon Chouinard, the patron saint of American ice climbing, had said, quoting a French maxim, "He who drops his ax deserves to die." I was prepared to die in the best French fashion—hence no wrist loop. Leigh and George wore hard hats; I was bare-headed. But then I had scars on my head; they didn't.

Our crampons were also different. George and I had rigid chromium-molybdenum Chouinard crampons with front points filed to razor sharpness. Leigh wore hinged, soft-metal Grivel crampons that were about as sharp as erasers. Worse, he had cut the stitching out of the back of his ancient boots to make room for his bone spurs. His pants were baggy—probably army surplus—and his checked shirt made him look like a Maine canoe guide. Climbing across the slabs of ice, he seemed a figure out of World War II. But could he cut steps! The ax moved effortlessly, the ice chips flew, and he progressed with the grace and the precision of a master craftsman. I did not know how to cut steps; given my equipment, I didn't need to, but I wish now I had learned from him.

In short, Leigh's spirit was marvelous, his technique superb, his equipment antique. Unfortunately, the route above us could not be climbed with antique equipment.

When the time came to cross the Black Ice Couloir proper, it was George's lead. I belayed; he led it with no protection, standing on his front points with one gloved hand on the 50-degree ice and the other hand on the top of his ax, the pick at waist level. I followed in the same fashion. Leigh cut steps. I teased him, and he teased me back. It had always been that way between us.

We continued up the Enclosure Couloir until we reached the base of the buttress. Leigh made short work of the first lead, which ended behind a pillar. I led the next pitch over an overhang, where I used two pitons for direct aid, and up into the main crack system. I climbed past a big chock stone into the wet and slightly icy off-width crack and arranged a hanging belay (standing in web stirrups) from several shallow, tied-off pitons on the left side of the crack. I was freaked out. The weather was collapsing, I didn't like my belay, the next lead looked grim, and everywhere I looked I saw white shafts dropping straight into Valhalla, not a propitious spot for those of the heroic persuasion. I was glad it was George's turn to lead.

The memory of George's lead that day still makes my heart sing. Off-widths are not fun under the best of circumstances, but there he was, in heavy, rigid boots and a down parka, climbing rapidly up a hard, icy, wet shaft at over 12,000 feet. He tried to get in protection but couldn't. Finally he was out 80 feet, with no protection. I was standing in slings, with the rope clipped to the highest piton and circling my waist—these were the days before climbing harnesses and belay devices. He thrashed a bit, he rested, breathing hard, and then he thrashed some more—thrashing being intrinsic to off-widths. He stemmed, he jammed his elbows, and he canted his boots sideways in the crack. The lead went on and on. Finally he was up.

My turn. I clipped my pack to a sling hanging from my waist and went at it. Same thing: thrash, thrash, rest, thrash, thrash, rest. During hard climbing, the world shrinks to touch, pressure, kinesthetics. The mind is not separate from these. Your body is doing so many things at the same time that separate intentions merge, and at the most difficult points, surrender to the body's memory, a body that is smarter than your mind. It was indeed a hard lead, but I managed to climb it without a fall. I was terribly pleased with myself.

There was not much time for self-congratulation, however. The next lead looked just as hard—another off-width. Since Leigh was still below, I took the rack from George and kept going. It was cold. The sky was black with sooty clouds that had been building since noon. We were going to get nailed.

I climbed a ways until I reached a nice ledge. There were more ledges above, but I couldn't see them. I decided to wait until everyone was up and we could attempt a meeting of minds. When they arrived, we didn't need a meeting: The weather had collapsed—high winds, graupel, the usual. As Leigh was pulling his rain parka out of his pack, we were hit by a fierce blast that knocked him down. The parka flew into the storm like a crazed bird. We huddled together. I had on a double-layered French down parka and a rubberized French cagoule that came down past my knees. My feet were thrust into my pack, boots on but unlaced—after reading how Herzog lost his boots on Annapurna, I never take off my boots on a climb. George was arrayed in similar fashion; Leigh was going primitive. It started to rain hard, driving rain that did not stop. We told stories, nibbled at food, and waited.

In the last light I looked down into the dreary space of cold rock and steep ice and wondered again, Why am I here? What possible chain of events could lead to this absurd moment? Ortenburger—it was his fault. I sent forth my best blast of excoriating vituperation. Leigh smiled. He loved it.

The temperature dropped rapidly; the water on the rock turned to ice. Snow fell; the wind blew. It was a long night, but we managed to catnap in the midst of chaos.

Waking at dawn was like waking up inside a freezer. The world was white with snow, rime ice, and verglas. It was clear, the storm gone. When we could see, we put on crampons and began to rappel down the route. Alas, we soon discovered that ice had filled the cracks, making it hard to place pitons. Finally we reached a point where we simply couldn't place pitons. George had a large triangular nut slung with a single piece of 9mm rope. We clipped two carabiners into it and reversed the gates so the rappel ropes would pull cleanly—it was not a place to hang your ropes.

Nuts were still relatively new in 1969 and more traditional climbers didn't yet trust them. And rappelling off a single nut—or any single anchor—is not something one likes doing. In Climbing 101, you learn never to rappel off a single anchor. Nonetheless . . . what to do? Leigh let us know in no uncertain terms that he was *not* going to rappel off a single anchor, especially a single nut, more especially yet a single *British* nut. We teased and argued. Leigh couldn't imagine how George and I had made it to graduate school.

Finally George went; then I followed. The argument was that since I was a good deal bigger than Leigh, if the nut held me, it would hold him. It did. We pulled the ropes and rappelled again into the Black Ice Couloir.

Rock along the edge of a couloir is often fractured and loose. The spot we landed on was no exception. We placed four or five pitons and tied them all off with a web of nylon slings. We were all a bit freaked: Although the rappel was short—we doubled one rope—it was not going to be easy. We would have to rappel at a roughly 45-degree angle across steep ice to reach the only point of rock in the area. We didn't have the anchors for rappelling off ice, so we had to reach that rock. I belayed; George rappelled with a friction device constructed from carabiners. He held the rope in one hand, his ice ax in the other, and reversed the technique we used climbing up. It was dicey. If he fell, he would, despite my belay, pendulum across the couloir into a rock wall—an unpleasant prospect. Also, the sun was up, warming the summits above us and loosening chunks of ice and rock. Soon they were roaring down the couloir, whistling as they passed. I pondered my bias against hard hats while Leigh lectured me on the fragility of the human skull.

As always, George made it look easy. Soon he had a good anchor in the rock outcrop. Since Leigh's crampons were so dull, we decided to belay him from both sides. Also, Leigh was addicted—it is the only word—to rappelling without a friction device. Instead, he wrapped the rappel ropes between his legs, around his hip, across his chest, over his shoulder, and down his back— where he held on to it with one hand. This does indeed provide a lot of friction, but it is rather hard on the crotch. I reminded Leigh that the body rappel had led to the decline of the Austro-Hungarian Empire.

I was worried, because when one rappels at an angle in a body rappel, the force is not up into the body, but across the upper leg. This throws one off balance. Sure enough, right in the middle of the couloir, Leigh flipped upside down, coming completely out of his rappel ropes. His hard hat came off and bounced several thousand feet in long arcs down the Black Ice Couloir toward Valhalla. Hanging upside down and belayed from both sides, Leigh looked like a slam dancer doing a jig. His ice ax hung from his wrist loop, though, and I decided right then and there to forever abandon French maxims as a guide to life.

George and I were amused, Leigh less so. He cursed me in particular because we kept a list of one another's mistakes and foibles. George pulled, I let out rope, and Leigh finally reached the anchor.

I rappelled across the couloir belayed from below as occasional chunks of ice clattered down the face.

Once we were all on the rock outcrop, a cloud lifted from our minds. We were off, free. After another rappel and some scrambling, we reached Valhalla, the Hall of the Brave. But we were alive, we saw no Valkyries, and we did not dine with Odin.

We left a fortune's worth of gear on that route. Several weeks later, George went back with Exum guide Mike Lowe and completed it—not least to collect all the iron we had left. We had climbed the crux leads, but there was still lots of hard climbing to the summit.

When completed, the Lowe Route was the hardest route in the Tetons; thirty years later, it remains among the hardest. Exum guide Jim Donini and his friend Rick Black are the only team to have climbed it since then—twice. The second time, Donini led the whole route without direct aid—a remarkable achievement. To my knowledge, the Lowe Route has not been climbed since 1977.

Leigh was the great elder of our Teton climbing tribe. No one was respected more. At the time of our climb he was forty years old, much older than we were, a mathematician who worked all year at an office job. I guided all summer; I climbed frozen waterfalls and hard rock during the winter. George was a climbing ranger and among the most talented climbers of his generation. The apex of his long and brilliant career was the first ascent of the great Kangshung face on Everest. Because George led the hard leads, the most difficult section is known as the Lowe Buttress. But as we descended Valhalla and Cascade Canyons in that giddy summer long ago, Leigh walked us youngsters right into the ground. And of course he teased us about it. We loved him.

The descent from the Upper to the Lower Saddle is circuitous, but if you know the route, it's easy. Most of the time we scramble down a trail, but there are two steep, exposed cliffs where we rope up again. Because Lisa is the strongest climber, I send her down first. I bring up the rear.

At 12,500 feet, in cracks and sheltered depressions, we find flowers again: yellow draba, purple saxifrage, the ubiquitous alpine smelowskia, and, lower down, smelly sky pilot. Martin wants to take pictures, so we stop, strip off extra clothes, and drink the last of our water. The morning cold is a distant memory; now it is so hot, I'm back to shorts and my Hawaiian shirt.

We cross the Black Dike and follow the trail down to the hut. It is noon, the sun absurdly hot. The wind is blowing; the clouds are coming back—Kanzler was right yet again. I wash dishes, eat lunch. I take my usual dose of ibuprofen—we call them "Rocky Mountain M&M's"—then grab a bag of garbage. Time to head home. Lisa, Jim, and Martin are caught between conflicting desires: to stay at the beautiful place they worked so hard to reach, to get the long trip down over with as fast as possible, or to lie in the sun and sleep. I know we have to leave; another group of guides and clients are on their way up, so we must go down. And the sooner the better.

Our packs are light now, but we've already been at it for nine hours, and it is still eight miles and 5,000 feet back to the parking lot. When we reach the fixed rope, we are out of the wind, hot, and suddenly tired. I keep everyone moving, losing altitude, decreasing the distance over which something can happen. Going down the talus when you are this tired you can easily sprain an ankle, and I've seen people do face plants on the trail from sheer exhaustion. Afternoon thunderstorms with lightning are coming and we are exposed on fields of talus—the usual guiding situation: Hurry, hurry, hurry.

We stop briefly at Teepe Creek to refill our water bottles, then descend the steep drops to the Petzoldt Caves and the Meadows. We rest on grass beside the stream, happy to be among a rainbow of colors again. I eat a Snickers, share another with Lisa and Jim— no use carrying food out of the mountains.

The first drops of rain arrive as we traverse out of Garnet Canyon, but I do not put on my parka. The big cold drops feel too good on sunburned skin. The storm breaks, returns. Our legs become wooden, our feet swollen. The wind blows so hard we are frightened. Once four clients and I had to run the last several hundred yards of trail and out into the parking lot while perhaps a hundred trees blew down in the forest around us. Good old Wyoming. As a young woman wrote as the last entry in her diary, "God Bless Wyoming and keep it wild."

Then it is over. We drive to the Exum office and say our goodbyes. Everyone is happy. In a day or two they will return home. In a week I will barely recall their names or the little charms and riddles of our climb. I will have climbed the Grand again, perhaps twice, with other people, in other conditions. Things change. Only the mountain abides.

## 9. The End of Summer

After the middle of August, the sky changes. The sun sinks to the south, its lower rays sharply illuminating the southern buttresses of the peaks. The great northern faces darken. Shadows in the canyons deepen, becoming shadows worthy of de Chirico. The light of spring and summer is limpid, gentle; the light of autumn has an hallucinatory clarity, crisp and brittle. When it is particularly hot and dry and the snow is gone, the peaks glitter with the metallic sheen of schist and mica—the color of isinglass. Nights are chilly.

The leaves of serviceberry turn yellow—the first sign of autumn and so ubiquitous that its message cannot be ignored. The aspens and cottonwoods turn. The year rolls on. And we respond in counterpoint to its deeper theme, striving for harmony but always subordinate, mere obblagati to a grander motif.

I teach climbing classes and climb the Grand. The vast snowfields of spring are reduced to dirty seams of snow, buried in the deepest cracks. The days are hot, in the eighties, which is as hot as it usually gets in this country—the record high is only 95. We go for days without seeing a cloud. Then come the late-summer thunderstorms, destroying our potlucks, sending everyone into the cabins. The thunderstorms here are one of the wonders of the world—a recent one near the town of Douglas dumped six inches of rain in two hours and pounded the residents with hailstones 2.75 inches in diameter. When we have to be out in such storms, we hide in the trees or in caves. On climbs, we put on all our gear and put our packs over our heads. The storms pass as rapidly as they arrive—the light changes, the birds sing, steam rises from the rocks, and you climb on.

My friend Casey visits with her son Weston and his climbing partner, Andrew Hockwald, who is also thirteen and a competitive climber. They are training for the Nationals. They work on the boulder problems at Jenny Lake, and they change the handholds on the climbing wall at the back of the Rescue Cache to make the moves harder. They boulder with Rolo and talk with him, and about him, for hours—he is their Michael Jordan. In the evening they stalk pronghorn and elk along the edge of the meadow, studying them with my spotting scope and taking photographs.

I run up and down the Grand, the boys climb, and Casey writes in the cabin, interviews my neighbor Dick Dorworth for *Wild Duck Review,* the journal she publishes, and cooks elaborate dinners. At night we lie in the hammock and watch the Milky Way with binoculars, drink tequila, and eat chunks of fresh salmon our Chilean guide Rodrigo Mujica has flown in from Alaska. Life feels so full and complete that the prospect of change, any change, brings anguish.

Driving home from a day at intermediate school, I pass a collection of Park Service vehicles and a truck loaded with jet fuel. The near meadow looks like a landing zone, as though we are at war. People I do not know stand around the Rescue Cache, forlorn, stricken. Men and women assemble gear. Some are in yellow or green flight suits, some in yellow fireproof shirts; everyone wears hard hats; some have a radio tucked in a harness across their chests. When Ken Johnson lands his L-3 Long Ranger helicopter, climbing rangers move loads to the open door, their bodies bent slightly away from the down-blast created by the rotors. I pick out Tom Kimbrough and Renny Jackson. Mark Magnuson is sitting at a desk inside the Rescue Cache with his head bent, holding a phone. He must be the rescue coordinator. People I don't know are milling about. Nearby, a child is riding a bicycle fitted with training wheels. He pedals slowly, with intent, oblivious to the roar and chaos.

Unless the injured is one of our own, I seek emotional distance. Every year, there are between twenty-five and thirty rescues in the park and fatal accidents average three a year, although in 1997 there were six fatalities, including an experienced member of the Jackson Hole Mountain Guides. I feel it, though, in my chest and stomach. I try not to feel it in my head or think about the details. I tell myself that thousands of people died every day, most of them children. It doesn't help much.

The chopper comes and goes during dinner, ferrying rangers and equipment. We carry on normally, take showers, and cook. Later, Casey and I linger at the picnic table next to the creek, drinking red wine, talking with Dorworth—ideas and writing being a common passion—and discussing the many ironies and the controversies in Jon Krakauer's *Into Thin Air*. Several Exum guides were present during the climb Krakauer recounts, and most of us know climbers mentioned in the book—both living and dead. Rolo knew the Russian climber Anatoli Boukreev, who later died in an avalanche on Annapurna, and he vociferously defends him against all criticism. Dorworth and I contemplate the commercialization of climbing, the decline of wildness. As usual, we do not agree completely, but in general, we think guiding Everest with clients is slightly less rational than Russian roulette.

The helicopter continues to make its trips. Casey has not been anesthetized by hundreds of rescues, and through her we feel vicariously the whine of the helicopter as an unnerving reality. Weston and Andrew have been practicing on the climbing wall, but eventually their rope hangs slack from the carabiners in the ridge beam and they stand in the parking lot, riveted to the scene before them. Mostly they have climbed in rock gyms, on boulders, and on short cliffs with a top rope. Here things are serious: Life is at stake. As I look at them, I realize this is what is riveting: that something is at stake.

Dusk. We can hear the helicopter's whine somewhere on the face of the Teewinot. I search for it with binoculars and find its red taillights blinking in the falling darkness. It hovers at 11,500 feet near the edge of a crevasse, rocking gently. It's rather late to be flying a chopper next to a mile-high mountain face, but Johnson is an exceptional pilot, our favorite, and a local hero.

Later, at dark, the helicopter returns. We have gone to bed and lie buried beneath a down comforter. The chopper's lights flash against the window and the blades clatter. A cloud of dust blows across the parking lot and the trees sway slightly, the way they do before a storm. A rubber body bag in a net hangs from a cable beneath the belly of the helicopter, like a victim in a spiderweb. Gently the chopper descends, lowering the bag to the ground while rangers below direct it with upstretched arms and flashlights. Then it lands nearby and the engine is cut. The blades collapse with a sigh.

Another fall on snow. Another fatal head injury. The chill of moats.

The number of people in the mountains declines sharply through the last week of August. There is a blip of interest over Labor Day weekend and then it's pretty much over. Depending on the weather, Exum will guide the Grand for two or three more weeks. Parties tend to be smaller, and up at the hut we rise at 5:00 A.M. instead of at 3:00. The mountain is always cold this time of year, solemn and strangely silent, though I cannot say what sound is missing. We climb only in good weather: Any storm this time of year is serious. As Dan Burgette likes to say, "After the middle of August, you can have winter in the Tetons."

Some time in early September Exum hosts its annual end-of-summer dinner, the only time during the year that all the Exum guides are together in one spot. We usually have it at Dietrich's, at the Teton Village Ski Area. Everyone goes—guides, spouses, lovers, former guides, friends of the guide service. People dress up in the way that counts as dressing up in Wyoming: Women wear dresses and real shoes; men wear cowboy boots, Levi's, sometimes a sport coat. There are no ties—few of us own ties. We mill around at the bar for an hour, talk shop, catch up with people we haven't seen all summer. Then we have dinner.

Al Read is the master of ceremonies. The Exum owners sit at the main table with Glenn and Beth Exum. Glenn is in his eighties now, still courtly and handsome. Al congratulates us for a safe summer, thanks us, makes a few jokes. We eat. After dinner, Glenn tells stories of the early days of the guide service—the thirties—stories we've all heard before that are part of our tradition. My favorite is the one about the time two dogs followed Glenn and Paul Petzoldt up from the valley, then up to the bottom of the climb. They put the dogs in their packs and climbed to the summit—probably the only time dogs climbed the Grand Teton until climbing ranger Scott Berkenfield climbed it with his dog Sunshine, which was many years later.

I leave early—partly because I am uncomfortable in large

crowds, partly because I've seen and heard it all before. Also, a faint pall of mortality fills a room of climbers, the presence in my mind of those no longer there in body, the stark recognition that many here—laughing, with one arm dangling idly around the neck of a loved one, the other swirling a glass of wine—will also die in the mountains.

There are worse ways to die.

Exum guide Fred Ford died on June 28, 1935, after being hit by a rockfall in what is now named the Ford Couloir on the Grand Teton. His clients got him off to the side, tied him to the rock, and went for help. Somehow he untied himself and fell.

Art Gilkey died on K2 in 1953 after contracting phlebitis at 25,000 feet. The other members of the climbing party made a valiant effort to evacuate him, but he was lost in an avalanche.

Jake Breitenbach died when a wall of ice collapsed on him while he was climbing through the Khumbu Icefall on Mount Everest as a member of the 1963 American Everest Expedition. Jake's remains are buried on a narrow ridge west of Thangboche Monastery. I visit him when I pass through. A pole flying Tibetan prayer flags marks the site; beneath is a piece of rock carved with his epitaph: LONG LIVE THE CROW.

Willi Unsoeld died in an avalanche on Mount Rainier in 1979. Willi was undoubtedly the most famous of the Exum guides. His list of achievements is long, both in climbing and in public life, the most stunning feat being the first ascent of the west ridge of Everest with Tom Hornbein. Since they bivouacked on the descent of the normal route from the south col, they also became the first, and as far as I know the only team to traverse Everest.

Willi played his harmonica at the belay ledges on the Exum Ridge. Sometimes he would secretly carry a bottle of beer to the summit and announce, "I'd give five dollars for a cold beer." Someone would say, "Me too," and out would come Willi's beer. "Where's your five dollars?" he'd ask.

He also had a saying that is no longer politically correct but which rings like cold, hard truth: "Mountains are like women— they have many moods. If you're going to love the mountains, better learn to love their moods." Few loved the mountains with such constancy. When he died, Willi was fifty-three years old, a white-haired professor of philosophy, and for some people, a prophet. He had earned his wisdom. Willi's daughter, Nanda Devi, died on the mountain he named her after. He had no toes; he limped. He was in constant pain. And still he wandered the mountains, seeking.

Harry Frishman died on January 18, 1981. While climbing unroped with Mark Whitten near the top of the northwest couloir of the Middle Teton, he slipped and fell 2,000 feet to his death.

A few months before, Harry and I had been members of the first American expedition to China, an attempt to climb 24,900-foot Minya Konka on the border of China and Tibet. The Chinese allowed us to bring two kinds of presents into the country: buttons imprinted with political logos and postcards of our home landscapes. Harry brought hundreds of buttons saying SEX, DRUGS, ROCK'N'ROLL. Since no one read English, everyone Harry gave his buttons to wore them. I have pictures of Chinese army officers saluting proudly with while sporting the buttons on their uniforms. As for postcards, he brought pictures of the jackalope—a mythical rabbit with horns—and of trout the size of trucks riding on railroad cars. He showed them often, always with a straight face.

One day on Minya Konka, when I was carrying a load up to camp 1, an avalanche swept Rick Ridgeway, Yvon Chouinard, Jonathan Wright, and Kim Schmitz 1,200 feet down the mountain from a point slightly above the camp. Kim, who was last, turned and drove in his ax, but it was pulled out of his hands. They went past me a couple hundred feet from where I stood, tied together into one rope and fighting to stay on the surface as they rode a slithering mass of wet snow over several cliffs, then disappeared from sight. Seconds later—it seemed like hours—they appeared again, far below, on a crest of avalanche debris. The avalanche wiped out a thousand feet of the tracks we had just been climbing up.

Badly shaken, we climbed on up to camp 1 to use the radio to call base camp. Harry was there—he hadn't climbed that day because he was sick. We were addled, in shock, stuffing things wildly into our packs. We headed down as the light dimmed, moving slowly. We had forgotten our crampons, our rope; we had only one sleeping bag and a stove but no pot. Addled.

When we reached our friends, we found that Jonathan was dead. Rick was injured but ambulatory. After doing all he could for Jonathan, he had gone down to base camp for help. Yvon had a concussion, was in shock, and didn't know he was in China. Kim was a mess: crushed disks, broken ribs, smashed teeth.

Harry helped Yvon down to base camp. I stayed with Kim, getting the foam pad under him, then hugging him for warmth while I covered us with the sleeping bag. I pleaded with him not to die. He screamed and screamed.

Inexplicably, lightning and thunder surrounded our 25,000-foot peak—the only time I've seen that on a peak that size. Avalanches came down around us in the dark, making muffled, slushy sounds that stopped as abruptly as they started. We waited.

A rescue party reached us from base camp around midnight. Al Read, the leader of the expedition, spent hours cutting a platform in the ice large enough for the four-person tent he had hauled up. The expedition doctor, Dick Long, shot Kim up with painkillers. We wrapped the foam pad around Kim's midsection, taped it rigid, and started down with former Exum guide Jeff Foott supporting

Kim under one arm while I supported him under the other. Long belayed us. When we reached Al's tent site, it was nearly morning. Since there weren't enough sleeping bags to go around, we huddled together, shivering, until dawn.

Harry, possessing endless energy and, like Odysseus, clever in all ways of contending, kept going after he got Yvon to base camp, hiking down to a monastery miles below. There he commandeered the monastery's flagpoles and hired a crew of Tibetans to carry them up to the mountain. Just after dawn, as our rescue party made its way onto the steep talus above base camp, Harry arrived with Tibetans, flagpoles, and ropes to make an enormous litter for Kim. The Tibetans carried it on their shoulders while we belayed the contraption with a long rope. Soon we were all back in camp.

We buried Jonathan on the mountain, under a chorten that Rick Ridgeway built for his friend—a lovely stone structure on a ridge out of the paths of avalanches. Prayer flags sang in the breeze when we left. The view is unsurpassed.

Kim's trip home was long and harrowing. But true to character, he made a first ascent on Amne Machin, a 20,610-foot peak in eastern Tibet, the following spring; a week later, he led the first guided ascent of it. A year later, he was on the west ridge of Everest.

Harry died a few months after the Minya Konka accident. Friends held a memorial service on the sagebrush flats above Blacktail Ponds, overlooking the Snake River and the Tetons. Tibetan prayer flags snapped in the wind, grown men wept at their own eulogies, and Harry's Scottish climbing friends sang in brogue. Ski-patrol friends threw twenty-one two-pound explosive charges off the mountain. Dozens of his former students at Southwest Outward Bound sat in the snow in silence. After it was over, we went to the bar at Dornan's and danced, sang, and drank into the night. On Harry's tombstone is a quote from Washakie, last great chief of the Shoshone: GOD DAMN A POTATO.

Leigh Ortenburger died tragically in the great Oakland firestorm of 1991. He was visiting friends for dinner when the fire swept through the hills, destroying three thousand houses and killing twenty-five people.

Astute, argumentative, stubborn, witty, tireless, and possessing an astonishing memory, Leigh influenced generations of climbers in the Tetons. He climbed in the Himalayas and in Peru. He knew the Teton Range better than anyone ever has, or ever will. He walked everywhere; he climbed everything. He wrote the definitive climbing guides to the range and a lengthy history, still unpublished, of its exploration. He photographed the Tetons from an airplane with a four-by-five-inch camera. He developed his own film, made his own prints. Together with his writing, they constitute the canonical interpretation of the range.

Hemming. The name is singular, like the man. Gary Hemming died of a self-inflicted gunshot wound to the head on the night of August 5, 1969, near the old Guides Hill at Jenny Lake. The circumstances of his death are fugitive. There was a party, drinking, a fight, physical and spiritual put-downs, then silence and a gunshot. Some guides lay in their cabins and listened to the whole fiasco. After the gunshot, no one went to investigate. The next morning, his body was found and the rangers were called. He was thirty-five years old, anguished beyond reason, a legend.

Hemming was the most famous American climber in Europe during the sixties, famous not only for his climbs but also for his lifestyle. There are many stories about him, some apocryphal, my favorite being his supposed traverse of the Matterhorn in shorts and tennis shoes in one day. In France he was a celebrity, featured in *Paris Match;* young girls followed him down the street. His climbing clothes were as tattered and patched as the robe of a Chan monk.

Hemming was unusually tall and strong; he liked to fight and often lost. Once three cowboys beat him with ax handles in the alley behind the Cowboy Bar in Jackson. Myth has it that the hospital in Jackson refused to accept him, so his girlfriend tried to drive to Idaho Falls, a hundred miles away. Unfortunately, she drove off the road and there were further injuries. When I camped next to him at the old Teton climbers' camp in the sixties, he carried a bowie knife and a revolver.

In an essay on mountain rescues in *The New Yorker*, Jeremy Bernstein described Hemming's features: "Hemming's face was absolutely remarkable. It had something of the beauty of the Christian saints, and it was crowned with an incredible foliage of long dark-blond hair, so thick that it must have afforded not only considerable thermal insulation but also substantial protection from falling rock. . . . He had a delightful smile, an air of inner strength, and great serenity."

In the European climbing world, Hemming was famous for first ascents of the American Direct Route on the west face of the Dru and the south face of the Fou, difficult routes in the Mont Blanc region of France. He soloed difficult routes on the Aiguille Verte and the Triolet. And in 1966 this impoverished American climber, who had been kicked out of the elite aspirant-guide course in Chamonix for refusing to cut his beard, led the French teams that made the spectacular rescue of two German climbers on the Dru, an event that is, let us say, unique in French alpine history.

Hemming's death was noted in the French papers and Pierre Joffroy published an appreciative essay in *Paris Match* entitled "Gary Hemming: La Fin Tragique d'un Poète." Bernstein's essay on Hemming, "On Vous Cherche," in *The New Yorker* followed in 1971 and James Salter published a novel, *Solo Faces,* based broadly on Hemming's life. Recently, Mirella Tenderinni published a biography, *Gary Hemming: The Beatnik of the Alps.*

On the day he died, I gave Hemming a ride from Teton Village to Jenny Lake. I was on my way to guide the east ridge of Mount Owen with a client, Elizabeth Cook, who had traveled often in

France and knew his reputation. She was amused that the famous beatnik was clean-shaven, polite, and witty. He was on his way to Africa, he said. When she asked why, he replied, "Well, you know, you can't call yourself a man until you've killed a charging lion." I looked in the rearview mirror; he was smiling his serene smile. When Elizabeth and I returned from Mount Owen the following afternoon, Hemming was dead.

The funeral took place at the Valley Mortuary in Jackson. The room was musty and a scratchy record of a Bach concerto droned from behind a curtain. Hemming's mother had flown in from Hawaii. She sat, alone, at the end of the left row of pews, tight against the wall, a big blond woman with a stricken face. The rest of us sat in the pews to the right of the aisle. Glenn Exum and Al Read wore suits and represented the Exum Guide Service. Dave Craft, Jim Greig, and I were there because we loved the man. Several guides' wives were present. Noticeably absent were the people Hemming thought of as his friends, the people he had come to the Tetons to visit.

The mortician served as preacher, donning clothes to match his labors. He read from the Psalms, and referred to Gary as Gareth— the only time I'd heard anyone use his actual name. The service was short. Lacking the necessary number of men, the mortician changed into a suit and served as the sixth pallbearer. Few cars followed the hearse to the Aspen Cemetery at the bottom of Snow King Mountain.

A plastic carpet of bright green grass surrounded the grave; the coffin rested on two straps attached to a small motor. The mortician, transfigured back into a preacher, read from the Bible as he nursed the motor lowering the coffin into the ground. The only man I have known who deserved his myth then rumbled into the earth to mumbled words alien to the freedom and the struggle of his life.

When the service was over, the preacher transformed himself into a grave digger. He changed into overalls, balancing on one foot while firmly gripping a shovel. We left when the first clods hit the coffin.

Every year I visit Hemming's grave. An ice rink, parking lots, and a ski tow now crowd Aspen Cemetery. A line of Douglas firs obscures the view of the Tetons from block D, plot 16. A tangle of plants conceals the small, flat gravestone. The engraving is simple: GARY, GARETH H. HEMMING, DEC. 13, 1934–AUG. 6, 1969. On the upper left is a rendering of a stack of books; on the right an alpine hat with a feather. In summer, the grave is surrounded by wild fruits—chokecherry, serviceberry, rose hips. There are no flowers.

Alex Lowe died in an avalanche on Shishapangma, a 26,291-foot peak on the border of Nepal and Tibet and the fourteenth-highest mountain in the world. He was at 19,000 feet, scouting a route for what would have been the first ski descent with several other climbers and cameraman Dave Bridges, a friend of Dick Dorworth who had often visited Guides Hill. What happened was, in the most exact sense of the word, an accident.

At 9:20 A.M., on October 5, 1999, a section of ridge 6,000 feet above them fractured and fell into deep snow, starting an avalanche. Alex noticed it first. He, Bridges, and Conrad Anker ran. Another group of climbers, including Exum guide Hans Sarri, was on the other side of the glacier in a more protected position. Saari says that when the avalanche reached them it was 500 feet wide and traveling at 100 miles an hour. Alex and Bridges were buried; Anker was thrown 100 feet and partially buried, but he survived. An extensive search failed to locate the buried climbers. Finally the rest of the party retreated to base camp.

Alex was famous, his death a national event. NPR reported the accident and gave an account of Alex's life. Tom Brokaw did the same for NBC television. Al Read appeared on *Good Morning America*. *Outside Magazine* devoted an issue to Alex.

But Alex was not only famous; he was loved, beloved. Family and friends descended on Bozeman, Montana, to console Jenny Lowe and their three sons. A memorial service was held after the other members of the expedition returned home.

Alex was the best of us, the best climber at Exum, the best climber in America, probably the best climber in the world. He was a gentleman. His presence and energy were a joy. We all stood in awe of Alex. We always will.

After leaving the Exum dinner I drive back to Lupine Meadows along the back road from Teton Village to Moose. It is dirt most of the way, and narrow, winding through forest. Finally I break out onto the sagebrush flats again. Even though it is late, cars with the windows rolled down are parked in the turnouts. A few bull elk are bugling. The rut is beginning and the bulls' calls are the definitive harbinger of autumn. People sit in their cars in the dark and listen to them, something I find incurably romantic.

Nineteen degrees this morning. A storm dumped snow above 9,000 feet. The first autumn snow is a revelation. Since everything is bare, the snow seems sifted onto the range like powder onto a fingerprint, revealing its fundamental structure.

The high mountains are cold; the temperatures approach zero. The Grand Teton spews clouds like a geyser, and the high winds twist them into circles. The flowers in the meadow stand withered, the grasses tan and fallen. Along the creek, the alders and cottonwood are wreathed with hoarfrost. A flock of white pelicans drifts south over the meadow, their wings extended, barely moving. Cottonwood Creek is a sleepy mountain stream with the first autumn leaves circling in eddies, shoaling among the rocks.

I wait for a good day to walk up to the hut and retrieve my climbing gear for the winter. To the Saddle yet again. I remind myself it could be the "L" into Chicago. I usually take it easy, loaf, and enjoy the solitude of autumn in the Tetons. Some years the good day doesn't come and I go on up anyway. This looks like one of those years. The storms continue. I wait for a break, but finally I can't wait any longer.

Late in the afternoon, I leave the parking lot under baleful skies. The cloud level hovers at 11,000 feet and squalls are blowing through, carrying rain and sleet. I carry a light pack with two bottles of hot tea and a handful of Snickers bars.

When I reach the Meadows, two inches of snow covers the trail and things look grim. Sheets of blowing snow veil the lower walls of Nez Percé, the Middle Teton, and the ridges of Disappointment Peak. The summits disappear into a mass of dark clouds. I put on gaiters and another layer of clothing and head up to the Petzoldt Caves.

By the time I reach the caves, snow conceals the trail. Two other guides are several hours in front of me, but I see their tracks only occasionally. Soon I am muddling my way upward through snow-covered talus and boulders. Visibility is down to half a mile and diminishing rapidly. Everything is okay, I tell myself, just a bit slower than usual. But the light is fading; the world is turning gray. The snow is the color of old pearls; the wet rocks gleam like pewter. Even the shrouds of blowing snow are gray. Above me, miles away, the wind rips through the towers on the Exum Ridge, moaning like a siren.

At the caves, I finish a bottle of tea and refill it with water. The long section up to Teepe Creek is disorienting. I can't stay on the trail. There is just enough snow covering the rocks to make walking difficult. Stones roll underfoot; I fall. Ridiculous.

I climb straight up the hill, abandoning the trail and searching for the dwarfed pines where I should turn west toward the creek. I can't find them. I am absurdly lost. I know where I am, but not exactly. I know where I want to go, but not exactly. Eventually I hit Teepe Creek a hundred yards above the trail. I drink more tea and consider going down—it's nearly dark now. I cannot see the Headwall through the blowing snow.

The boulder field leading to the Headwall is a mess of cobbles, talus, and VW-sized rocks covered with fresh snow. Visibility is a hundred yards. The last steep stretch to the fixed rope is covered with crotch-deep snow the size of BBs. Falling snow, blowing snow, snow pattering down the steep slopes, spindrift snow blowing off the cliffs above me. I am no longer climbing, but wading: I push the snow aside with my hands, drive up with my knees, then try to stomp the sugary junk into footholds.

Since I'm not equipped to survive a night out and no one knows where I am, my mind becomes a melee of paranoid images. I see my body frozen like the Sioux at Wounded Knee. I obsess about who will find me, who will be called first. Or whether, if the storm continues, I will not be found until spring. All of this is useful, I think, an evolutionary adaptation for survival. Maybe. One part of the mind says, "Only the paranoid survive." Another part summons William Burroughs: "A paranoid is someone who knows something other people don't know yet."

A line from Tu Fu drifts through my mind: "Swift, urgent snow dances in whirlwinds." Then the great poem by Hashin:

> *There is neither heaven nor earth*
> *Only snow*
> *Falling, endlessly.*

I reach the fixed rope in darkness, in a blizzard. When I turn on my headlamp, a cocoon of brilliant light perhaps eight feet in diameter envelopes me and the scintillations from the blowing snow destroy my sense of place and direction. I turn it off, preferring darkness, with its vague but familiar forms. After all, I know this place—I've been here hundreds of times. I can picture everything with my mind's eye.

The fixed rope is coated with ice. Gripping it with my left hand, I climb upward, one foot on the rock, the other stomping steps in a chimney filled with bottomless sugar snow. The rock is greasy with half-frozen water. In the summer this section is so easy that we don't belay clients, but on this dark night I am exhausted and off balance and oh so keenly aware that even a short fall here could be deadly.

Then, in the darkness, without thought, my right hand searches the right wall of the chimney, brushing away snow. My fingers sink into a great handhold, a handhold I know as well as I know the difference between hot and cold. Yes.

As I climb on, my fingers find more handholds, each buried under snow, each waiting for me like an old friend, each, I want to say, greeting me. Whoever knows a reef or river or mountain intimately knows, at some point, this feeling. It is among the gifts that flow from returning, again and again, each new return enriching the cycle forever. At another time and place, each handhold would have a name and I would greet them. This is my home, these rocks, as much a home as I shall ever know.

Above the chimney, I set out at an angle toward the Lower Saddle. I am wading again, but no longer in a hurry. I stop and drink the last of my tea. I down a Snickers. Then I wade on, taking my time, relishing that lush privacy found only in great storms at night.

Suddenly the wind is stronger, the ground is flat, and I know

I am on the Saddle. To my left, light from a lantern glows faintly through the Plexiglas door of the hut. Rod Newcomb and Ron Matous are having tea. I join them.

The next morning the Lower Saddle looks like the Arctic. We dismantle the hut and put it in the big metal box, wrap it with plastic, and tie the whole thing down with a climbing rope. Matous leaves, running down the trail—off to a chess tournament in Montana. Rod and I take our time wading down to the fixed rope. I remember my friend Max Lyon being trapped on the Lower Saddle after a big storm with terrible avalanche conditions everywhere except on the level section of the saddle. Wisely, they stayed put, prepared even to burn the outhouse to melt snow. Rod is completely comfortable under these conditions; I am always paranoid about avalanches. He goes first; I follow.

The sun has melted the ice on the rope. We go down hand over hand and I smile at my friendly handholds, now clear of snow. We wade again until we reach the moraine, shed layers, and eat, admiring the mountains in all their winter beauty. Then we descend yet again to Lupine Meadows.

The climbing season is over and Exum is closed for the winter. The guides and rangers are gone, the meadows empty. The intense work that defines our lives for three months is forgotten—the constant presence of people you must watch like a hawk, the stress of group interactions, the risk. I am again free to travel alone or with a small group of friends, folks who can take care of themselves. I am free to return to plants and animals, my paints and journals.

I turn my mind to other matters, travel other paths.

# 10. Snowshoe Canyon

Late September. The aspen and cottonwood are in full color. The temperature drops below freezing at night. The park is empty save for locals on the year's last day hikes, a few fishermen trolling the lakes, and knowledgable dry-fly buffs drifting the Snake for cutthroat trout. Hunting season begins and gunshots occasionally echo across the valley. The pelicans are gone, the ospreys; the smaller birds are flocking, heading south. The meadows are a pale brown and filled with grasshoppers. I watch two small black bears spread-eagle in the branches of a chokecherry, gorging themselves and looking sheepish.

It is still early to fish for spawning brown trout in the north, but I hunt the Gros Ventre for deer and elk and plan trips to the northern Tetons, the country north of Mount Moran and west of Jackson Lake. Remote, beautiful, rarely traveled, filled with game and solitude, the northern range fully equals the majesty of the major peaks, even if it is majesty in a minor key. The peaks are thousands of feet lower than the Grand Teton, and most are walks, not climbs.

Few people know the country well. Most of them are park biologists and rangers, people who are in some sense paid to know it well, though that in no way diminishes their love of the place. Poachers know it well for quite different reasons. Few travel its heart for reasons intrinsic to the place. Fewer still—I imagine less than a dozen—wander there alone, solitaries, Melville's *isolatoes*. Peter Koedt, Ron Matous, and John Carr probably know it as well as anybody.

Not all the northern country lacks trails. Moose Creek, Owl Creek, and Berry Creek—at the northern tip of the park—have trails, though they are rarely traveled, and Berry Creek and Moose Basin—a vast collection of meadows at the head of Moose Creek—have patrol cabins. A ranger uses these cabins while patrolling the area during the summer and fall.

From the patrol cabin in Moose Basin south to the trail in Paintbrush Canyon lie approximately eighty square miles of wild country devoid of trails. Though much of the park is managed as wilderness, this is the only section I believe deserves that classy appellation. The heart of this wilderness is Snowshoe Canyon, its two forks, and the peaks marking its watershed: Raynolds, Traverse, Bivouac, Rolling Thunder, Doane, and Eagles Rest.

One morning Dan Burgette calls. "Want to go looking for critters and poachers up Snowshoe?" he asks.

"And come out Webb?"

"Yeah."

"Sure, Dan. I'll keep you out of trouble."

This is one excuse. Another is bushwhacking for four days with heavy packs while we extend our long-running discussion about wildness and wilderness—a subject about which we fuss with the passion of medieval logicians. But the truth is, I want another trip into the northern mountains—one cannot make too many.

Getting around in the northern Teton canyons without trails is a practice for masochists. Even to reach them, one must either cross the range from the west, through the Jedediah Smith Wilderness, or arrange to be dropped off and picked up on the west side of Jackson Lake. The bottoms of the canyons, near the lake, are bogs of subalpine fir, lodgepole pine, and Engelmann spruce, and piles of downed logs—like a giant version of the children's game Pick Up Sticks. You walk a mile to make a half mile of progress; or rather, you climb over trees, around trees, and through limbs. Higher, where the canyons narrow, you are forced onto steeper terrain, often with poor footing, overgrown with thickets of brush beneath which is mud, oozing and slick, moss, oozing and slicker, or talus—the kind that turns your ankle. There are cliff bands to skirt, streams to cross. In short, it is wild.

One of the nice things about going into the northern mountains with Dan is that a Park Service Boston Whaler drops us off at the northwest end of Moran Bay. When I go alone, I have to kayak across Jackson Lake. As we approach shore, three loons lift off the water. They are big birds, up to a yard long, that can dive to depths of two hundred feet. Though not common, a few summer here on the lakes each year and breed in the northern end of the park. The loon is a symbol of the wild, and justly so. Its cries are varied: wails, moans, howls, yodels, hysterical laughter. In *The Maine Woods,* Thoreau describes the loon's cries as "sometimes singularly human to my ear." For me, a loon is always a good omen.

We shoulder our packs and cruise through old-growth timber at the mouth of the canyon—a shortcut that allows us to avoid bog for a while. The forest is open, inviting. We watch a coyote hunt mice in a meadow, a moose lounging in a bog, and we find an unfortunate number of bull thistles—one of the many exotics that have invaded the park.

When the canyon narrows, we play one of bushwhacking's many games: how to stay off the cliffs above without wallowing in the bog and marshes below. After an hour, we admit we are too high, but since we don't want to lose altitude, we fight thick brush and cliffs all the way to our destination, Dudley Lake, a small pool beneath the north face of Bivouac Peak, at 8,243 feet. There is a charmingly picturesque island in the middle. By the time we arrive, the lake is shaded, but the air is warm. Slabs of gneiss slant into the water, the autumn colors weave about the forests and cliffs, and the view north to Rolling Thunder, Doane, and Eagles Rest is stunning in the evening light. The lake is still as glass and covered with reflections.

Neither of us has been here before; in fact, I don't know anyone who's been here. We find a place to camp and look around for separate places to cook and hang our food. There are moose and pine marten tracks on the shore, old tracks, hard. A pair of golden-eyes cross the lake as we approach.

Since Dan is a carver, he notices wood. Now, looking at a burl on a white-bark pine, and knowing of my desire to carve Buddhas from stumps, he says, "Burls would be good for your Buddhas."

In a dry marsh stand delicate grasses, grasses fine as hair. I stoop to figure out their ambiguous color, not yellow, green, or tan. Among them is a Mormon cricket, an archaic creature that looks more like a toy than an insect. I walk around the lake to admire the tormented whorls in the slabs of gneiss. Bear sign is plentiful: turned rocks, smashed logs, and scat filled with the pits of choke-cherries.

We eat a simple dinner. Then we wander away from each other, wanting to be alone. Dan lies down on a slab of gneiss near the lake to stare at the stars. I work on my journals. Dan is a perfect companion in the mountains, capable of both prolonged silence or interesting conversation, possessing much practical knowledge, and strong as a horse.

The sky is clear, the stars bright—a western sky. Bare trees stand like rows of candelabra on the ridge above us and I hear a breeze whispering among their branches. We do not put up our tent. The ground smells too rich and fecund and the air is too warm, the forest bright with starlight, its shadows muted, complex. Shades among shades. In comparison, the darkness of a tent is barren. One dreams differently under starlight.

The next morning, we eat our traditional breakfast of oatmeal, raisins, nuts, and maple syrup. Then we hang our food and gear from trees and hike up the left side of the south fork of Snowshoe Canyon. It has a reputation as the worst bushwhack in the range, a reputation it deserves. The indefatigable Fryxell passed this way in 1933 while returning from the first ascent of Rolling Thunder with Phil Smith. Later he wrote in his *Mountaineering in the Tetons: The Pioneer Period 1898–1940*: "the canyon narrowed to a gorge, one of the deepest in the range that have been cut by water since the glacial epoch. Here we made slow progress in the half-mile of heavy brush along its south rim."

Nothing has changed. The steep northern face holds snow late in the year, the heavy brush provides a tangled mass of roots that releases water slowly. The result is a precipitous morass of mosses, chokecherry, serviceberry, willow, and alder. A fall would send you over cliffs into a narrow canyon filled with icy water. Those who have skied this section in spring speak of it with awe: a steep snow slope interspersed with cliffs, a mound of avalanche debris at the bottom, and in it a deep slit through which flows a narrow black stream.

We pass into a forest of whitebark pines with an understory of grouse whortleberry, country that is open, magical, country for wandering wherever one will. We lunch in a high, spacious valley amid meadows and talus fields. Five streams merge here and a small cascade gurgles in the distance. White boulders the size of trucks lie scattered among a mass of autumn alpine colors—mats of yellow, gold, russet, and coral. At the edges of the valley are stands of spruce, fir, and pine. Above is a barren ridge layered with gray and reddish rock. Perfect elk habitat; perfect grizzly habitat. The Tetons are relatively safe—no rattlesnakes, no black widow or brown recluse spiders, no scorpions, only one patch of poison ivy, no poison oak, no killer bees—just grizzlies.

This time of year grizzlies like to feed on whitebark pine nuts, a major source of fat for winter hibernation. A grizzly does not have direct access to the pine seeds because the cones do not drop and grizzlies rarely climb trees; their claws are long and straight, designed for digging, not climbing. To get whitebark pine seeds, the grizzly needs the help of the red squirrel. The red squirrel, in order to put in its hoard of winter food, snips off the pinecones intended for its storehouses, or middens. The bear eats the ones the squirrel doesn't hoard fast enough.

Because of their legendary ferocity, grizzlies are thought of as carnivores, but they are omnivores. Further, with 80 to 90 percent of their diet consisting of flora, they are mostly vegetarians. In addition to whitebark pine nuts, grizzlies eat grass, sedges, corms, tubers, berries, the inner bark of trees, mushrooms, moths clinging to the undersides of talus, fish, ants, gophers, marmots, squirrels, deer, elk, moose, bison, other bears—anything in North America they wish to eat. John Muir said they eat everything but granite. Occasionally, only very occasionally, they eat us.

I work on my journal, Dan sits on a boulder, glassing the slopes for sheep, bear, and poachers. Suddenly he calls softly to me and motions for me to join him. Dan is more attuned to wildlife than I am, more aware and watchful. I'm the romantic, painting and mumbling about metaphysics. The softness in his voice tells me he's spotted bear.

Three grizzlies are feeding on a meadow above us, a big sow and two cubs, a quarter of a mile away, at 9,600 feet. The sow is black, with a tan, almost whitish, porcine snout. The cubs are cinnamon, with classic silver-tipped guard hairs over their shoulders. Since grizzlies remain with their mothers for two years, sometimes longer, the word *cub* does not accurately describe a two-year-old grizzly. They may weigh only a pound when born, in the middle of winter, but by summer they weigh thirty pounds, primarily because of the high fat content of their mother's milk—ten times the fat content of human milk. By the time the leaves fall, they weigh over a hundred pounds. By the end of their second year, grizzly cubs can be as big as adult black bears. These cubs are big, healthy, and so fat they jiggle when they run.

All three are feeding on succulent greens next to a rill that tumbles off the western ridge of Rolling Thunder. We watch them until they disappear into a clump of pines. Then we discuss what we are going to do about them.

Most encounters with bears and mountain lions are like this— benign. Movies and nature films lead us to expect the ever-charging grizzly or the lion hurtling from a tree, so most people believe danger lurks behind each bush in the country. On the contrary— sighting big predators in wilderness is rare, and what the film cannot record is precisely what I find most precious: their presence, a presence that heightens experience. It is as though the oldest and deepest area of our heart/mind—the Pleistocene heart/mind—is nourished.

We drop our plans to continue up the valley to the ridge crest, since it is right where the bears are—had Dan been less observant, we could have walked into them. Instead, we climb the ridge to the left, staying out of sight and keeping the entire valley between us and the bears. We climb until we are across from where we last saw them, then move back over the ridge and sit in a little grove of spruce. They are still directly across the valley, the sow feeding, the cubs playing. For a while they disappear behind a few dwarfed firs, a clump so small that it couldn't have concealed three bears, so I think they must have a den. Dan doesn't think so. Soon they are out again, frolicking. We watch them patiently, with delight.

There are 200 to 400 grizzlies in the Greater Yellowstone eco-system—of which Grand Teton National Park is only a small part. Some say there are fewer than 200, some say there are more than 400. It doesn't matter. Since they are cut off from populations farther north, and since the World Wildlife Fund calculates we need roughly 4,000 bears to have a self-sustaining population for a hundred years, all estimates of our grizzly population are far below what is required. Most people don't care. Even though they are classified as a threatened species, hunters clamor to hunt them everywhere in the West. Grizzlies were hunted in Montana until 1991, when a court action finally stopped the hunt.

I am not as infatuated with grizzly bears as are some of my friends; I'm too infatuated with mountain lions. But given its position at the top of the food chain, the grizzly is not only our greatest symbol of the wild but an indicator of wilderness health, and I love it for that. To watch a grizzly walk the mountains is like watching a fish in water—a being completely, unconsciously, at home in the world. As predators, they are magnificent. A grizzly can outrun a horse from a standing start, they've been filmed doing somersaults, and I've watched one shake a large tree like a broom. Adult males can weigh over 700 pounds—approximately twice the size of an African lion—and stand eight feet tall. They can roll boulders with one paw that we can't budge. Someone watched a grizzly shaking another 600-pound bear like a rag doll.

When they do come after us, the result can be grim. One man

who was mauled required a thousand stitches to sew up his wounds. However, given their strength, it is remarkable they often treat us so gently, especially when we are their only enemy. They rarely kill us, even though they could easily do so anytime they wished. Since people began making records, grizzlies have killed only seven people in the Greater Yellowstone ecosystem, an area of 12 million acres, much larger than the park. No one knows how many grizzlies we have killed, but during the same period, humans have killed 100 million of their own species.

Our fear of wolves is similarly ill-informed. There is not a documented case of a healthy wolf attacking a human being in North America. Every year, 3 million people suffer dog bites and twenty of them die from their wounds. Nonetheless, as we all know too well, the irrational persists in the face of facts.

We watch the grizzlies for two and a half hours. They never know we are watching, or rather, never let on they know we are watching—a grizzly's sense of smell is so acute it can smell an elk carcass from forty miles away. But the behavior of these bears never varies. They eat, they frolic—happy bears.

We climb on up the ridge. From a withered whitebark pine at timberline hangs a tiny lump of red, a collapsed balloon with the ribbon still attached, the remains of some child's birthday party. Some people would put it in their pack and carry it out. I leave it where it is: The karmic juxtaposition of birthday balloon and grizzly is too pleasing.

We kick steps up a snowfield, then scramble through shattered rock to a col littered with the droppings of mountain sheep. Below us is the south fork of the South Fork of Snowshoe Canyon, the worst boulder field I've ever seen. We don't mind. We have seen grizzlies and we are indulging in that exquisite pleasure—the freedom of the hills.

We reach camp at five-thirty. Dinner is quick and easy. Then we settle in for another night under the stars, among the shades and shadows.

The next morning we thrash our way down to the bottom of the canyon and up the north fork of Snowshoe. As usual, the area we bushwhack through gets the best of us. We go up the right side of the creek and slither around on steep mud, holding on to branches of trees for support.

Noon. We are at two of the most beautiful lakes in the park. The lower one is unnamed, though we call it "Garnet Lake" because of all the black garnets embedded in the gneiss around its shores. The upper one is Talus Lake, tucked under the north face of Rolling Thunder.

In the afternoon we wander north along the divide between Snowshoe Canyon and Webb Canyon at 10,000 feet, heading for another unnamed lake west of Doane Peak. We find what we believe is wolverine scat. Wolverines are rare in Wyoming. The authoritative *Mammals in Wyoming,* published in 1987, shows no sightings in the Tetons, but recently both Peter Koedt and park biologists have seen a number of wolverines in the park. They have probably always been there—a few.

The air sharpens with the smell of rain and I put on my parka. A storm is moving in north of us. We stop and sit out of the wind with our backs against our packs and watch the play of lightning on the peaks. The sky is dark with rushing clouds. We move on a few hundred yards, but the light is so beautiful, I stop again and paint a small watercolor of Elk Mountain and Owl Peak veiled with rain and cloud. Dan is patient, always happy to be surveying the landscape with his field glasses.

We move again and finally reach the lake. As we put up the tent, the clouds descend. Soon it is snowing lightly.

Another cloud has descended, too. Although we don't think the bears saw us, we saw them—unfortunately. We lie in our sleeping bags discussing the fact that Dan is required to report a grizzly sighting. I don't want him to. A reported grizzly is a hassled grizzly.

Here is a healthy, happy sow with two cubs in a part of a national park so remote it had not been visited all summer. According to park biologists the habitat is as good as anything in Yellowstone, perhaps better. She is a smart old sow who has found a good place and is minding her business. And yet, because we saw them, they could be trapped and radio-collared and then, of course, trapped again, tested, poked with needles, measured, harassed, and if the researchers don't actually kill them with all the trapping and drugs, they might grow accustomed to people, lose their fear, become "good bears"—and be easily poached. This is not an idle fear. It has happened in Glacier National Park.

Both of us are troubled: Dan by what he has to do; I by the fact he is required to do it. It is my primary disagreement with the Park Service, indeed with any bureaucracy. As a good Thoreauvian, I believe I am obliged to do only what I believe to be right. I am not obliged to do anything else—regardless of what the rules or laws say I should do. Rules are not about order; they are about obedience. Indeed, I may very well be obliged to resist rules and laws. Thoreau's famous essay, "Civil Disobedience," was originally entitled "Resistance to Civil Government"—a healthy attitude, I think.

There is considerable public resentment toward wildlife biologists intruding into the lives of wild animals, toward the complex laws and rules governing their lives, the intricate management of populations with no care or attention to individual animals, and the elaborate law-enforcement apparatus that protects it all. It may be unjust, but disliking wildlife-enforcement officers is a tradition in Wyoming.

Once I was waiting for a haircut in the Teton Barbershop in

Jackson, the best place in the valley to touch the pulse of social reality. In the chairs were an old cowboy and a Wyoming Game and Fish officer. The cowboy had buried his upper body in a *Casper Star Tribune,* as though protecting himself. The barber accidentally nicked the officer with a razor and he bled a bit. After the officer left, the cowboy said softly into his newspaper, "I'm surprised he had any blood in him."

But then, cowboys don't love grizzlies, either. Indeed, it is hard to find someone who lives around these bears who does—and that's the problem. Most people, say from Florida, love the *idea* of grizzlies, but they don't want to live with them. Yet that's what we must learn to do—live with them, live among them.

The legal status of grizzlies in a national park is a thorny issue for many reasons. The thorniest is the fact that male grizzlies have territories of 1,500 square miles: Sometimes they are in Montana, sometimes Wyoming, sometimes Idaho. Furthermore, they are sometimes in national parks, or national forests—federal lands not usually subject to state laws—sometimes on state lands, sometimes on private lands. Given this complexity, who owns grizzly bears? Does anybody? Doesn't the idea of anyone owning or controlling a grizzly, our great symbol of the wild, sound a bit nutty? Unfortunately, most people believe—and some who know better say—that wildlife is the property of the state. The Supreme Court has consistently thought otherwise.

In *Toomer v. Whitsell* (1948), the Court decided that the theory of state ownership of wild animals was "a fiction expressive in legal shorthand of the importance to its people that a State have power to preserve and regulate an important resource." In *Douglas v. Seacoast Products, Inc.* (1977), it ruled, "It is pure fantasy to talk of 'owning' wild fish, birds, or animals. Neither the State or the Federal Government . . . has title to these creatures until they are reduced to possession by skillful capture." Unfortunately, in *Huges v.*

*Oklahoma* (1979), the Court decided that although the states do not own wildlife, they can control them pursuant to their general police powers, just as they regulate other natural resources.

Wyoming, a states' rights state if ever there was one, ignored the highest court in the land, either out of ignorance or obstinacy—both are possible—when as late as 1986, in *O'Brien v. State,* the Wyoming Supreme Court held that "the declaration of ownership and preemption by the state of the management and control of all wildlife in Wyoming has constitutional sanction." Finally, in 1994, Judge Clarence Brimmer, in *Clajon v. Petera,* decided, "Thus, even though claims of ownership may be 'pure fantasy,' the state's ability to exercise its police power to regulate this resource is unaffected."

In short, the state believes it can act *as if* they own grizzlies. The result, says my lawyer, is "completely disingenuous, an unhappy, contradictory status for wild, free creatures." Right.

Recently Wyoming Game and Fish removed grizzly bear number 209 from the park for killing eleven cow calves *in the park* in sixteen days. It was taken to Lander and lethally injected, sort of like a serial killer. Even though grizzly bear number 209 was radio-collared, it took three weeks to catch him, with the team of biologists working through the night. One smart grizzly, number 209. Too bad his genes are no longer in the pool, but then, modern wildlife management has in many cases taken the place of evolution, and it doesn't select for smart bears, it selects for nice bears with good manners.

Needless to say, for many of us, this is less than satisfactory—thus my fit in the tent beneath Doane Peak. I am still raving after Dan drops off to sleep. He's heard it all before.

It snows all night; the morning is cold and wet. We are glum. Then we spot seven mountain sheep above us on the talus—they are easy to see against the fresh snow, and they lift our spirits. Later, while following an old game trail down Moose Basin we see two black bears and our spirits return to normal. We reach the Webb Canyon Trail at noon, eat a quick lunch, and keep going eight more miles through wet snow to Jackson Lake. Somewhat casually, I count seventeen piles of bear scat along the trail, mostly black bear, but one is grizzly. The difference in size is all too obvious.

At five-thirty we reach a small boat rangers have left for us at the Berry Creek estuary. It is still storming and the lake looks wild, so we wait. The glassy blue lakes of summer are history; now the water is gray and green and tipped with whitecaps. The storm blew many of the leaves off the local aspen into the lake and the waves washed them back to the beach, where they flow in lines, rocking gently. While we wait, I try to paint rocking leaves.

At dark the wind drops somewhat and we bounce nearly two miles across the lake, dodging waves. Dan runs the motor; I lean on the bow to keep us from flipping. When we reach shore, I am soaked and my arms feel like rubber.

As I drive back to Lupine Meadows, snow is sticking to the road. It snows all night. In the morning the mountains are white and ice rims the shallows of Cottonwood Creek. I put on a ski hat and gloves to split wood. Summer is a memory.

With so much fresh snow in the mountains, the issue of finding and radio-collaring the grizzlies does not arise. Happy bears, happy me.

## 11. A Cougar and a Chase

e have had a herd of elk in Lupine Meadows all summer. In late September with the rut in full swing, we can have as many as a hundred. During the day they sleep in the forest, but at dawn and dusk they come out into the meadows. The bulls bellow, challenge one another, and try to increase the number of cows in their harem. Mostly, they posture. Occasionally, they fight and I hear the clack of horns. The cows make sounds, too.

The sound the bull elk makes during the rut is, everyone agrees, difficult to describe. The word *bugling* leaves too much to the imagination, but attempts to be more specific usually end up being humorous. The early English hunters were particularly eloquent and fanciful. Sir Price said: "It is a decided whistle, not unlike a soft note on a clarinet, ending with a very mild sort of grunt at the finish—a most difficult sound to describe, but one which I am happy to say we became very familiar with before the hunt was over. It is the most gentle musical sound that emanates from any animal I ever met with."

Not to be outdone, Baillie-Grohman said: "It is very hard to imitate, or to describe. It is neither a whistle nor a bellow. Not unlike some tones produced by an Aeolian harp, it might also be compared to the higher notes produced by the flageolet, and of course is entirely different from the red deer's call."

Olaus Murie's description in *The Elk of North America* is, in the best tradition of American pragmatism, more prosaic, but it rings true: "The call begins on a low note, glides upward until it reaches high, clear, buglelike notes, which are prolonged, then drops quickly to a grunt, frequently followed by a series of grunts. The call may be very roughly represented thus: 'A-a-a-a-ai-e-eeeeeeeee-eough! e-uh! e uh!' "

Whatever the description, if you live among elk, the rut can keep you awake. Sometimes they make such a ruckus, I go to bed wearing earplugs. I forgive them because once in a while they put on such a stunning show as I sit dazed at the edge of the meadows. The stage is always early morning. The tip of Teewinot is white, but everything beneath it is dark blue and purple. Frost covers the meadows. An inversion leaves a line of fog that hides the lower slopes of the mountain. The owls hoot, the coyotes howl, and bulls wander in the fog, bugling, fighting, protecting their harems. One senses, besides the beauty, that the world gets on just fine without us.

With the hunting season open, poaching becomes a problem. Hunting is legal right up to the park's boundaries. Occasionally someone decides to wander over the boundary, especially in the seldom-traveled northern mountains. Slowly throughout

September, the rangers begin to deal with hunters instead of climbers. As Dan says, he likes to keep some men in the field. Whenever possible, he leaves his desk for the mountains; whenever possible, I go with him.

Dan and I make another trip into the northern mountains to help count mountain sheep and patrol for poachers. The park worries that the sheep population is declining—both in numbers and possibly in physical size—so it has mounted an effort to count them. They have already searched the southern half of the range; now there will be teams of biologists in the north. Since Dan is also on poaching patrol, we won't have as much time as the biologists to sit and look for sheep, but we will cover country they may not visit.

I arrive at Dan's office at the Colter Bay Ranger Station at 9:00 A.M. At 9:30, we load our packs into a nineteen-foot Boston Whaler sporting a 150-horsepower Mercury engine. It looks like a fast, mean machine to me, but the driver, a woman named B. J. Clancy, says it will go only thirty-two to thirty-five miles per hour, while Jet Skis—the biggest patrol problem on Jackson Lake—can go sixty miles per hour and (impossible!) there are no speed limits on Jackson Lake. Despite the public impression that the government is all-powerful, it often appears to me that the park is understaffed and underpowered.

Clancy is dressed like the other rangers: bulletproof vest, .357 Magnum, the usual collection of sprays, bullets, and Asp on her belt. Dan and I bundle up in parkas and stand behind the steering column while B. J. cruises down Colter Bay into Jackson Lake. As we swing west into the lake, she hits the throttle and the bow rises. A merganser hen and her four young swim off to our right. Female mergansers always appear in a hurry, in part because their distinctive crest streams behind their head, suggesting roadrunner-like speed.

The ducks are close, bouncing in the wake. In the strong sidelight I can see the hen's hooked and serrated beak, a salutation from a wilder world.

B. J. heads five miles northwest toward Colter Canyon. Dan has memorized the western shore of Jackson Lake, so we head directly for a small bay north of where Colter Creek enters. B. J. nudges the Whaler to the beach and we jump to the sand without even getting our feet wet. The beach is strewn with driftwood. There are no human tracks; it feels to me like the Yukon or Northwest Territories. After we unload the packs and ski poles, B. J. backs out into the lake with finesse and heads south. Soon we are enveloped in silence.

We lean our packs against a log and get out our binoculars— ten-by-forty Zeiss, the best in the world for mountain travel. Dan knows of an eagle's nest, but no one is home.

We shoulder the heavy packs and head into the canyon. Bear scat—from black bear—is everywhere. We walk in silence, choosing our own paths instead of following each other so as to have less impact. We talk only when we rest. It's hot. We are in shorts and T-shirts; I would rather scratch up my legs than wear long pants.

Faint noises occupy my attention against the background of greater silence: Grasshoppers flutter around cracking their wings, summer-dried twigs snap underfoot, the pack harness creaks, the heart pounds. Time slows; the buzz of human events drops away. Empires are being created, but they will not endure as the cracking and snapping will endure.

In 1974 a wildfire swept Waterfalls Canyon to the south, then jumped the ridge and spread across the lower slopes of Ranger Peak into Colter Canyon. The fire started as a lightning strike on July 17; smoke was not noticed until two days later. With no one to control it, the fire burned itself out according to its own self-organizing principles—as wildfires are supposed to do. It was the first prescribed "let burn" natural fire in the park, one of the first in any national park. By October 24 it had burned 3,700 acres and went out only after winter snow arrived. The fire was quite controversial in its day, since it filled the valley with smoke through much of the tourist season—yet another of the many conflicts resulting from the Park Service's conflicting mandate: On the one hand, preserve the resource in a natural state; on the other, allow visitors to recreate without having to deal with the messier aspects of natural process.

Wildfire is intrinsic to this habitat, shaping soils, vegetation, and wildlife patterns. When T. S. Brandegee of the U.S. Geological Survey visited the area in 1897, he noted: "It is only occasionally that tracts of timber of merchantable size are found . . . due simply and solely to fires that have swept over the country so completely and persistently that scarcely any part has been exempt from them, while nearly all portions have been burned again and again within a generation." The American public's adverse reaction to the 1988 fires in Yellowstone demonstrated how consistently we confuse the scenic with the natural. Despite public opinion, huge wildfires are quite natural. They are also marvelous and beautiful.

The Colter Canyon wildfire changed this habitat according to an ancient order. The slope is open now, filled with berries. The berries of the Oregon grape are petite globes of cold manganese blue. Thimbleberries are still out. With the first frosts, their leaves are turning aubergine. There are huckleberries and thickets of currents. We nibble as we walk.

Like most canyons in the northern Tetons, Colter has no trail, and since the park manages the area as wilderness, it will not have a trail. We make our way slowly, following an irregular path westward several miles into the canyon. North of us are the steep cliffs of Peak 10,075. Only the highest peaks have names here; the others are designated with their altitudes. The peaks in front of us at the head of the canyon appear a muddy pink. It looks like limestone instead of granite.

"What kind of limestone?" I ask Dan.

"Sandstone. Flathead sandstone."

Lower down are bands of gneiss, Precambrian gneiss pushing up Cambrian sandstone as the range continues to grow. When I check the map, I find that a fault line runs across the head of Colter Canyon.

Halfway up the canyon, around 8,500 feet, the cliffs converge. With less sun, the snow stays longer, so the forest is richer; and since the fire did not reach this high, we are in an old-growth forest. The understory is thick with low plant cover. Meadow rue is common. The remains of western cornflowers are level with our shoulders. Engelmann spruce are common, and so are elk beds. We cross a circle of matted grass twenty-five feet in diameter where two bulls have sparred.

At one spot, thimbleberry, huckleberry, blueberry, currant, and gooseberry are all within an arm's reach, and we stop to gorge ourselves. A fat mule deer buck wanders past, noticing us when he is fifty feet away. His rack has only three points, but the tines are thick. He stops to watch us, then circles around to the north, alert, ears as long as his face tracking us like radar, but eating too, not indifferent, unafraid.

A while later, Dan calls me over and points with his ski pole. He doesn't have to say anything. Grizzly scat.

"This is healthy land," says Dan. "Wildfires, all the predators except the wolf, old-growth forest, a full range of flora and fauna. And the wolves will soon be here." They are already in Jackson Hole. One of these springs, they will follow the elk back into this northern wilderness. All of which makes Dan happy. He wishes nothing more from his tenure here than to leave the northern range in better shape than when he arrived.

We move more cautiously now, studying the meadows before we cross them. Lunch at 1:00 P.M. Above us and to the south lies a high open cirque beneath the minor summits running east from Ranger Peak. Where the snow has only recently melted, bright grass glows beneath dark cliffs. It is still spring in parts of the high country. We glass for sheep and bear but see nothing.

"Do you know anyone who has ever been up in that basin?"

"No. Do you?"

"Nope."

Another time. There is high cloud cover and we still have a long ways to go to camp.

Before us is a high buttress that divides Colter Canyon into two forks. We climb steeply into the south fork. I search for a little lake, but it is hidden in a small moraine that was not obvious on the map. The stream is small now, a rill flowing through dense displays of alpine flowers, many just now up, even though it is late September. Lower down, on Blacktail Butte, these flowers bloomed in May. Some—the monkeyflowers, Parry's primrose, Indian paintbrush, elephant head, are common throughout the range, so I've seen them all summer. Others—spotted saxifrage, a single blue gentian—are firsts for me this year and I want to spend time with them, but it is late and cold and we are still in shorts. We keep moving.

The wind is up. Ragged clouds are blowing through with occasional squalls of rain and graupel. The landscape is sublime in the sense of the English Romantics: the towering peaks, their cliffs partly veiled with clouds, the various subtle grays, like ash in a wood-burning stove. The pines on the ridge above us are barren snags flagged with witch-fingered limbs streaming leeward, shaped by a thousand storms.

We can't see the extent of the storm because of the high cirque in front of us, but it does not look good, so we step up the pace.

Camp is at the edge of a small meadow among one of the last

stands of big whitebark pine. A light rain is falling. While I put up the tent, Dan walks a hundred yards away, builds a windbreak with a small tarp, and starts the stove. I am amazed to find arnica still blooming among the grouse whortleberry. Three Clark's nutcrackers arrive to examine us and caw.

Climbers rarely agree about what to eat in the mountains, so we have each brought our own food. Dan has tortillas with fresh onion, tomato, cheese, and instant bean dip. I fix instant mashed potatoes and cover them with dehydrated black bean dip, plus crackers and cheese. The cuisine is not quite up to the Ritz, but, as usual in the mountains, we eat every bite. For dessert we have homemade cookies baked by Dan's wife, Pat, and tea. We wash dishes and wash our hands, trying to keep the smell of food minimal, especially around the tent. We've learned not to sleep in the clothes we eat in; you want to be clean in bear country.

A black bear stepped on me one night in Yosemite, and another time I awoke and found him sniffing my ear. But that was long ago and the bear was so well known, he had a name: Spartagus. I told Spartagus to go away, and he did. I don't want to ask a grizzly to go away.

At dark, we rig the famous bear-proof hanging food bag. Dan finds a whitebark pine about a hundred yards from the tent with a thick, more or less horizontal limb about twenty-five feet off the ground. He puts a stone in a small stuff sack and clips it to a carabiner at the end of a length of nylon cord. After several tries he succeeds in throwing the sack over the limb about six feet out from the tree trunk. He then unclips the stuff sack and replaces it with our food bag. I haul the food bag up until it reaches the limb. Dan ties another loop in the cord about shoulder height and clips another stuff sack into it with another carabiner. He fills this second bag with rocks until the two bags are roughly the same weight. Then we fold the excess cord into a sash and wedge it loosely under the loop with the carabiner. Finally we push the second bag up into the air with a ski pole until both bags are about nine feet off the ground. In the morning we will knock loose the excess cord, pull down the sack of rocks, unclip it from the loop in the cord, and lower the food sack to the ground. I do not know how many years it took *Homo sapiens* to perfect this procedure.

The rain patters on the tent. Dan puts his Sig semiautomatic next to his pillow; I put the pepper spray beside mine. We have no illusions: Neither would protect us against a grizzly. The pepper spray would affect us inside more than a bear outside, perhaps providing spice for its dinner. The Sig is for law enforcement, not for defense against bears. Even at close range, the hollow-point bullets would be ineffective against a grizzly. They cannot penetrate deep enough to hit vital organs and will flatten if they hit large bones. Even when shot several times with high-powered Magnum rifles, grizzlies have been known to live for hours and often still manage to maul their assailant. It has always been thus. Meriwether Lewis, writing in 1805, said: "These bear being so hard to die reather [*sic*] intimedates [*sic*] us all; I must confess that I do not like the gentleman and had reather fight two Indians than one bear . . ."

Besides, neither of us wants to hurt a grizzly. I sometimes wonder if Dan would die rather than protect himself from part of his "resource."

Nonetheless, as members of an irrational species we prepare our meager defenses. Then we try to sleep. The wind moans, the pines creak, the tent flaps, and the rain changes from a patter to a barrage. *Dark* fails to express the Stygian blackness that envelopes you at night inside a small tent during a storm. Our Pleistocene brains reassert their wisdom. Better a cave, a fire, a spear than pepper spray and a Sig inside a nylon casket.

We awake to a few billowing clouds moving fast out of the southwest. It is warm. We eat our oatmeal, then head up the south fork. The rill continues, bordered by more wildflowers. In places, there are still patches of snow in the shadows under the northern cliffs. On a long snowfield we find elk droppings and then a frozen bumblebee curled up like a cat in a shallow depression. I pick it up and brush its rigid hairs with the back of my fingers. Then I put it back, exactly as I found it.

We stop for rest beside a tarn at 10,000 feet; it is shallow but still filling with water from a large snowbank. Mats of bright yellow and orange heath surround slabs of rock that lie about like sarcophagi. The dry sedge bog is so spongy we sink several inches with each step. The stonecrop among the heath is now a brilliant red and I am reminded of the moors in England. Even here at timberline there is autumn color.

The alpine tundra in the Teton Range stretches from roughly tree line, about 10,500 feet, to around 12,500 feet. The tiny plants with sparse venation and simple forms contain jewel-like colors of intense lucidity, especially in autumn. Everything seems brighter here, more vivid, and it is not just the imagination: There is 25 percent more light at this altitude than at sea level, the air is less polluted, and the winds scour everything clean.

Dan looks for sheep while I study plants. On a nearby hill, islands of Engelmann spruce and whitebark pine grow among fields of talus. Nowhere are they more than five feet tall, and usually less. They look more like big bonsai than trees. In the middle of the meadow is a patch of dwarfed willow that blends into the heath subtly and with such similar colors I first think it is a *mound* of heath. I suppose a mountain spirit has been practicing the topiary arts.

Technically, these dwarfed trees are called krummholz, a German word the *Oxford English Dictionary* defines as "crooked wood," or, more charmingly, as "elfin-wood." Their size and shape is a function of the alpine environment. Wind shapes the tiny forest and flags its upper branches; cold interferes with photosynthesis, stunting growth; and water evaporates more rapidly at high altitude, further stressing the plants.

Dan arrives, and as we examine the willow krummholz, he finds an elk's tail. And it doesn't look like it's been there long.

"Stranger than science," Dan says.

Although there is a bit of grass around the edges of the tarn, there is not much here to attract an elk. The slopes above us are steep and barren. What's an elk's tail doing here? We search the area and find a set of elk tracks but no carcass. Another mystery. It suggests a story for a children's book: *The Elk That Lost Its Tail*. We search for the elk carcass; Dan finds an owl pellet with the remains of a rodent's jaw visible on one side, probably a shrew's.

But we are loitering and having too much fun. Time now to grunt five hundred feet to the head of the cirque. We head diagonally up the talus slope to the west, aiming for a small subsidiary ridge that projects off the ridge to the east. Although the talus slope looks bare from below, it is littered with flowers—cinquefoil, purple mustard, columbine, waterleaf, and thistle. At the saddle we find white daisies, phlox, rock jasmine, and one set of elk tracks. The intrepid elk seems driven to extremes, though animals do occasionally get into trouble on the high peaks. Dan knows of a moose that climbed Disappointment Peak but couldn't climb down and so died there.

Sheep tracks surround the grasses; their incisors have clipped them short. We eat lunch and survey the surrounding slopes for an hour. An osprey soars past, migrating south, a red-tail hawk, but we see no sheep. This is worrisome, because perfect sheep country is all around us.

Stretching north a mile is an undulating ridge ending in Peak 10,881. We follow a pleasant sheep trail just to the west of the crest and gradually make our way to the summit along a shattered, rocky ridge. Near the summit we find a hole so large it could only have been dug by a grizzly. At the bottom are the remains of a marmot hole. One pities the marmot hiding in his maze, the beast above digging, digging. Kafka wrote a brilliant short story on the subject—"The Burrow"—really an essay on paranoia pretending to be a story. But this marmot was not paranoid.

The summit is worth the walk. Yellow clumps of grass and flowers cover the sedimentary gravel. Mount Moran is just visible far to the south; the view of Owl and Elk peaks—close to the northwest with their radical, uplifted stratification—is sublime; farther north rise the plateaus of Yellowstone National Park. Straight down is Webb Canyon.

We drop into the north fork of Colter Canyon and arrive at a small lake where park biologists are camped for the night. For the next couple of days they will be counting mountain sheep. We talk sheep and owl pellets with Mason Reid for a few minutes and then move on.

We reach our own camp late, cook, eat, and crash.

The next morning we load the big packs and climb to the col west of Ranger Peak. Ranger is the last of the high peaks in the northern Tetons, remote from the usual paths of mountaineers. The summit is an easy walk. Beneath us to the east is Falcon Canyon with its chain of four delicate lakes—a place I've always wanted to visit. We lounge on top enjoying the views north and south and soaking up what remains of the sun. Clouds fill the western sky, but they are not thunderheads. Somewhat anxious, we descend southwest toward a small tarn. On the way, I notice krummholz high on the south face of Ranger at close to 11,000 feet, what may be an altitude record for the Tetons. Then a bit farther down, I find pale yellow, dwarf alpine paintbrush, a flower I've only seen on the saddle between the Middle and South Tetons.

As we descend along a rivulet that glistens with emerald green moss, the air becomes heavy, the sky sullen. There are no birds. We stop often and glass for sheep but see nothing. The tarn looks like a nice camp, but the ground around it is lumpy and wet so we set up the tent a bit higher, behind a big boulder and an adjoining wall of krummholz. Then we head off in the opposite directions to look for sheep. Eventually I get bored and end up sketching krummholz. Dan persists. Through my binoculars I see him sitting in the lee of a boulder, his back against the rock, his knees up, his elbows on his knees, the Zeiss buried in his face. He is looking intently at Doane Peak. When he finally returns, he is ebullient.

"Well, I saw a big critter," he starts off.

I wait, suspicious that I have missed something important.

"A mountain lion. A big one. Male. Probably eight feet nose to tip of the tail. He came up out of the talus and crossed the pass, right along the base of that snowfield."

He is pointing. We both study the area carefully. I am silent, green with envy. Dan, usually reserved, is bubbling over. "I was looking straight at him in the talus but I didn't see him until he was silhouetted against the snowbank. That's the first mountain lion I've seen in the wild."

This might seem surprising, because Dan has spent a great deal of time in the wild looking at animals, but the mountain lion is a most elusive beast, and unless you are trapping or hunting them, it is rare to see one.

I manage to act delighted for him, even though I've missed an incredible sighting. Dan calls the biologists on the radio to tell him about the lion. More elation. They have found tracks of a small lion—probably a female. Until recently lions have been rare in the park; now Dan might have a breeding couple in his bailiwick.

Sheets of snow drift through the high valley. The wind is up, of course. To the south, the summit of Mount Moran is buried in clouds. We hide in the tent and nurse the little cooking stove. As the storm picks up, the tent sags under the load of wet snow until I'm claustrophobic enough to go out and shake it off. Later the wind drops, but the snow continues to fall; as we fall asleep, its patter is barely discernible, like distant music.

We awake to snow and cloud cover, visibility less than a hundred yards, but we decide to climb Doane Peak anyway. It's on my list of must-do peaks. Dan has never climbed it from the east, and neither of us wants to head home. I find it difficult to leave the mountains. Even after months in the Himalayas with meager rations of lentils, chapatis, mountain tea, and an occasional turnip curry, even with longings for friends, books, the world of showers, fragrant soaps, warm beds, hammocks, cold salads, elk steak, pesto, Chopin, the smell of laundry, of baked bread—even then I find it difficult to leave the mountains. We pack and leave for Doane.

On the pass north of the peak are canid tracks: too small for a coyote, probably a fox—another rare critter in this country. The ascent—merely a walk—is faintly Himalayan, the windblown ridge, the fresh snow, the poor visibility.

Just as we reach the summit, the storm lifts. Beneath us lies a mat of cottony clouds with peaks and ridges poking through here and there. The wind blows, the clouds fracture, and to the south, the north fork of Snowshoe Canyon emerges from the vapors like an apparition, its meadows powdered with snow. Although the temperature is well below freezing, we tarry, studying another perspective of our world and looking for tracks that should now be visible in the snow. We see sheep tracks to the north, and to the west, we spot what might be lion tracks. We descend to take a look, but no—a coyote wallowing in deep, drifted snow.

We spend the afternoon descending Waterfalls Canyon to Jackson Lake. Along the way, we pass another unnamed lake and two

of the finest waterfalls in the park—Wilderness Falls and Columbine Cascade. The going is steep, the terrain maddening. My quads
burn even though I've been guiding all summer. At the mouth of
the canyon, there is another endless bog, of course. Dan says it's a
quarter of a mile to the lake.

An hour later, as we scramble over logs and through muck over
the tops of our boots, I ask, "Dan, is this the fifth quarter? The
third? The fourth?"

We trudge our separate ways until I smell the lake. There it is,
gray, fringed with whitecaps. Dan is north of me, a hundred yards
up the beach. "What took you so long?"

Dan calls B. J. and she heads out to pick us up. After ten minutes
she turns back to Colter Bay to get a larger Boston Whaler. I see
its spray long before I see the boat. The ride back is rough. We
roar down the troughs, then back off the throttle as we drop over
the crests. After we reach Colter Bay and sort equipment, I drive
back to Lupine Meadows, put a Stouffer's dinner in the microwave,
eat it, and crash.

Unfortunately, rangers, like doctors and firemen, are always on
call, and the meaning of "on call" has expanded with the
advent of modern communications. All the rangers are connected
via radios, and more and more backcountry users call rangers with
cell phones. A quarter of the rescues in the park are now initiated
via cell phone. Climbers call rangers at night to ask detailed questions about their route up the Grand Teton; then they call back
later to ask more detailed questions about how to rappel off the
mountain. Ah, wilderness!

At eight o'clock at night, Dan was at the firing range shooting
for his fall firearms qualifications when he received a call from Steve
Cain, the park's chief resource biologist. Steve was counting

sheep from the ridge of Elk Mountain, north of Webb Canyon. Through his spotting scope, he saw three people on horseback leading four packhorses across Forellen Peak. Dan knew where they were heading: a small, well-hidden lake on the east ridge of Forellen, about four miles inside the park—a well-known poaching camp. The area around Forellen is such a superb elk habitat, the locals call it "the Elk Factory."

Dan instructed two rangers, Jeff Rader and Scott Guenther, to ride up Berry Creek. At four o'clock the next morning, Dan paddled his seventeen-foot canoe a mile across a now-calm Jackson Lake and hiked eight miles to the Forellen Divide, a broad saddle between the peak and the park boundary. Around eleven o'clock he found horse tracks entering the park from the west, either via Conant Pass or Jackass Pass. He followed the tracks over the summit of Forellen, walking on grass and stones so as not to leave tracks of his own. Using their radio, Rader and Guenther reported that four riders on a grassy meadow east of the peak had just passed within eighty yards of the hidden rangers. Knowing their camp was unoccupied, Ranger Burgette walked in and looked around.

It was a mess, but messes are misdemeanors, not poaching offenses: camping in an undesignated area; fire in an undesignated area; illegal disposing of refuse; illegal grazing of livestock; injuring plants; off-trail horse use. Without falling into the trap of an illegal search, Dan noted the obvious. One packhorse was white, the rest brown. Their tent was made in Idaho Falls, Idaho, white with a zippered door. Covered panniers, blue halters, trash, an ax, and a case of Busch beer. No guns, but they could be with the riders or in the tent. Then, careful not to leave any tracks, Dan climbed three hundred yards above their camp and bivouacked. Meanwhile, two more rangers, Chris Flagherty and Kevin Killian, hiked into the Upper Berry Creek patrol cabin. Five rangers were in place, waiting for shots.

But the evening passed and there were no shots.

In the morning, the rangers heard bugling, strange bugling—it went in a straight line heading east. Then Rader and Guenther reported three riders with three packhorses heading down into Owl Canyon. The rangers went to the camp, documented the damage, and took off after the riders, who had a couple-mile head start up Owl Canyon toward Horse Thief Pass at the top of Moose Basin.

Fortunately, the riders didn't know they were being followed, and they took a break. Rader, on horseback, caught them just below the divide. Dan, in a bad mood from running several miles, caught up a few minutes later. When they refused to be cooperative, his mood got worse. Dan said later, "They didn't know their names, didn't know where they lived, didn't know anything, by golly!" Dan is the only person I know who can get away with saying "by golly."

"Okay, there are two ways we can handle this," Dan told them. "You can tell me what we need to know, we will issue mandatory citations, and you can talk to the magistrate. Or you can sit in jail until you decide who you are." They gave their names but still couldn't remember their addresses.

Finally, Dan said, "They fessed up."

Sort of. They started lying. They claimed they camped near Survey Peak, outside the park. They denied they had ridden off-trail and that they had traveled with a fourth person.

Dan started asking questions. What kind of tent did they have? They described a white pyramid tent with a zipper, made in Idaho Falls. One of their pack animals was a white horse. They had Busch beer. Dan went down the list. Everything checked out. Then he told them exactly where they had camped, what it looked liked, and exactly what they had done the previous day. They looked glum—it wasn't exactly a Godfather-style criminal operation.

Dan cited them for the misdemeanors and added a new one:

providing false information. The total was around eight hundred dollars in fines. Then the rangers let them go.

Where was the fourth person, the one the rangers probably heard bugling that morning? Ranger Rich Baerwald contacted a man at the Hominy Peak Trailhead, several miles outside the park across Jackass Pass, who had just loaded two lathered horses into a horse trailer. He had a rifle in his truck. He was anxious and wanted to leave, but he submitted to a voluntary search, which revealed no blood or hair under his nails, so he was not cited. The ranger did note, however, that he was drinking a can of Busch beer.

The case dragged through the courts. There was no U.S. attorney in Jackson; and the closest one, 285 miles away in Casper, didn't want to start a trial in Jackson over a collection of misdemeanors. The defendants wanted a trial, but they wouldn't enter a plea of guilty or not guilty. The case drifted into limbo. The U.S. attorney wrote a letter; the defendants ignored it. The U.S. attorney got angry and filed charges in the U.S. District Court in Cheyenne, five hundred miles from where the defendants lived. The defendants hired a local attorney who had been caught illegally snowmobiling in Grand Teton National Park and convicted for timber theft. They all drove to Cheyenne and pleaded not guilty—by golly.

Plea bargaining began. Finally the young couple paid fifty dollars each and the old man paid five hundred. They were also ordered to stay out of the north end of the Tetons for a year. Not much, given all the hassles, but no one will use that poaching camp any time soon.

Still, it is little wonder that poaching in the park is common and casual. Until the fifties, Ashton, Idaho, threw a free annual banquet featuring elk and venison poached from Grand Teton National Park. For many locals the park is just a line on the map and an elk is an elk. They were here before the park existed; some fervently believe they will be here after the park ceases to exist. Some small part of me admires them.

My grandfather—I called him "Pop-Pop"—was part owner of a hunting camp on Buffalo Mountain in eastern Pennsylvania—a reminder of how far our bison once roamed. The men in my family hunted and fished all year. I never ate store-bought meat at my grandparents' house. My grandmother tended a large garden and ran an extensive canning and jam operation, so I didn't eat many store-bought vegetables or fruit, either. The Depression hurt them (the local bank folded and all my grandfather's savings were lost), but they were never desperate. They could always, as they said, "make do." Even as a young boy, I knew that deer season was in the fall, so when we had fresh venison in the summer, I would ask about it. Pop-Pop would say, "Jackie, meat is meat." My uncle Bubbie, his son Pud, and my dad would smile.

Perhaps it is my Appalachian heritage, or perhaps I've read too much modern French philosophy, but I cannot help but relish the irony of having half the ranger force in Grand Teton National Park chasing elk poachers at the north end of the park while the other half of the Grand Teton National Park ranger force is checking the permits of 2,800 hunters who the park has "deputized" as short-term "rangers" to kill 927 elk at the south end of the park.

Dan's position is clear: "My duty is to enforce the law. And besides, they don't just poach elk; they poach sheep and bear. You don't want that, do you? And do you want to talk about those folks we caught with the fresh bear heart?"

No, I don't. *Quad erat demonstrandum.*

But . . . but . . . I cannot help noticing the distortion between all this and what used to be.

In another world I would wait for the rut to end, then make my preparations. Perhaps one evening I would pass my rifle through sage smoke from sage picked down along the creek where the local elk leave and enter the forest. Then one morning when it was wet and foggy, after the fallen leaves no longer rustled underfoot and before the first noisy, crusted snow, I would wander down the side of the meadows before first light and wait behind a cottonwood until the elk left the forest. I would shoot the first young bull or cow that offered a clean shot. I would cut off the feet and head and place the head on the feet, facing Teewinot. I would butcher the carcass there, haul the meat to the cabin, and eat the liver for breakfast, like my father and grandfather before me. Many others would feast, too. The hooves and head would remain for many years. I would visit them from time to time and offer thanks.

## 12. Moose Basin

October is my favorite month in the Tetons. The nights are in the teens, the days in the fifties or sixties—sweater weather. The elk are ending their rut; the deer and pronghorn are prominent. They are bunched and easy to see. The songbirds are gone, the last mountain bluebird. Flocks of geese and ducks are flying south. The forest along the creek is naked again. The mountains wait for the first winter storm, the storm with snow that will not melt until next July. We are always trying to get in the last trip before that storm. One day Dan calls—this time we're going up Moose Basin, a vast rolling meadow punctuated with islands of conifers and home to the greatest variety of game in the park.

We leave Lizard Creek Campground at the north end of Jackson Lake around eleven o'clock—Dan, his son Lane, and his friend Toby Carman. The lake is calm, but Dan's 16-foot aluminum boat with its 9.9-horsepower engine grinds along slowly, the gunwales low and slopped with water.

We're heading for the bay beyond Wilcox Point, where Berry Creek and Moose Creek empty into the lake. The west end of the bay is a bog of willows and mud flats pierced by several deep, clear channels. Stumps from the cleanup when the dam was finished in 1914 still clog the end of the bay, making progress difficult. Lane is standing at the bow, searching for the route. We nose in, push with oars, back out, try again. There are beaver lodges around us; the aspen and cottonwood are dropping their last leaves. They edge the channel like gold filigree. Finally we reach the entrance to Berry Creek and tie the boat off to a clump of willows.

The ground is boggy, filled with thick grasses, sedges, and an occasional mountain gentian, its deep blue flower a welcome contrast to the brown meadow. There are many well-worn trails, the work of elk. In his field notes for 1910, the biologist Merritt Cary remarked that Webb Canyon was crisscrossed with elk trails, "from the dense willow thickets along Moose Creek up to the limit of trees at 10,000 feet." Fortunately, this is still true: Webb Canyon is elk paradise.

At noon we stop and strip to shorts and T-shirts, thankful for the absence of mosquitoes and deerflies. Dan points to a huge thistle, five feet tall. "Canada thistle. Probably arrived with hay."

Canada thistle is an exotic—not indigenous to the Tetons. Unfortunately, it is now quite common, along with several other exotic thistles. Until recently, wranglers threw hay off a boat and fed it to their horses before heading up Webb. Horses are still allowed on this trail, but no grazing is allowed, and the horses must be fed processed horse feed, pellets certified to be weed-free. Exotics are the bane of the resource biologist. During the summer, two park biologists are devoted to eradicating them.

Toby and Lane are in the tenth grade. They've lived most of their lives in Jackson Hole and are happy to be in the mountains. There're both fit as SEALs. I once watched Toby hang by his knees from a rope ladder set at forty-five degrees and do sit-ups for so long, I got bored watching. I ask them what sports they play at school.

"None," says Lane. "We just climb and ski." Lane is carrying the biggest pack. He's beginning to haul his dad up hard climbs now. As Dan says, "Grim."

We hit the trail up Webb and turn west into the mountains. It's nine miles to the patrol cabin at 8,500 feet and the days are shorter now. We walk spread out, alert, the way you walk in country where something can eat you; we study the meadows before we cross them.

At one o'clock, we stop for lunch and talk about formative books, books that might help explain why we are hauling heavy packs in the wilderness on Saturday instead of watching football on television. The books that made the greatest impression on me were T. E. Lawrence's *Seven Pillars of Wisdom* and R. M. Patterson's *Dangerous River.* I can be a bore about the merits of *Dangerous River,* but Dan tops me with *Caruso of Lonesome Lake,* his favorite book in high school, upon which he is quite willing to expound. Finally the boys wander off to look for boulder problems and study the white water in the canyon below. Dan and I turn to our journals.

We visit an old mine cut several hundred feet into solid basalt, a hard blackish igneous rock composed of hornblende, iron, and feldspar that is of marginal interest to miners. John Graul, a hermit, worked it alone for twenty-three years with a four-pound sledge, a chisel, and dynamite. No one knows what he was looking for in his mine. The Tetons did not produce much of interest to the mining fraternity. They searched for gold and silver in the southernmost peaks, lead in Death Canyon, and asbestos in Berry Creek, but they found nothing of interest, except, of course, the place.

Graul helped build the Jackson Lake Dam. After that, he

worked his mine each year from July through October. He worked six days a week from exactly 8:00 A.M. to 5:00 P.M., and being a religious man, he didn't work on Sundays. Nor did he hunt or fish. Every week, a boat crossed Jackson Lake with a supply of beans, sowbelly, and reading material. Graul was a handsome, well-dressed man. He lived with his dog, his books, and his work. Since I've lived that way myself, I think of him with empathy.

After years without luck, Graul temporarily went to work the mines in Colorado, where he took a long fall in a shaft and died. With surprising gusto, Dan notes that Graul was working on Sunday. I worry about what happened to his dog.

The entrance to the mine is well hidden. We walk the length of the shaft using headlamps. It is perhaps seven feet square and two hundred feet deep, a marvel of labor—though one wonders at the mind that could work alone for years in such a black pit. There is water on the floor, old boards over puddles, and, remarkably, a few mosquitoes. It is wet and cold—a place for trolls. On the walls are clusters of moths a pale reddish brown. None of us has seen them before. Since I suffer from claustrophobia, I am happy to leave.

After the mine, the sunny autumn landscape is suffused with color and life. Huckleberry leaves are variations on salmon and coral pink; rattlesnake plantain is brilliant green; the mountain ash is bright red.

The canyon narrows where Moose Creek cuts through hard veins of quartz in the gneiss bedrock, its contours serpentine, almost fleshy, the line between animal and mineral strangely fuzzy. There are cascades and falls and deep pools with mayfly hatches dancing in the sunlight. The cobbles on the bottom of the creek glow with the colors of prehistoric cave paintings. Suddenly, the colors fade. High, milky altostratus moves in from the west.

In the late afternoon we watch two small birds chase a bald

eagle. A bit later, I hear an owl. Lane watches it disappear into the forest. "It's a long-eared owl," says Dan.

We are standing in a forest of giant green gentian, five feet tall. Each is filled with hundreds of dead flowers. I pick a single pod and count forty-nine chocolate-brown seeds. We argue over how many miles it is to the patrol cabin. I think it's quite a ways, since whitebark pine are still above us. Lane says two miles, Dan says more. I suggest we look at an incredible object one can buy in the stores—a map. Lane is right: two miles.

We cross a fresh avalanche path, probably from last spring. It came down the north side of the canyon, crossed the canyon floor, and climbed 150 feet up the other side of the canyon, leaving a wreck of mature logs like the flotsam a wave leaves on a beach. Avalanches this size are not common. You remember them.

The sound of a jet breaks my reverie. As it passes overhead, its contrail drifts rapidly to the northeast. Big winds up high.

We go on, then stop again at sundown in a meadow Dan wants to explore. I put on my DAS parka and arrange my Crazy Creek chair for a good view of the mountains. Then I search for sheep and bear. Dan and the boys look along the creek for signs of an old campsite where Dan thinks Dr. Steward Webb and his party camped in 1897 while hunting mountain sheep in Moose Basin. According to Major Sir Rose Lambert Price, who accompanied Webb and describes their hunt in *A Summer on the Rockies,* Webb camped for two weeks in the canyon named for him and shot four sheep, one of which "carried a good head."

This was a spur camp. The main camp was down on the Snake River. (Jackson Lake Dam had not been built yet, so there was just the river at the entrance to Webb Canyon.) It consisted of 150 men—officers, noncommissioned officers, troopers, civilian employees, enlisted teamsters, packers, Indian guides, and servants— 113 horses, and 164 mules. There was a chef. Champagne was

available every night. According to Price, the Webb party killed
forty-three elk, thirty-seven antelope, fourteen mountain sheep,
and "various sorts of grouse, sage hens, wild ducks, and some few
thousand trout." It is enough to make me bow down in humble
thanks to the ghost of John D. Rockefeller for giving the country
Grand Teton National Park.

Even though Webb Canyon, Moose Basin, and the surrounding area is part of Grand Teton National Park and the Jedadiah
Smith Wilderness, and even though it is among the least-visited
places in Wyoming, the mountain sheep population is barely hanging on, and grizzlies, cougars, and wolverines are rare. Without this
protection, they wouldn't be here at all, and there probably
wouldn't be many elk, either. To read Price is to glimpse the bleak
path not taken.

Despite a careful search, Dan and the boys find nothing. We
move on, arriving at the patrol cabin at 6:30. The temperature is 44 degrees and falling rapidly. The cabin faces east in an
open meadow at 8,500 feet. Dan says that sometimes during the
winter when the weather is bad, it can be hard to find. "Right,"
says Lane. "Once I had to dig down to find the top of the
chimney."

There is a stream that begins at a fine spring two hundred yards
uphill, a pool worthy of Narcissus. It never freezes. Even during
the coldest winter nights when the temperature reaches 50 or 60
below, it flows beneath twenty feet of snow. Sometimes there is a
hole; sometimes one must break through the crust. In either case,
you lower a bucket attached to a rope—not quite like turning on
the tap.

The Moose Basin cabin was built to assist Olaus Murie's research on elk, a study that resulted in his masterly *The Elk of North*

*America.* A sign on the front says MOOSE BASIN PATROL CABIN, GRAND TETON NATIONAL PARK. Horses and mules hauled the materials and furnishings nine miles up the trail from Jackson Lake. It is a simple mountain cabin, twelve feet wide and fourteen feet long, with a nicely pitched metal roof. The walls are batten and board over plywood. Thick panels of sheet metal and plywood cover the door and windows, offering further protection from bears and humans. The window panels are bolted close through the frame; the door is secured with a heavy hasp and a serious padlock. The cabin has been broken into several times over the years, and backcountry rangers have been forced to make major repairs. The door and frame have been ripped out several times; once an entire wall was torn off. Bullet holes in the door are evidence someone tried to shoot the lock. Poachers and snowmobilers are the main suspects, since both despise park regulations.

Inside, we remove four-by-four posts bolted to the cross beams to help hold the winter snow load. The furnishings are spare. There is a small table with a propane stove, a Coleman lantern, a fold-down table concealing a pantry, two metal lockers for food storage, and a small Waterford wood-burning stove. Mattresses and folding chairs stand against the wall. Sleeping bags are stored in the rafters, buckets for hauling water stand just inside the door, and antique pots and pans hang from nails. The lid on one says GTNP, CCC.

And there are tools, tools that were common sixty years ago, tools that were known and understood and used with great specificity. Now they would appear mysterious to most visitors: a Pulaski, a double-bite ax, a bow saw, a picket, a sledge, a maul. The proper place for each tool is written on the wall above a pattern of nails indicating where it should hang. There are written instructions for using the lantern, the stove. Everything is neat and functional, like the cabin of a sailing ship. Perhaps a bit too much so. On the door a wit has written "Door."

Toby is making a large cheesecake in a pan. Lane puts on water for spaghetti and works on a tomato sauce mixed with a pound of ground elk meat from the spike bull he killed at the north end of the National Elk Refuge last month. I kid him about hunting on a refuge, shoving the irony at him, as usual. He smiles, impervious.

Meanwhile, we change into warmer clothes.

Dan is on the radio.

"Seven zero zero, four seven zero. Radio check."

"Four seven zero, loud and clear."

"Copy."

The park dispatch number is 700; 470 is Dan. Dan is required to keep his radio on, and all the channels are open (you can hear everyone talk), so we fix dinner in this remarkable cabin in this wild place to the monotonous drone of law-enforcement talk—license plates, car types, names. More irony, I think, but I am bored with irony, and soon our talk turns to our favorite subject: wilderness and wildness and all the rare critters in this area—wolverine, lynx, cougar, fisher (possibly), grizzly, and, recently, a few wolves.

We are up at dawn. I go outside to meditate, then make oatmeal with dried cranberries, cinnamon, milk, and maple syrup. Dan and the boys are going to patrol along the upper edge of Moose Basin and the headwaters of Owl Creek, in the next canyon to the north. I'm going to stay at the cabin and enjoy the solitude. They leave; I wash dishes, fill the wood rack inside the cabin, and turn to my journal.

After a while, I notice an old map. It turns out to be the 1948 topographic map of the park, a map I've never seen. Placed next to the current map, the old one shows pentimenti: Ranches emerge, dirt roads crisscross the valley, reaching every lake; trails penetrate now trail-less canyons and circumambulate lakes now wilder and less traveled. Like the lavish hunting expeditions portrayed in Sir Price's book, the pentimenti on the 1948 map represent possibilities that we as a people changed our minds about, just as painters sometimes change their minds. Had we not done so, the park's lovely piedmont lakes would resemble the south shore of Lake Tahoe, a warren of fast-food joints, motels, amusement parks, trailer courts, monster homes, condos, huge movie screens, and marinas. The old map is a reminder. I bow again to the ghost of John D. Rockefeller.

I paint sketches of the stream, the pool, and Peak 10,881. I glass for sheep and bear. There are still grasshoppers about, mountain chickadees, Clark's nutcrackers feeding on the seeds of whitebark pines. Robins pick at the dirt next to the cabin. Jet stream clouds sail northeast. At two-thirty I spot the patrol on the slopes of Peak 10,333, directly north of the cabin—a perfect mountain from which to scan ten miles of park boundary, and they are doing just that. With my binoculars I can see them sitting among blocks of Madison limestone, bodies bent forward, looking through field glasses.

I study the guest log. The number of guests has increased dramatically over the past five years, but still: how many trails in our national parks are overgrown with grass? The day passes uneventfully, oblivious to events in the outside world. The patrol returns. We eat a simple dinner of macaroni and cheese and go to bed early. If the weather holds, we plan to climb Elk and Owl peaks tomorrow, October 14.

Alas, Elk and Owl will continue to elude us. It snows during the night, the temperature drops to 22 degrees. Sheepishly we admit we should have brought our heavier boots. We sleep in and banter through a late breakfast.

At eleven o'clock the world looks brighter, and we head west to climb Moose Peak, traverse the divide south, visit Horse Thief Pass, perhaps even reach the north ridge of Glacier Peak.

The day is cold and bleak, with storm clouds breaking up around us. The ground is frozen, heaved by frost. We watch a lone immature bald eagle flying south. Dan and I climb up to the divide through talus and scree; Toby and Lane elect to climb a rotten snow- and ice-filled chimney—unroped. Occasionally, dainty pika tracks inscribe the snow patches among the talus, making it look like lace. They are still gathering grass for winter. Tracks of a long-tail weasel wind between the pika tracks—the food chain made visible.

Moose Peak is nothing to boast about; a mere bump on the divide, but it's a good place to glass for poachers. Both north and south are wide saddles easily crossed with pack animals. After half an hour of surveillance, we drop south down the ridge to Horse Thief Pass, probably the least-used pass in Grand Teton National Park. Horse Thief Pass boasts a sign and trail mileage, even though it doesn't appear on the topographic maps.

The divide south of Horse Thief Pass is a solitary ridge of lime-stone shards, mats of brown and desiccated grasses, tufts of phlox, still white as snow, and occasional islands of krummholz, dwarfed and distorted by gales. Ice storms have blasted clean the stumps of dead trees, fretting some, polishing others smooth as metal. They glow with a soft silver sheen. The walking is easy, the views the essence of grandeur.

Below us lie the western slopes of the Teton Range, the Jedediah Smith Wilderness: the South Fork of Bitch Creek, Hidden Corral Basin, Camp Lake, Dead Horse Pass, Carrot Ridge. I can see the braids of Bitch Creek and above it meadows with thick stands of aspen.

I killed an elk on the south face of Carrot Ridge. I was working for the Linn brothers, Gene and Ben. I had just spent part of two days searching for a wounded elk. I found where he had slept both nights, wound to the ground, leaking only a trace of blood. I let him go.

I was riding Tail Feathers, one of Ben's horses, up the South

Fork of Bitch Creek, looking for Ben and his client. Above me was a small herd of elk. I tied Tail Feathers to a tree and stalked the herd, wanting a better look at the bull. Suddenly, above me, the client shot perhaps six times, wounding the five-point bull, though he was still running. His harem of seven cows ran too, leaving him to his fate. I yelled to let them know I was there. The client yelled, "Shoot the son of a bitch, Jack. I'm out of ammunition."

I ran on the level through the sagebrush, knowing a wounded animal will drop downhill. After several hundred yards I crossed a knoll, and there he was, gulping air, bleeding, staring at me. I shot him just above the heart with a .270 at forty yards. Chunks of rib and lung spewed into the sagebrush behind him. He hit the side of the hill hard, managed to get his front legs under him, and tried to stand, but he couldn't. He rolled downhill, stretching his neck and gently tucking his rack back along his rib cage so it wouldn't catch on the ground. He tried to stand again, but he failed. He rolled a second time, again stretching his neck and tucking his rack, tucking it with grace. Then he was still. I walked up to him with my grandfather's voice playing in my mind: "Careful, Jackie. There're not dead till they're dead." I knelt on both knees in front of the bull, my rifle across my thighs, as if in supplication.

He was still alive. A fine mist of blood sprayed from his nostrils. He licked it off slowly, carefully. He looked me right in the eye. Then Ben walked up, his right arm bent in a cast—the result of a horse accident. His left arm hung straight, my grandfather's .45 Colt in his hand. Ben holstered the Colt and knelt beside me without a word. Then he took the single-shot Ruger rifle off my knees and lightly touched the elk's eyeball with the side of the barrel. Nothing. He handed the rifle back to me. After several minutes of silence, he said, "That's the way it is down in Texas."

The country is whole. We have divided it with our minds. In one sense, the line between designated wilderness and designated park is invisible, a legal fiction. In another sense, it is quite visible: It follows the top of this ridge, a division by watershed. That it also marks where we can kill and where we can't kill is inscrutable, at least to me, and most certainly to the elk. To kill here is to become a violator; to kill there is to procure meat for your family or earn money or swell your ego, become an instant hero to some, to others a blood-tainted slaughterer of innocent beings. As a Buddhist, I struggle with our first vow—"No killing"—and another: "Beings are numberless," we sing; "I vow to save them." For a long time I thought these vows were literal, but I was wrong. As my teacher once pointed out to me, to save the many beings requires saving your car keys and asteroids, which suggests a deeper inquiry, deeper than the issue of how we obtain our food.

Dan is still glassing. We lie in the sun, lazy, until I begin to fall asleep. A shadow moving across my face wakes me, and we move on down the ridge until we drop off the divide to a tarn just inside the wilderness boundary. In the space of several hundred yards, we have passed through two kinds of Cambrian sedimentary rocks, Death Canyon limestone and Wolsey shale, past Quaternary talus probably only 20,000 years old, into Archean layered gneiss and magnetite nearly 3 billion years old. We've crossed a point where the Teton Fault disappears under the debris of old seas.

Whitebarks and subalpine fir surround the tarn. There are splendid slabs of gneiss pitted with garnets; in the tarn are freshwater shrimp, caddis larvae, water beetles; around us are Clark's nutcrackers, piles of bear scat, and two golden eagles, heading south.

The boys skip stones. I know a woman who teaches her students to ask the stone's permission before they move them, and I approve, but now I say nothing. I fill my water bottle in the tarn. I think of Zen master Dogen filling a cup with water and always pouring half of it back. I pour some water back into the tarn, though not half. Dan is studying bear scat. Some contains cambium, the inner bark of a tree, which is filled with nutrients. Bears strip the outer bark with their claws, then rip off the inner bark with their teeth. Other scat contains the hulls of whitebark seeds. Black bears.

We cross back into the park and traverse Moose Basin toward the patrol cabin. Little rills course down through the limestone; brown stalks of green gentian fill the meadows. Elk graze the eastern slopes of Webb Canyon. The sun is down, it's cold, and the wind has picked up again. We stomp through snow that still lingers on the northern sides of the rolling meadows.

"I love seeing snow on the ground," Toby says.

"Me too," I reply. "I love bad weather."

Toby smiles. "So do I."

We arrive late. Dinner has gone downhill: Rice-a-Roni with canned chicken. Dan saves the evening with another cheesecake.

Next morning the sky is overcast. At nine o'clock it is snowing lightly, so lightly that you can still see the summits of the peaks. We pack, clean up, put the posts back under the cross beams, and bolt the windows. Dan leaves the stove filled with kindling and twisted paper—a one-match fire. Even so, he wedges two matches into the vent on the stove door. The lantern is full and two matches rest against its base in a small triangle. The stack of wood reaches the ceiling. This may be the last time anyone visits before winter, and when you arrive at this remote outpost in winter, you want warmth and light—you want it easy and you want it fast.

We reach the lake at four o'clock. Five trumpeter swans lift off as we cruise out of the bay, then a bald eagle. It is calm here, but farther south the lake is dark and tipped with whitecaps. At Lizard Creek, Dan lets Lane and Toby take the boat south to Leek's Marina while we drive, but it is so rough he soon waves them in from the highway. Then Toby and I drive south in my truck while Dan and Lane pound down the lake through snow squalls, Dan running the engine, Lane standing with one knee on the bow to keep the boat from flipping in the waves. The fifteen-minute trip takes forty-five minutes. When they reach the marina, I ask Dan if he had a nice voyage. He allows he wouldn't want a nicer voyage on that lake. I head home. Dense clouds are pouring down the canyons, flowering over the peaks. I count 231 elk on the sagebrush flats between Jackson Lake and Lupine Meadows.

## 13. Early Winters

I n country where it can snow any day of the year, it is difficult to say exactly when winter begins. There are calendar winters and scientific winters, but in Lupine Meadows winter begins when snow remains on the ground. Slightly before this happens, eagles arrive at Cottonwood Creek on their migration south. Slightly afterward, weasels and hares change their summer browns and grays for winter coats of white. The actual date varies, though it is usually some time in November.

Until the fifties, the road through the park was the only road north to Yellowstone, and the park kept it plowed all winter. Until recently, the road remained open until deep snow closed it—what we might consider a natural closing. Now the road is gated the night of October 31. Thus the season for the interior of Grand Teton National Park is six months long. Sometimes the closing coincides with the arrival of winter and sometimes not. One Thanksgiving I walked nine miles up to Lake Solitude, at 9,035 feet, in the north fork of Cascade Canyon. Except for a dusting of snow in the deepest shadows, the trail was clear. Snow level was 10,000 feet and the peaks were frosted like ice-cream cones, but the canyons were dry.

But that is rare; usually the storms in late October and early November close the mountains and the few souls that venture there are alone—I do not believe this is accidental—people seeking solitude, people who know that nothing so magnifies solitude as a storm in the mountains. The storms will not last long—a couple of days. They will drop a foot or so of snow, more above 11,000 feet, but they will be wilder storms, winter storms, storms of what is still the Wild West.

The American West has the wildest weather of any place on earth. There are colder places and hotter places, places with higher winds, places with more snow, but no place can match the variations between Death Valley's record high of 134 degrees and Montana's record low at Roger's Pass of −70 degrees—a distance of only 800 miles. Paint a broad line between the two and you will also mark one of the lowest population densities in the country. The cowboys and Indians may be gone, but the Wild West remains.

Changes in temperature mean changes in pressure; changes in pressure mean wind and storm. During the winter, winds in the Tetons can approach a steady 120 miles per hour. Add the low temperatures in the park and you have a place of snow. The lowest recorded temperature in the park is −63 degrees at Moran, the second-coldest recorded temperature in the contiguous states. At 9,500 feet in these mountains, snowfall averages five to six feet a month from December to March. In December 1996, it snowed twelve feet at the base of the range. When I skied to the cabin that winter, I could ski directly onto the ridge of the cabin's roof.

Given the solitude of November, my attention turns again to

the animals, although few remain. The pronghorn have left for the Gros Ventre Range and their winter grounds in the Green River Basin; the deer have headed south to the Gros Ventre buttes. Most of the Lupine Meadows elk, poor beasts, are running the legal gauntlet of hunters on their way to the National Elk Refuge, though a small herd may still graze the lower slopes of Teewinot. Moose are still common, and tracks in the snow allow more intimacy with smaller critters.

Birds are still migrating. Flocks of mallards crowd the remaining pools of Cottonwood Creek; lines of northern pinheads stream south, and occasionally I see snow geese or tundra swans. The feeling of the meadows is harsh, barren, rather like one of Andrew Wyeth's pitiless winter scenes. Hence the eagles are a welcome presence.

J ust before dawn I awake to the cries of eagles flying up Cottonwood Creek. I lie in bed and listen to their calls, which to my ear resemble the shrieks of gulls, shrieks that can wake me from my dreams. I can never decide if they sound like distress, alarm, or despair. Or perhaps their calls have evolved to frighten and intimidate. I do not know. At times, when I do not hear them, I believe I can feel their presence. We have lost the language of presence— we are reduced to speaking of "vibes"—but the sense of animal presence remains, implacable as touch or smell.

I get up in the dark and walk out onto the porch, my bare feet stinging from the coat of ice. I look down the creek with the binoculars. I make them out even in the hazy light—wedges of black, their heads shining dully, like dark sentinels waiting for I know not what.

I start the stove and wait for light. I know where the eagles will be: they return to the same trees, the same limbs—indeed, it seems to me, the same perches—year after year. I can go for eleven months without seeing an eagle on Cottonwood Creek; then one morning I hear their cries, get up at dawn, and find them on their ancestral limbs, looking at me just as they did before they left the previous winter. Initially two or three will arrive; then the number grows to eight or ten, though one memorable morning I counted nineteen from my porch.

I make coffee and peer into the pearly ice fog rising off the creek; it has coated the cottonwoods, alders, willows, and grasses with rime. On a snag across the slough are two eagles in their usual spot, one immature—it looks about two years old. The young bird is preening; the mother stares south, not deigning to dignify my presence with her attention. But when I set up the spotting scope, I can see she is studying me, obliquely. There is rime along the edges of her feathers; even the tiny feathers at the corners of her eyes are coated. She is venerable, imperial.

An eagle's immobility is as impressive as its size and bearing. Eagles rarely move when they are visiting the creek—a slight turn of the head, no more. Then, for no reason I can discover, they fly to another tree and settle onto another tribal perch. Once, I timed one perched in the snag for an hour and ten minutes—sitting, staring, as though something important was about to happen. But unlike in the movies or, say, *Wild Kingdom,* nothing happens, no drama, and after a while you realize that this nondrama of nature is one of its enticing secrets. These eagles are the Taoists of the bird kingdom, the masters of nondrama. And when they actually do something, it is usually decisive.

I'm told they are here because the whitefish are spawning down from Jenny Lake—the whitefish being the park's only native fall spawner. When the lake temperature drops to just above freezing, they descend into Cottonwood Creek. Schools of them swarm in pools beneath shallow riffles—often the same pools that are filled with mallards. Occasionally a big cutthroat will follow them and hold several feet downstream from the school, feeding on ova and milt. But in the many years I've watched the eagles, I've never once seen them attempt to catch a fish. Sometimes they sit in trees along the edge of Jenny Lake, but I've never seen them fish the lake, either. And yet they must eat.

I'm told they spend the days along the creek and feed at night on piles of elk guts in the killing fields at the south end of the park. Perhaps, but there are many lines of cottonwood trees between the killing fields and Lupine Meadows. Native eagles are around, it's true, but not that many. Even if they are feeding on offal, why do they return here? And why are they sometimes here until January, a month after hunting season has closed? Perhaps there was once a reason that time has overturned, or diminished, but they still return, either from habit or for deeper reasons, reasons more akin to rituals. I prefer to believe this and its attendant mystery.

Only once have I seen a migrating eagle attempt to take food from the creek. An immature bird dove into a narrow pool packed with mallards, the mallards exploded in ten directions, and the eagle, talons braced, hit the water with the eagle equivalent of a belly flop. It returned to the tree and perched next to its mother, fluffed its feathers, and stared into the distance. The mother stared too, as though to say, Fool.

My attention turns from the eagles in the snag to a set of weasel tracks. Weasel tracks are distinctive—you cannot mistake them. The tracks are parallel—as if you had touched a dumbbell to the snow—with an eighteen- to twenty-inch hop between them. This weasel hopped across the dry slough of the creek, sniffed my meditation platform, then nonchalantly hopped across my porch and slid under Jim Williams's cabin. I follow the tracks, binoculars in hand, hoping to see it. From the cabin it goes to the bathhouse, across the parking lot to a lodgepole pine, up into the pine, down, and thence under Kim Schmitz's cabin. There are no exit tracks, so it probably discovered a week's worth of our always-plentiful cabin mice.

When I return to the cabin for breakfast, the two eagles are still in the snag, watching. They will remain along the creek until December or early January, then one morning they will continue their cycle of returning—south and north, spring and fall.

I pack for my last walk of the year around Jenny Lake. A few other folks have walked it too, so a path has been stomped down in the snow. The loop is a little over seven miles, cabin to cabin.

Everything has changed. The Moose Ponds are covered with black ice, the boat dock is gone, the cascades of Cascade Creek are now a mere trickle, filled with slush. There is ice on the boulders, ice at the edges of the stream, icicles hanging from the bridge, and sheet ice with elaborate crystal patterns over the few remaining pools. The shallow bay where the creek enters Jenny Lake is frozen solid for several hundred feet, with blue water lapping at the outer edges.

I visit favorite places in my private geography, I write, I paint, and I watch the mountains. There is not a cloud all day. I pass three people. The walk around the lake is the final ritual of my life in the meadow, another circumambulation.

Usually the walk is uneventful, another immersion in nondrama. Once, however, it was quite dramatic, though I realize more and more, in retrospect, that the drama was of my own making, a manifestation of our human proclivity to dramatize the world.

The autumn of 1992 was dry in the Tetons. Since little snow had fallen, the Park Service kept the road open, and though from eight to ten inches of snow lay on the ground, people continued to drive into the park. In late November, I drove to my cabin and set off around Jenny Lake. The temperature was 2 degrees and an icy fog hung low. From the cabin I crossed a quarter mile of meadow to reach the lake trail. Using ski poles, I walked on what was in summer a dirt road to a little parking lot just west of the meadow. From there, I struck north on a path to the main trail and wandered around the lake, trying to paint watercolors before the water froze. When the fog cleared, the day became cloudless, calm, and cold.

When I recrossed my trail at the bridge over Cottonwood Creek that evening, I saw large cat tracks with tail-drag marks in the snow. The edges were crusty from the afternoon melt. They were the tracks of a mountain lion. I had seen him earlier that fall when I was driving home from dinner with a friend. A Yellowstone ranger climbing Guides Wall saw him in Cascade Canyon, and twice tourists watched him walk calmly through the sagebrush near the Windy Point turnout.

I walked to the cabin, got a tape measure, a headlamp, and my old green copy of Murie's *Field Guide to Animal Tracks*. The paw prints varied from three and a quarter to four inches, but I realized that the lion was stepping in his own tracks and also, no doubt, the melting had enlarged them. The straddle measurement was thirteen inches, and the stride varied from twenty to twenty-eight inches, with one jump of thirty-eight inches. From the prints and tail-drag marks, I figured the lion was nearly eight feet long from his nose to the tip of his tail.

After wandering about near the bridge, the lion had followed me across the meadow, walking right over the marks made by my right ski pole. He was intent: The prints were so consistent, they could have been laid down by a tractor. I did not like the fact this was the second time I had found him on a road and I did not like that he had tracked me, most likely in the early-morning fog. I did not like the fading light. I remembered his ribs. He was probably on his last legs and having difficulty hunting.

I followed our tracks across the meadow. As I left the little parking lot and the path narrowed, the tracks moved left, over my footprints. I was wearing Vibram soles and the section under the ball of the foot was about four inches wide—I noticed the similarity in the size of our prints. Then his prints split a bit more, no longer in direct registration, as they say, but slightly behind one another and slightly off center, so the combined print of the front and hind paws merged and grew larger.

Then one paw had stepped directly into my boot track, mostly erasing it—like one signature canceling another. Just my toe stuck out in front of his print, like something hanging out of a mouth, I thought. I stopped, my foot in midair, and felt that cold stab of terror in the stomach that means something is terribly wrong.

I stepped backward carefully and looked around. The sky behind Teewinot was the palest blue and pink, the iridescence of opals. With the sun down, the wind was dispatching plumes of snow from the summit six thousand feet above. To the east, the sky was menacing, the gunmetal blue of the earth's shadow supporting banks of carmine clouds. In my paranoid imagination, the colors reminded me of a bad wound. There was no sound but the wind in the forest. For perhaps a minute I was paralyzed, my will absorbed by a presence.

Until then, I had had no fear of mountain lions. I knew that, statistically, I had little to worry about. During the hundred years from 1890 until 1990, there were only fifty-three recorded attacks on humans by mountain lions in both the United States and Canada, only ten people died, and 64 percent of the deaths involved children. So it seems reasonable to make room for lions.

But terror is not a matter of statistics. Confronted with Blake's forest of the night, I faltered. I had no sense of this lion, or any lion; no expectation of what he might do, no knowledge, no tradition to help me know how to act. Traditions bring the unknown into the circle of our lives and give it form and a practice that manages its otherness. Those who love wild predators lack such a tradition, thus our discontent. As Wittgenstein says somewhere, a man without a tradition, who wants one, is like a man unhappily in love. When I observe the great fascination that wild animals sometimes have for us, I wonder if they feel a similar discontent. Or are we always other to them, *their terror*?

We do not lack information about *Felis concolor*. The literature, both general and technical, is vast, and Harley Shaw's *Soul Among Lions* is a masterpiece of natural history. But information does not a tradition make, and virtually all of it the result of two activities: hunting and science. I am not interested in these ways of relating to mountain lions, so I find this vast literature mostly worthless. Instead, I am interested in a possible future tradition. I want to know how our relationship to wild predators might become, let's say, friendly and respectful—a peaceful covenant.

Since this strikes most people as absurd, an example is in order. "The Old Way," Elizabeth Marshall Thomas's remarkable essay on the Juwa Bushmen and the African lion, describes just such a peaceful covenant between humans and a large predator. Anyone who loves the wild should ponder it, assiduously.

Until the past few decades, the Bushmen and the lions lived among one another. They shared water holes. Prides occasionally came into Bushmen camps. A small group of four Bushmen hunters could drive a pride of thirty lions off a wildebeest killed by a Bushman. A lone and unarmed Bushman would often encounter a lion while out gathering, and both lion and human could handle the situation with what can only be called an etiquette.

The Juwa Bushmen could not defend themselves against a lion. Their spears, unlike the spears of the Masai, were too short. They carried no shields. Their bows were too delicate. They hunted primarily with poison arrows that took so long to kill, they offered no immediate protection, though they would over time kill a lion. Although Bushmen could kill lions, they choose not to; and although lions could kill Bushmen, they choose not to. A genealogical study conducted by Thomas's brother, John Marshall, and Claire Ritchie, involving more than three thousand Bushmen and going back nearly a hundred years, found only one instance of a lion killing a Bushman, and this was a paraplegic girl. And Thomas knew of no lion killed by the Juwa.

These salient facts suggest future possibilities for our own relations with the mountain lions, grizzlies, and wolves—especially in national parks. We cannot expect to have a friendly, respectful relationship with predators we hunt and kill—for whatever reason. Inhabitants of North America have rarely established a decent covenant with predators, and our current inability to go beyond historical forms of failure simply confirms the poverty of our imagination. No one has the slightest idea what to do about it.

The old lion and I shared no covenant, thus my unreasonable terror. With a mixture of sadness and fear, I turned tail and headed back across the meadow, nursing a bad case of over-the-shoulder-itis.

Late that night, it snowed. The next morning, I went back to Jenny Lake and searched for tracks. A small herd of elk grazed some tall grasses on the lower slopes of Teewinot. The snowshoe rabbits were active along the creek. There was an unusual number of weasels about, and a few mule deer near the Moose Ponds. But no mountain lion.

That night it snowed again. The road into the park was closed for the year. I skied out to the lake along the road—still a bit spooked, even during the day—as bad a symptom for an old mountaineer as walking paved roads was for an old mountain lion.

The elk had moved off Teewinot onto the sagebrush flats east of Timbered Island, their last waiting place before their dash to the Natural Elk Refuge. The deer tracks showed they had gone down Cottonwood Creek, toward the Gros Ventre buttes. I carefully searched the new snow with my glasses and spotting scope but found no cat tracks. The old lion was gone.

Early December. Clear, very cold. There is not enough snow to ski, so I walk up the road to the cabin to pick up a few books I forgot to bring out when the road closed and to board up the cabin for the winter. A storm is coming, but the weather folks say the worst of it will pass to the south. Besides, under clear skies it is hard to take storms seriously.

There is more water in Cottonwood Creek now than in October. A long spell of warm weather has made the country seem like early May—the snow no longer covers the sagebrush; there are patches of bare ground with small drifts in the lees of ridges and melt-out rings around the trees. The snow is a frozen crust. It is winter in the mountains, though, with fifty-two inches of snow at 10,000 feet. The summits of the highest peaks are rimed with ice.

A couple passes on Rollerblades, talking so intensely that they fail to see me until the last moment and nearly run me down. A woman on a mountain bike moves to the other side of the road as she approaches; she passes me, pedaling hard, unsmiling, her face down over the handlebars as if she were ill. Then the road is empty again, incongruously empty, a postapocalyptic emptiness. Streaks of cirrus are streaming out of the southwest.

Along the road are flocks of snow buntings, finchlike birds that summer in the Arctic, breeding farther north than any other land bird. One flock, perhaps a dozen birds, is eating seeds in the grass alongside the road. They are tame, perhaps because people in the northernmost communities make birdhouses and feeders for them. In flight they appear mostly white, with black wing tips; on the ground, their patches of tan and black are more obvious. They rise and land in unison, as though connected with invisible strings. When I reach the cabin, I study Audubon's painting of them: It is a miracle of accuracy.

Four downy woodpeckers chatter feverishly in the cottonwoods along the creek. Chickadees are still here—they will remain all winter. Moose are feeding on the snowy slopes of Teewinot; the pattern of their tracks appears random, like the scribbling of a child.

The elk have finally gone down the valley.

I nail plywood over the windows and settle into the bare gloom of empty bookshelves, empty closet, empty pantry. By noon, the sky is gray and clouds are settling around the peaks. I set up my laptop and check the AccuWeather Web site. Then I check Jim Woodmency's mountain.weather.com—the most accurate source of weather information for the Tetons. I pull up the Doppler radar and look at the time-lapse sequence for the past few hours. I look at the current satellite picture. Then I look at forecast maps for the next forty-eight hours. No doubt about it, the storm is moving farther north and I am going to get nailed.

At two o'clock, the sky above the mountains is heavy with lead-colored clouds moving in from the northwest, even though the storm is approaching from the southwest. At dusk it begins to snow gently. When I hold out my hand, I can barely feel the flakes; they are weightless and melt on contact. Just before I go to bed, I open the door and look at the porch: A layer of fresh snow covers it like a plush carpet.

It snows all night. By morning, six to eight inches of new fluff surround the cabin and some drifts are eighteen inches deep. I call the Bridger-Teton National Forest for the Avalanche and Weather Forecast and listen to Kanzler's gravelly, detached voice, a voice I always find consoling, even on a recording. Five inches of new snow, but that is down the valley. We always get more up here. The wind is out of the west, averaging twenty-three miles per hour, with gusts to eighty-five miles per hour. Snow is predicted for the next couple of days. That's enough for me. I hang up and check the thermometer outside the window: 17 degrees.

I pack and obsess about gear. Even the poorest guides have the best mountain gear in the world. Virtually all of mine is either Patagonia, Black Diamond, Marmot, or Petzl, the only oddity being a pair of Sorrel Pacs, but then everyone in Jackson Hole owns Sorrel Pacs. When I first came to the Tetons to live, Harry Frishman said, "Turner, the first things to buy are a pair of Sorrel Pacs and a toy rack for your car." How true.

I put on the bottoms of my Patagonia Capilene expedition-weight long johns, the top of my Patagonia Capilene expedition-weight zip-T long johns, Patagonia puffball vest, Marmot three-layer Gore-Tex pants, Patagonia parka, Smith goggles, Patagonia balaclava, Black Diamond gloves, and a Black Diamond pack stuffed with books, my ThinkPad, a stainless-steel thermos with hot chocolate, two Snickers bars, a bag of oatmeal cookies, and my Motorola cell phone. I put powder baskets on my Black Diamond expedition ski poles. Thus arrayed for my modern four-mile, two-hour adventure, I lock the cabin for the winter and head into the storm, musing about Scott and Shackleton and laughing at what a weenie I am.

It's not bad along the creek, but when I reach the road, the situation turns a bit polar, just enough to make the walk interesting. I see no one and no animals—indeed, few signs of animals except for mouse tracks. Since the blowing snow must erase them in seconds, I must be walking right up on them. I have no idea why they are about—perhaps they know this is *the* storm and are making the best of their final hours of autumn.

The snow buntings are still here, oblivious to wind and snow. As I approach, they skitter along a short distance and land farther down the road. After several encounters they fly east toward Timbered Island, tiny as a flight of bees before they disappear into the blowing snow. A lone raven perched in a cottonwood looks like a blot of ink.

Billows of snow blow across the flats. I can see them coming from half a mile away. When they reach me, I lean forward on my poles like a ski jumper, unable to move until the gust stops. Snow devils twist across the sagebrush flats to the east, like wanderers cut off from the main structure of the storm. Visibility is about a mile when things are calm, the forests on both sides but vague silhouettes. The only things I hear are the wind and snow drumming on my parka, hard snow the size of peas. The air is sharp with the smell of winter, a smell of absence like the white in the landscape. I suck it in, raw and delicious, intoxicating.

I plod on for an hour, then stop and drink hot cocoa, being careful not to lose gloves to the wind. It takes me only two hours and ten minutes to get out, yet during that time I am enclosed in a different world—even with the computer and cell phone. Many will say that these new commodities destroy the wildness of the experience, but I do not find this to be true. It is merely a new synthesis, one that I find pleasing. I labor in the wild storm; despite the contents of my pack, the road, and the waiting vehicle, its wildness suffuses me.

Except for my truck, the Taggart Lake parking lot is empty and drifted with new snow. It feels like the end of the beginning of winter, and it is—the end and beginning of a cycle always being the same.

## 14. Skiing to Jenny Lake

January. Four feet of snow on the sagebrush flats at Moose, the village at the entrance to the park, more up at the cabin. Temperature is −43 but warming. At least Kanzler says it's warming; it's even supposed to get above zero for the first time in nearly a week. The landscape has the ambience of an icebox.

Early morning, −8 degrees, and clear, good weather for skiing into the cabin. No one at the Taggart Lake parking lot. As the ski patrol clears the Jackson Hole Ski Area of avalanche danger, I hear the soft thump of artillery echo from down the valley. Later, there is the long-muffled roar of a jet flight taking off from the Jackson Hole Airport, the only major airport inside a national park and the object of ongoing battles between developers and conservationists. Happily, in this instance, the National Park Service is on the side of the conservationists.

The sole question before me is where I want to ski. Two ski trails lead to Lupine Meadows and Jenny Lake. One is simply the summer road. It has several advantages: It's out on the flats, with splendid views of the mountains, and since snowmobiles use it, the snow is usually packed—which makes for easy skiing. Furthermore, the road surface is raised somewhat above the surrounding plain and the wind blows much of it clear of snow. The disadvantages are equally obvious: At times, the wind is strong enough to be unpleasant and the snowmobiles are a bore.

The second trail snakes north along the western edge of Cottonwood Creek. You are out of the wind most of the time, with occasional views of the mountains, and, after several miles, the creek affords open water and the possibility of seeing dippers and kingfishers. It is also very beautiful. If a trail is set, the ski to Jenny Lake along the so-called Inner Trail is a delight. If there is no trail, you face four miles of breaking trail, sometimes through deep drifts—a trying day. But the Inner Trail is so popular there is nearly always a track.

Equipment makes little difference when skiing to Jenny Lake. People use old wooden touring skis, fancy, sleek waxed skis, waxless skis, telemark rigs, and snowshoes. There are usually three trails now, two for skis—one in each direction—and a trail off to the side for snowshoes.

The day is windless. With all the exercise of cross-country skiing, you don't need to wear much in the way of clothes. I carry a light pack with the usual Snickers bar and water, a windbreaker, binoculars, journal, and watercolor pencils. Watercolor paints don't do well at this temperature, but later one can use a wash over the pencil drawings. At the bottom of the pack is my DAS parka and Crazy Creek chair for long sits watching critters or for surviving a night out.

The trail heads north through a long meadow to the west of the creek, passing what in the summer is the Climbers' Ranch. There is no water in the creek here, not because it is frozen but because the flow from Jenny Lake diminishes so much the dwindled stream of water percolates down through the glacial till instead of flowing on top. Eventually you reach open water, where the flow is still sufficient. Cottonwood Creek never freezes.

Then there is deep forest as the path reaches the terminal moraine of the now-remnant Middle Teton Glacier below Bradley Lake. The creek is close and there is often open water here. I search for dippers but find none, so I move on.

More meadows and more cabins, the remains of a ranch. I keep going for another mile until I reach the point where the trail turns west at the bottom of Lupine Meadows. The osprey nest I visit each spring is now filled with snow. The clown-faced coyote is still here, though. I see her tracks mingled with the tracks of hares, mice, and red squirrels. I ski along the creek until I hear dippers.

Dippers remain all winter where water flows, singing heartily in the mornings as they court, much more so than during the summer molt. I listen for their songs, then ski along the creek until I find one with the binoculars. Then I take off my skis and sit in my Crazy Creek chair on one side of the snowy, steep canyon through which the creek flows. I watch the bird feed exactly as dippers do in summer, oblivious to the cold.

This one is clobbering caddis larvae. It dives into the water from an icy twig, stays under for about five seconds, then flies back to the twig, not even bothering to shake the water off its feathers.

Soon another arrives—dippers carve out breeding territories this time of year. They peck at each other, do some acrobatic flying, then return to feeding. I leave them, and being so close to the cabin, I decide to stop for a cup of tea.

Snow is piled three feet high against the door. Inside, it is dank and gloomy. I make tea but sit out in the snow—the cabin is simply too dreary. I watch chickadees and study the fresh avalanches on Teewinot with my field glasses.

I don't always go to my cabin when I ski to Jenny Lake. When I do, it is usually to check on how it's dealing with the cornice on the northeast corner of the roof. The prevailing wind from the southwest scours most of the snow off the west side of the roof and dumps it on the east side. Sometimes the cornice is six feet thick with snow and extends out from the cabin wall for five feet.

Today it is bad, so I put my ladder against the roof, climb up, and make my way to the northeast end. I shovel and pound, trying to break it off, but it is dense wind pack, hard, and not inclined to fracture. Even getting some of it off is hard labor. I jump up and down on it until it breaks and it and I fall to the ground—fortunately only about two feet.

Because all the cabins are angled in slightly different directions, each roof and snow pattern is unique. The west side of Al's roof is especially problematic. Despite ingenious wedges, sliding snow and ice knock the chimney pipe off the roof nearly every year, and I often have to climb up and put plastic and duct tape over the hole. If I don't, there are problems with pine martens.

Kim Schmitz and I once watched a pine marten dive down the broken-off chimney pipe on Al's roof. What we saw was a classic marten event.

Even with considerable snow on the ground, it was eight feet to the top of the snow on the roof. The marten crouched in the soft snow beneath the overhanging cornice at the north side of the cabin. Then it vaulted eight feet onto the overhang, clawed desperately with all four feet for a hold, and fell off. Not deterred, it tried again. And again. Finally it clawed its way over the top and promptly disappeared down the pipe into the cabin. We waited. Perhaps five minutes passed. Fortunately, the door to the stove was closed, so after thoroughly examining the ash in the stove box, the marten shot back up the pipe, bounded across the roof, and, without hesitation, leapt off the roof into the snow. It disappeared for a moment into the fluff, then emerged with a new white coat and hopped off to the next marten escapade.

Martens are brash animals. I've had them sit on a windowsill and watch me carefully from a distance of eighteen inches. I've had them wander into the cabin when the door is open, look around, study me, and walk back out. I've had one jump onto a barbecue grill, lusting after my salmon fillet. At the same time, I've never seen one aggressive toward a human being. To me they are among the animals that seem particularly conscious, their eyes veiling souls of considerable complexity.

Only once has a winter storm trapped me at the cabin, and fortunately Kim and Thekla Von Hagke were along. We skied in, and it snowed with what can only be called fury. The next morning, we were in a whiteout of blowing snow as fine as flour. We buried ourselves in our cabins, plunging back and forth through waist-deep drifts only to share meals and Thekla's freshly baked cookies with chocolate chips, oatmeal, and raisins. We drank tea and reminisced about Nepal—the three of us had spent a month together in Khumbu one fall. Then I would fight my way back to the cabin and feed the stove, thinking of other huts and cabins and caves I have seen—in the Yukon and Peru, in the mountains along the Mexican border, in China, Nepal, and Tibet, and in Wyoming, Montana, and Colorado—dwellings where people have spent long, cold winters alone, or nearly so.

I have done a bit of that myself. One survives a winter as one survives solitary confinement, the mind pouring back over itself in tangled ruminations. My little cabin was a luxury in comparison with that, even with the windows boarded up. With little to see and nothing to do, I migrated to the bed, where I meditated, snuggled into an old Chinese sleeping bag I leave at the cabin, and reverted to my habit of reading poetry.

I stacked the books beside me and wandered through them

randomly, visiting old favorites. For the classics, I have my frayed copy of the *Mentor Book of Major British Poets*. Inside the flyleaf is written "sixth copy." Earlier ones disintegrated during years of mountain journeys, long nights in tents with a headlamp, long days of storms, weeks camped at airports as I waited to fly in or out to someplace unknown, or weeks lying naked on a bed under a palsied fan during monsoon heat as I waited for bureaucrats to sign papers so I could proceed into the mountains. Pages were ripped out and given to fellow travelers, used for toilet paper or for starting fires, written over with ink as emergency messages, or sent as letters home. The sixth copy was going too; the cover was gone, the binding broken.

Nothing travels as well as poetry. I've tried novels—I've read *War and Peace* three times—but one grows bored with narratives. Poems retain their vigor, their interest. One finds acceptance in strange places, as in Matthew Arnold's lines:

> *Come, let me read the oft-read tale again!*
> *The story of that Oxford scholar poor,*
> *Of pregnant parts and quick inventive brain,*
> *Who, tired of knocking at preferment's door,*
> *One summer morn forsook*
> *His friends, and went to learn the gypsy lore,*
> *And roamed the world with that wild*
> *brotherhood,*
> *And came, as most men deemed, to little good,*
> *But came to Oxford and his friends no more.*

I read until I slept. Then I awoke and read again. There is no sense of time in a dark cabin in winter. I turned to the moderns, starting with Rilke's *Elegies*. I read a few of Ponge's object poems, moved on to Snyder's *No Nature*, then Merwin, then Harrison's *Theory and Practice of Rivers*.

There was just the whoosh of wind in the trees. The kerosene lamps glowed; the flames on the candles stood erect, unwavering. I read, the storm blew, and at some point—I don't know when—I fell asleep again.

Later I opened the door. The light was gray. The snow—finer, it seemed, than flour—had woven an intricate latticework that covered the doorway. It seemed a shame to destroy it, but I needed fresh air. I puffed my cheeks and blew a jagged hole through it that gaped like a hole blown in a wall by a cannon. Then I destroyed the rest of the filigree with my arm and shoveled snow so I could get out the door and onto the porch. The wind was still fierce, visibility less than a hundred yards. No birds, no tracks—nothing. I wallowed around the porch for a few minutes, finding no sign of the path I had waded through to and from Kim's cabin the previous day; then I went back inside, fed the stove, and returned to my stack of poetry. The dark hours flowed on as indistinguishable as in a fever, the world gone.

The next day the storm had lifted, though it remained overcast, with occasional snow flurries. We decided to tromp out through the waist-deep powder. Thekla is a tall, strong, lovely woman, stronger at times than either Kim or me. That was one of the times. Kim had something wrong with an ankle; all the snow depressed me. Thekla, disgusted with our whining, broke trail for the first two miles; Kim and I did one mile each. Our cars were buried at the Taggart Lake parking lot. No one else was around—they were too smart. We shoveled out our cars with avalanche shovels and headed home. It was still snowing.

Today it is difficult to believe in such storms. There is no wind; the sky is clear. The temperature is up to 20 degrees, the world is inviting. After tea, I pack and ski another half mile north to Jenny

Lake, following the trail around the lake to look for birds, but without much luck. People begin to arrive. On a good day, a hundred people might ski to Jenny Lake. Many of them ski out onto the lake or cross it to Cascade Canyon and follow the summer trail up to the spectacle of a frozen Hidden Falls. If the conditions are right, skaters—ice-skaters or ski skaters—have a ball on the lake. I work on getting up enough pluck to ski across the ends of shallow bays.

I want to study the ice, to see the lake frozen, to see how it froze, for it is rarely the same, especially early in the season. It will have frozen in mid-to-late December. I've never seen it freeze, though I've always wanted to. But I've never been present at the right time, and I feel a strange sense of loss because of this, as though I've missed an important event in my private world, a natural sacrament, the outward sign of a process holy to this cold place.

The freezing process borders on the mysterious. The lake cools as the air cools. During the summer the water in the lake is a layer of temperature gradients, with lighter, warmer water on top of cooler, denser, deeper water. There isn't any mixing of layers. With cooler air temperatures, the water on top cools until the lake is roughly the same temperature; then the surface and deeper water can mix. This is called fall turnover.

The mixing of layers is important for the fish in the lake. Windy autumn days create whitecaps that add oxygen to the surface water. It is absorbed and the mixing of surface and deep water distributes it throughout the water column. Thus a winter supply of oxygen reaches all levels of the lake and the fish can survive.

When water temperature reaches 40 degrees, its specific gravity goes down; if it didn't, the ice forming on the lake's surface would be too heavy and sink to the bottom. The lowered specific gravity allows ice to float. As the days get colder, the lake continues to lose heat until its surface water reaches 32 degrees. In order for this surface water to change from freezing water to ice, the lake must dump a lot of calories. This requires nights of 10 to 20 degrees below zero. Until freezing there are fog banks over the streams and lakes that form during the night when the warm water is steaming into the cold air. At sunrise, these wispy layers produce some of the most spectacular views of the range, the mountains rising through and around them like islands in the sky.

With colder weather, the lake first freezes around the edges, where the water is shallow and the ice is thickest. Eventually it freezes several hundred feet out. Then one of two things happens. If it remains relatively warm, open water remains in the middle, or deepest parts, of the lake. If the temperature plunges, then the entire lake will freeze in one night. When you awake, there will be no fog and you will know the lake has frozen. Once Dan found that Jackson Lake froze in six hours during the day—from 9:00 A.M. to 3:00 P.M.

Each year the ice on Jenny Lake has a unique history. The clear ice that forms with the initial freezing is called water ice or black ice (because of the deep, dark water beneath it). If it doesn't snow and the temperatures remain very cold, this water ice increases in thickness. In the winter of 1992–1993, it didn't snow for a long time after freeze-up and we ended up with clear ice twenty inches thick—which is nice to know if you are crossing the lakes in winter on skis.

If snow falls on the ice when the ice is thin, the weight of the snow depresses the ice and it eventually cracks with an intimidating sound. Rod Newcomb heard it crack one winter when he was caretaker at the Jenny Lake Lodge, a crack so loud that it woke him from a deep sleep.

Since water underneath is under pressure from the ice above, water floods through the cracks and forms a new surface of liquid water above the clear ice. The flooding turns the lower section of the snowpack into slush. Since dry snow insulates it from above, it may not freeze right away, or only some of it may freeze. When it does, it solidifies into white ice because it contains both air and snow. The cycle repeats itself until the lake is covered with an accumulation of clear ice, white ice, slush, and snow. Thus each year the ice on Jenny Lake presents a different profile.

Dan has studied the ice profiles on Jackson Lake. He says a typical ice-strata profile for Jackson Lake would be four inches of black ice, three inches of slush, six inches of white ice, five inches of slush, three inches of white ice, two inches of slush, ten inches of white ice, and, on top, eight inches of dry snow. It is all very complicated, and anyone traveling the lakes must know the layers and their vicissitudes. Ignorance is not bliss.

Ice fishermen are not a patient lot and they pursue their sport as early in the season as possible. This often puts them on the lake ice before it is solid—with amusing results. Dan likes to tell the story of two fishermen who, despite being warned, drove their new, unpaid-for, uninsured snowmobile a hundred feet out from the shore at Colter Bay. Suddenly a hole appeared beneath them and a lake troll swallowed their machine. They scrambled off in time, with a renewed humility.

Slush is a special curse on snowmobiles. The tracks start throwing slush into the tunnel the track travels through, and if it is cold enough, the slush freezes, filling the tunnel with ice until the track won't move. Then the machine stalls in a foot of slush. If it is not removed soon, it freezes into the slush. Once I saw two snowmobiles out on the lake covered with fresh snow, looking like casualties of a war. I am always delighted when the lake trolls win. After reading Jim Harrison's essay, "Ice Fishing, the Moronic Sport," I can only wonder why victory doesn't always go to the lake trolls.

Fortunately, snowmobiles aren't allowed on Jenny Lake, and today no ice fishermen are in sight. In most places the ice is a pale whitish blue with two inches of fresh snow blown into the same sinuous patterns one finds on sand dunes. In other places, it is all white on white, like marbled fat in a cheap steak. The ice looks solid, but I do not ski far from shore. I am willing to ski around the edges of the lake, but when it comes to crossing it, I turn chicken, especially when I am alone. I have this nagging memory of terror.

Twenty years ago I was exploring the country south of Everest with three Sherpas. Two were well-equipped Mountain Travel Nepal climbing Sherpas, Dorje and Ang Tsering. The third was a none-too-clever fellow from the village of Phortse whose name I could not pronounce, so I called him Phortse. He had lied about having boots, so now he was scrambling around on snow and ice in oversized tennis shoes filled with layers of socks. I was not amused. We were crossing the Mingbo La, a 19,000-foot pass leading from Khumbu to the Hunku Valley. The last 500 feet of the pass is a climb up 40-degree ice. We were moving slowly, it was getting dark, the wind was blowing at hurricane force, and I was worried. We were being hammered, but we were not in a position to do anything but suffer it out.

We reached the top of the pass in the dark, crawled over the top and down the other side until we were protected, then struggled to put up the tents. We tied them together with a climbing rope and I buried my Haliburton camera case to serve as an anchor for the whole mess. We did not eat, nor did we sleep. It was a time of prayer. In the morning, the tent poles were broken, but the wind had dropped.

We hurried down the Hunku Nup Glacier until we reached an ablation valley with a partially frozen tarn. Exhausted and hungry, we stopped for tea and breakfast. While we busied ourselves with the stove and food, Phortse wandered onto the ice to get water without uttering a word. We heard a crack, a scream. And there he was, hanging on to the edge of the ice with the tips of his fingers and his chin. I remember looking around: The sky was blue and lonely, the world silent, minding its business. I thought of Bosch's painting of Icarus.

We had two ropes. While the Sherpas yelled encouragement and I cursed him from the bottom of my soul, I tied a hand loop in the middle of one rope, put it over my left wrist, and walked out onto the ice with the other still-coiled rope in my right hand. The Sherpas dug their heels into hummocks of alpine turf and belayed me. As I reached Phortse, the ice bent down under me and water slopped up over the edge. He could no longer hang on with his chin. His eyes bulged. I handed him the coil of rope to grab. He sputtered. I yelled at the Sherpas to yell at him, but he would not grab the rope. So I started hitting him over the head with it, forcing him to do *something*. He grabbed the rope, I pulled him, the Sherpas pulled me, the ice cracked, we all pulled with desperation, and then it was over.

When we reached shore, Phortse was hypothermic—shivering uncontrollably, unable to speak. I poured a liter of kerosene along an eight-foot swath of dry, grassy tundra and threw in a match. For the first time at that spot on the planet, there was a fire, and it was three feet high. We stripped off his wet clothes and placed him next to the fire on a sleeping bag. Dorje and I rolled him over and over like meat on a spit, roasting him until he was well done. Ang Tsering made tea. Then we got dry clothes on him and forced him to drink tea until he was bloated with warm fluids.

Dorje thanked me profusely for saving Phortse, though not exactly for the reasons I expected. No, Dorji was happy, he said, because if Phortse had drowned, we all would have had to go back there with the police and fill out many reports. The more I thought about his happiness and its rationale, the happier I got. Phortse was happy too, though for different reasons. That night we reached the lakes at Panche Pokhri and slept like lambs.

Now when I even think of going out onto lake ice, I see Phortse's fingers, chin, and bulging eyes. I see the bending ice, the clear sky, the splash of Icarus. Thus stricken, I slink around the shoreline, tail between my legs, waiting for a crack. When I regain the trail at the summer boat-launch site, I feel better. I cross the bridge at the boat dock and head east to the road, then south into the low sun sinking behind Static Peak. No wind, the sky is still clear. I pass hordes of skiers, but I do not mind. The track is fast, my pack is light, and the mountains stand aloft like monarchs—a perfect winter day.

## 15. *Deep Winter*

In late January or February, we usually have a thaw in the mountains. Temperatures go into the forties or higher during the day; at night the snow crust hardens till it is like rock and, if weather remains good, climbers run up and down the Grand Teton as if it were summer. The thaw can end with a storm or with the return of cold weather. If it turns cold, I like to take solo trips. Instead of carrying a pack, I use a small fiberglass sled with aluminum runners that moves as effortlessly over crusted snow as a train moves on rails.

I leave the Taggart Lake parking lot early to avoid skier traffic and reach the magic point where no one will catch me and I'll be alone. The sled is attached to a climbing pack with poles so that the pull comes on both my shoulders and my waist. My destination is nine miles north, a promontory on Leigh Lake. No wind, no clouds, 19 degrees below zero. I can feel the cold in my nostrils, in the first sharp gasps of exertion. Even the sunlight feels cold.

Despite the temperature, I am lightly dressed. Even with hard snow and aluminum runners, hauling a sled in cold weather is laborious; the only thing worse is hauling a heavy pack. With a pack you are at least inclined to eliminate items, but a sled is like a canoe and you tend to add and add until it's as bad as the pack anyway. I slug away, my eyes down, until I notice moose tracks crossing the road. I look up and see a cow moose staring at me only a hundred feet off the road. I smile and wish her good morning and keep going, as though acknowledging a slightly hostile stranger. A cow moose chased me once, and it wasn't funny.

I stop every twenty minutes or so to drink half a quart of diluted Gatorade kept inside a parka to keep it from freezing. It is all too easy to become dehydrated in these conditions: You not only sweat; you breathe fluid out into the dry air with every pant. I keep going, making especially good time on hard snow that has been packed by hundreds of skiers and snowmobiles, has then thawed, then has packed again. The waxless skis work well and a bit of wax applied under my foot improves the friction.

The road ends at the String Lake Picnic Area and I switch to the trail to Leigh Lake, a fairly level clearing through the forest. There is a bit of a track, but it has melted out; except for an occasional climbing party heading for a winter ascent of Moran, few skiers come this far north. After I cross the bridge between String and Leigh lakes, even the melted track disappears. Most people drop onto the lake here, but I head up into an open forest of old-growth lodgepole pine broken by snow-covered boulders. In late summer, acres of huckleberries cover this ground and bears are common. I stay a distance above the lake, where the terrain is flat, the sledding easy. Finally I begin to feel alone.

I am searching for a shallow pond that in summer is filled with mosquitoes and dense displays of wildflowers, some of which are rare. The pond is my beacon in what is otherwise an expanse of unmarked forest—there are no trails, even in summer, and the only navigation point is the summit of Moran. Without a compass (I hate them) one must trust senses we rarely notice—a sense of direction, a sense of distance, a sense of scale. I am delighted when I strike the pond, not only because camp is only a short distance but also because I need to believe I can still do this, that those senses are still functioning.

Camp is in a clearing just above the lake, with a superb view of the great south buttress of Mount Moran, the biggest continuous chunk of rock in the range—five thousand feet of clean gneiss and granite lined with some of the finest routes in the Tetons. Afternoon light is streaming down Leigh Canyon, backlighting the ridges. The sun is long gone behind the mountains above me; the sky's light is pale blue and cold, the light of a winter afternoon hardening into night. I pack down the snow by jumping around on my skis, though it is too frozen to make much of a pit. My tent is a simple pyramid with a single pole and no floor—floors are a pain in the butt in winter, a bathtub for melted snow. After the tent is up, I dig a trench several feet long and as deep as a chair leg. I can then sit on one side, put my feet in the trench, and use the other side for a table. I lay out a space blanket, then a thick Ensolite pad, then my down bag, fluffed and filling with more air. I melt snow for tea. The temperature is $-2$, comparatively warm given the circumstances. The stove heats the tent somewhat and I can handle my pot and spoon with bare hands.

The tea I make is Himalayan mountain tea. I boil black tea in water for five minutes, add lots of powered milk and sugar, and simmer it for another five minutes. The result is thick and sweet. I make a quart, pour it into my cup, and drink it all while I boil more water in the same pot for my package of Uncle Ben's boil-in-a-bag rice: food stuck to a pot is another pain in the winter. When the rice is done, I drain the bag, dump it into my cup, and cover it with a glove. Into the rice water goes an aluminum package of Tasty Bite Kashmir spinach. Five minutes and it's done; I cut the foil and pour it onto the rice. Before I eat, I pack the pot with snow from the floor of the tent. When I finish dinner, I drink another quart of mountain tea and clean the cup with the dregs. I go outside bundled up in my DAS parka and drink more tea while looking at the pale light on Moran. Finishing, I swish the final dregs around and chant my favorite part of our Buddhist meal sutra:

> *We wash our bowls in this water.*
> *It has the flavor of ambrosial dew.*
> *We offer it to all demons and spirits.*
> *May all be filled and satisfied.*
> *Om Makulavahsvaha.*

I toss the dregs into the trees.

Seven below zero. I crawl into my sleeping bag and put on my headlamp to read. But not for long. Cold drives me deeper into the bag. I cover my head with a fuzzy. By eight o'clock, I'm asleep.

I awake in the dark and brew more mountain tea. It feels warmer and actually is 7 degrees. I sense cloud cover, and sure enough, no stars. In the east is a well-defined narrow wedge of pink light.

At dawn I ski along the promontory and watch the first rays of sun strike the mountain through the wedge of sky in the east. The light is milky blue and pink; its contrast with the sullen sky above is dramatic. The sun's harsh angle renders each feature on the buttress with precision. I study the Direct South Buttress Route with my binoculars.

I came here for specific reasons: to see Moran at dawn, to remember, and to experience yet again an iteration. I love this enfolding of layer upon layer of experience, like the steel in a fine sword, for a sense of place is a function not of space but of time, an accumulation of experience and memory constantly renewed. To return to a place remembered is to consecrate it with the rites of return. Ordinary trees, climbing routes, camping spots, and fishing holes become natural sacraments, like bread and wine, yet always more. I want to consecrate the Direct South Buttress Route with ritual visits.

There are routes in the mountains that rise like gravestones in the mind. The Northwest Couloir on the Middle Teton will always be Frishman's Gully. The Lowe Route on the north face of the Enclosure will always be the Ortenburger Route. The south buttresses of Moran will always remind me of John Hudson.

Hudson and I hiked around Leigh Lake in the early sixties to climb both of the big routes on this buttress—the Direct and the South Buttress Right. We were young: I was twenty or twenty-one; Hudson was probably only sixteen, though in two short years he had made a name for himself in mountain circles for ascents of major new routes and two first ascents of peaks. He was of average height, with freckles and a dense crop of red hair. Difficulty and bad weather amused him no end. He had a strong will, the soul of an elf, the beatific gaze of a mystic. He lived the proverb "If there is no wind, row." John seemed graced—one for whom a red carpet is unfurled as he walks into life. He died too young.

We hauled heavy packs containing clothing, camping gear, and many pounds of pitons, carabiners, and ropes. In 1962, the old trail around Leigh Lake (shown on the 1948 map of the park) was still usable, though barely. The old-growth forest south of Leigh Lake continued to collapse with age; huge spruce and fir blocked the trail, causing tedious detours through muck and mosquitoes. There was no trail up Leigh Canyon to the base of the climb. We thrashed around, looking for a famous log over Leigh Creek. Walking the log was a cool thing to do in those days, but rain had soaked the log, and a fall would have been deadly, so we scrambled across ingloriously on our butts, struggling with our heavy packs.

We camped in a grove of fir beneath the route. The camp was typical of those days. The tent was a piece of construction plastic slung over a piece of nylon cord tied to two trees. We scrunched up small rocks in each corner of the plastic to make a chicken head, then tied it off and anchored the plastic to larger rocks on the ground. We had no stove. My sleeping bag was a Marine Corps–surplus feather sack held together with Scotch tape. We ate gorp, cheese, and summer sausage. John and I had worked at the Powderhorn Ranch in Jackson for a week to earn money for the food.

That night it rained, light but steady. The wind blew—right through the ends of our plastic tarp. By morning, we were soaked, and the buttress loomed above us, hidden in cloud. We ate Grape-Nuts soaked with Tang for breakfast. A smoldering fire dried our gear a bit, but we were subdued.

John excelled in such circumstances. He carved a chessboard in the dirt and found stones, sticks, and various kinds of cones—pine, fir, spruce—to represent chess pieces. He easily won the game— which I found disconcerting, because I was a strong player. Since we didn't relish lying around in our wet sleeping bags all day, we bushwhacked five miles in the rain to the head of Leigh Canyon, then northwest to a saddle near Maidenform Peak, where I peered for the first time into the wild depths of Moran Canyon. We arrived back at camp at dark, floundering in the forest—no headlamps in those days—just finding our tarp at ten o'clock, under a clear sky of starlight and the last rays of the setting sun.

We rose in the early morning dark, the sky clear, the tarp stiff with frost. More Grape-Nuts and Tang. We packed our gear. In addition to our rack, we carried two ropes, a light pack each with wool sweaters, cotton parkas, woolen watch caps, gorp, and two quarts of water each. When we reached the lower section of the route, the sun was up and we were lost on a vast face of granite, so vast that it seemed its own world. We climbed unroped until we reached the second of two large ledges that traverse the lower face. Then we worked left and upward, never quite sure we were on the route. Finally the possibilities narrowed and we found old pitons. We were on our way.

John and I swung leads. I had more rock-climbing experience, especially at direct-aid climbing, but John was already the better mountaineer, blessed with an uncanny ability at route finding. After half a dozen leads, the route became both obvious and intimidating. Above us was a huge roof that was obviously unclimbable. We knew that eventually the crack we were climbing would peter out and we would be forced to pendulum right. We climbed on, straight toward the roof. Finally we could climb no farther: A short, hard pitch led to a lousy bolt or piton—I can't remember—from which the leader would pendulum right. It was my lead.

First, I had to reach the last piton (or bolt) and clip into it with the rope. Then John lowered me about twenty feet down the face. I ran back and forth until I could reach another piton to the right. After clipping that piton, John lowered me again and I ran back and forth again until I pendulumed to a ledge leading up through the overhang. Reading about this in the guidebook was one thing; executing it over fifteen hundred feet of air was quite another— sort of like being lowered from a window at the top of the World Trade Center, running across the face of the building, and then climbing in another window three stories down and twenty feet off to the right.

After I set up a belay, I lowered John until he was even with me; then he ran like mad across the face, yodeling, until he grabbed me and the sling that attached us to the tiny ledge. Then he untied and we pulled his end of the rope through the two pitons above. He tied back in. I led the direct aid up the next lead; then John romped to the large step that marked the beginning of the descent routes. We weren't interested in the last three thousand feet to the summit—we thought it too easy. We had done the hardest part of the route; now we had to get down.

In the first (1956) edition of his *Climber's Guide to the Teton Range,* Ortenburger had written: "If desired, an easy method of descent off the ridge is the gully leading down westward from the north end of this first step." It is only in the most recent edition, the third, completed by Renny Jackson after Ortenburger's death, that we find this advice: "No matter what, do *not* try to continue all the way down the first southern couloir, for it is blocked by huge overhanging chockstones, and terrifying rappels into outer space are required." This change is due to our descent that day of "the gully leading down westward."

Exhilarated, triumphant, we set off. Unfortunately, the gully soon bifurcated. We went down the first one: down and down and down until it narrowed like a sieve, the piton cracks disappeared, and we were stopped by huge chock stones wedged in the narrow gully. Below was air. We couldn't see if our rappel ropes reached bottom—or anything—but it was obviously too steep to climb back up if they didn't. At least the weather was good: In a storm the gully would be a waterfall. Hudson, who had been subdued on the climb down, became elated—a real adventure was at hand. Ever the clown, he jumped up and down on the chock stone before we wrapped a sling around it. Off I went, dangling, to the end of the rope. Then I swung into the gully. Hudson came down. We pulled our ropes. Fortunately, the ropes did not hang up; if they had, we would still be there.

We took turns going first down the rappels, leaving a dozen of our precious pitons tied off with a web of slings. There was no going back up. Each time the ropes pulled, we were jubilant. The world had shrunk to our nasty little gully. We were kids on a lark, pulling off a stunt.

Eventually we made it down to a talus slope leading into Leigh Canyon, the longest talus slope I've found outside the Himalayas. It was dark, of course. Finding the tarp was pure luck. We celebrated with Grape-Nuts soaked in Tang—our last food. Hudson was ecstatic. He wanted to spend another night and climb the South Buttress Right, an even harder route, the next day. I couldn't wait to get back to Jenny Lake and get my hands on Ortenburger.

I think it rained and we walked out soaked and cold, but I am not sure. Staring at the ridge thirty-five years later, I want to remember, to be sure; as though being sure will make it real, a necessary part of the consecration. But even looking at the route, I realize my memory is horribly flawed, a collage with missing pieces. Alas, the past cannot be reassembled, only folded into the present.

Eventually I did the South Buttress Right; eventually I climbed the entire south buttress, bivouacking en route, then over the summit and down the northeast ridge in a storm, spending a second night lost in the forest west of Jackson Lake. But that was later, with other partners. I have not been on the south buttress in thirty years.

Several years later, in 1966, John Hudson and I overlapped at Cornell for a semester. He was completing a degree in geophysics; I was in graduate school studying philosophy. We climbed together once in the Shwangunks. He had far surpassed me as a rock climber, and I was impressed with his casual, bold style. His humor remained sharp. At one point I fell off a climb and found myself at the end of the rope, five feet out from the wall. He gazed down at me with his minimal smile: "Steep, isn't it?"

After Hudson graduated, he hired on with a oceanographic research team. While in port in 1969, he met friends and climbed in Patagonia, Bolivia, and Peru. While scouting a new route on Huascurán with Roman Laba, snow broke beneath his feet and he fell over a short cliff and was killed. He was twenty-three years old.

Thirty years later, I ran into Laba on the Saddle and asked him about the circumstances of Hudson's death. "We were not roped; the angle was not that steep," said Laba. "But the snow we were climbing on was friable. John fell and couldn't stop himself on the bad snow." We were both a bit choked up just talking about him.

> *The grasses in the garden*
> *Fall*
> *And they lie as they fall.*
>
> —RYOKAN

Today the wedge of clear sky has narrowed, and the summit of Moran is fuzzy with snow. I forgo breakfast, but I make two quarts of tea, then drink one and put the other in a thermos. Hauling a sled through fresh snow is too masochistic even for me, and I want to be as far south as I can get before the snow starts. I shake the tent, fold it, and put it in the bottom of the sled. Sleeping bag, pad, stove, fuel, extra food, and clothes go on top. I zip the cover and cinch the straps down over the avalanche shovel. What I will need for the day, I carry in my pack. I start with a Snickers bar.

I follow my track back through the forest to the bridge. The day is dark, the mountains hidden. The first flakes melt on my gloves as I leave the picnic area at String Lake and head down the road. Before long, I put on my goggles: The wind is up, visibility down. Two hours later, when I reach the Lupine Meadows turnoff, I am dragging the sled through four inches of snow. The road is empty, devoid of a track. I sit on the sled and drink tea and think about the next four miles. The sled is a pain; the wind makes me angry. I remind myself that for too much of my life I've had to do this sort of thing; now I don't. Nothing left to prove.

I turn right and haul the sled a quarter of a mile to the cabin. Five feet of snow blocks the door. I shovel down until I reach the doorknob; then I open the door and jump into my dark and gloomy home. The fire is laid. One match and it burns like a torch until the musty room is warm enough to wander around in naked. Dinner is pasta, pesto, and red-pepper flakes, more mountain tea, and a Snickers for dessert. I sink into the sleeping bag with volumes of Melville and Salter. It's eighteen hours to morning; life is good. To hell with sleds.

Dawn is clear and surprisingly warm. When I open the door, I'm met with a foot of fresh snow. I brush it around with a broom and clean the sled before hauling it into the cabin. To double hell with sleds. I dismantle it and load the few things I need into my pack. The new snow on Lupine Meadows glistens in the mid-morning sun. When I reach the other side of the meadow, Teewinot is shedding snow with dozens of avalanches.

After a thaw, the surface of snow is hard and smooth, with little adhesion, and new snow on a steep surface with little adhesion means avalanches—so here they are. Some of them are two thousand feet long. The powder hangs in the air after the crest of the debris has stopped, like dust settling from an explosion. These are big avalanches, but there are bigger ones around.

Many years ago, an avalanche came off the top of Hanging Canyon and dropped three thousand feet, shearing off full-grown spruce and fir and destroying hundreds of yards of Park Service trail. The final crest of debris was piled a hundred feet out onto Jenny Lake. When I arrived on May 1, 1997, the Lupine Meadows parking lot beneath Teewinot was buried under fifteen feet of avalanche debris, and some of it was still there in June. That year avalanche debris covered the Meadows in Garnet Canyon until late August.

The largest avalanche I know of in the range occurred on December 31, 1982, a little after one o'clock in the afternoon. I was eating lunch at Dornan's—a bar at Moose with the best view of the mountains in all of Jackson Hole—when the waitress wondered out loud what that strange cloud was over the mountains. It was billowing snow from a huge avalanche that began when a section of the east ridge of the Grand broke off, fell fifteen hundred feet to the top of Teepe Glacier, then another three thousand feet into the Meadows, and then spewed out the mouth of Garnet Canyon. The plume rose four thousand feet over the summits of Cloudveil Dome and Nez Percé, then down into Avalanche Canyon to the south. It went up and over Disappointment Peak and down in Glacier Gulch to the north. The Meadows were buried under a hundred feet of snow or more. It didn't melt until mid-September. The summer "growing season" lasted two weeks.

A skier down on the flats near Cottonwood Creek took a picture of the cloud, which duly appeared in the local newspaper—a reminder, as it were. Dan was fortunate enough to watch the show from the Taggart Lake parking lot. The day before, he had skied through the Meadows on patrol. Dan describes this collection of events as "interesting."

Since the avalanche on Minya Konka in 1980, I've been as chicken about avalanches as I am about lake ice. I will venture into the canyons when snow is as stable as concrete. I will ski in the mountains when I get my Ph.D. from Rod Newcomb's American Avalanche Institute, a likelihood that diminishes daily, though Dick Dorworth is doing his best to teach me how to ski and Newcomb keeps offering me free courses. In truth, I am afraid of snow and ice—too many deaths, too many close calls. As Pratt warned me when I was a nineteen-year-old rock climber, death comes from clouds. And yet I am obsessed with mountains and bad weather—a moth to the light.

I cut through the trees to avoid the Lupine Meadows parking lot—only the paranoid survive. Soon I meet skiers coming up the Inner Trail. I'm not particularly happy to see them, but I'm very happy to stop breaking trail. In an hour I'm at my truck. The Taggart Lake parking lot is filled with people, grown-ups and kids, dogs, and a million dollars' worth of ski gear. It pleases me to see no sleds.


Dan calls. He's been chasing illegal snowmobiles up Berry Greek with six other Park Service employees, and he caught one on February 27. The patrolers were on skis, of course, which is a disadvantage if you're chasing snowmobiles. As they were climbing the divide between Forellen Peale and Red Mountain, they heard snowmobiles—seventeen snowmobiles, to be exact, seventeen doubly illegal snowmobiles, since they had entered the park through the Jedediah Smith Wilderness. Ah, wilderness! It ruined Dan's day, so he set out to ruin their day.

The snowmobilers were heading toward Moose Basin. Dan and the others gave chase. Suddenly he noticed a snowmobiler above him at the lip of a seventy-foot cliff; he had gone down steep snow and knew he was in trouble, but the snow was too steep for him to ride back up. He was trapped. Dan took off his skis and climbed up to the fellow, carrying his pistol and ticket book.

"Need some help?" asked Dan.

"Yep."

"What's the deal? All your buddies left you?"

"They'll be back. But I don't want my snowmobile to fall off this cliff."

"Well, actually," said Dan, "I am a ranger and we're going to have to do some paperwork."

Dan asked if he knew where he was. No, he didn't have a clue. Didn't know east from west. He didn't have any idea he was in the park or had entered it through a wilderness area. Didn't know his name, either. "I've heard you're not supposed to tell the cops anything," he said.

Dan explained that he could arrest him but that he didn't want to. He would give him a citation; then he could show up in court and deal with it there. An arrest for misdemeanors is well outside the park's budget for helicopter use.

"I think you just ought to arrest me," said the snowmobiler.

"Wait a minute—I've already said I don't want to arrest you. I don't need *you* to say anything. I've got all the elements of the crime I need for conviction. You're in the park and here's your snowmobile."

He caved and gave Dan his name, date of birth, and address. Dan called it into Park Dispatch and it was confirmed. Then the other sixteen snowmobilers came back. Their license plates were covered with duct tape, they wore Darth Vader–like crash helmets that concealed their faces, and they had no intention of stopping for the rangers down below. They tore through the group, missing one ranger by only three feet. They all gave their fellow snowmobiler a thumbs-up.

"Personally, if I had been down there, I would have tackled one of them," said Dan. And it's true. I have no trouble imagining Dan going head-to-head with a snowmobile.

By the time they got the snowmobile out, a storm was brewing. Most of Dan's party dropped into Moose Basin and dug out the patrol cabin. Dan and Rich Perch helped the snowmobiler get his machine out; he joined the other snowmobilers—they were waiting for him just out of sight on Red Mountain.

But the matter didn't end there. Dan didn't just give him a ticket—a fifty-dollar fine for snowmobiling in an undesignated area—he issued the snowmobiler a summons to appear in court, which meant the magistrate could put him in jail for six months or a year and fine him up to five thousand dollars.

Dan attended the proceedings. The magistrate read the charges and asked the U.S. attorney if the government considered this to be a serious case. He said no.

Dan sat there thinking, I think this is serious. If the government doesn't consider it to be serious, there won't be jail time, just a monetary fine.

Just then the U.S. attorney said, "No, we are not looking for jail time, just money." Fortunately, the snowmobiler hassled the judge and the judge got irked. After a lot of legal gyrations and several court appearances, the defendant ended up with a plea bargain, agreeing to pay $2,500, with $1,500 suspended, and being put on probation. Instead of a $50 ticket, the guy paid $1,000, had to hire a lawyer, went to court several times, and ended up on probation. Dan was delighted.

Still, catching him was a matter of luck. Illegal snowmobilers roam the park and adjacent wilderness all winter with virtual impunity, often threatening those who discover or report them. From Driggs, on the other side of the range in Idaho, you can watch the headlights of snowmobilers plying the wilderness area at night. No one does anything about it.

There must be a better way. After Dan's call, I consult my favorite ecoterrorist on methods of preventing illegal snowmobiling in the park.

"Mono," he replies.

"Mono?"

"Fishing line. The heavy stuff they use for sharks and marlin. The snow maggots gotta come up narrow canyons of forest to reach the passes leading into the park. They use the same trails over and over. String mono in the trees. Works just like a cheese slicer."

"Any other ideas?"

"Finnish snipers. Everything they have is white—skis, guns, everything. Take out a couple snow maggots as they approach the park and . . . no more problem."

I mention these suggestions to Dan the next time I see him. He creases his brow the way he does when I'm particularly dense. "Illegal snowmobiling is a misdemeanor, Turner. And their approach is outside the park. The Park Service frowns on killing people for misdemeanors they have yet to commit."

"Picky, picky."

# 16. The Open Road

Spring, at least the spring of calendars. The peaks are hidden under a bank of cloud reaching from roughly 9,000 to 15,000 feet. The valley is clear, the sky above the band is clear, but the bank hangs there like a wave. Occasionally the wave breaks and clouds fill the canyons and blow out into the valley like spume. Then, yet again, it snows, though only for a few hours. Soon the wave retreats. But it can hang above the range for days.

For the past week, giant Norland or Snowblast rotary plows have been eating through the four or five feet of snow covering the park's roads. Two plows, driven by John McAvoy and Bob Martinez, work north from the Taggart Lake parking lot. Another, driven by Frank Lynch or Lowell Schierkolk, clears the road south from Signal Mountain. They meet at the Mount Moran turnout. If you are out at the north end of Jackson Hole, you see a rooster tail of snow advancing slowly along dark forest at the base of the mountains. The whine from these monsters fills the valley. The whole operation takes ten days. Often the calls of the first flocks of geese heading north accompany the whine.

When April 1 arrives, the road again winds like a canyon through the park, surrounded by plains of snow. The road is plowed early so the asphalt can dry until May 1, when traffic resumes, and so people can wander the park's roads without traffic. Since the lakes are too mushy for snowmobile travel, the month of April is a vacation from the roar of machines—no monster motor homes, travel buses, motorcycles, cars, trucks, Jet Skis, speedboats, or snowmobiles. Just hordes of pedestrians enjoying the park. Many local people spend more time in the park during April than during any other month of the year. The government ought to think about that.

Removed from their machines, people become more social and the road becomes a promenade, a great parade, especially on weekends. The Park Service puts picnic tables in the summer turnouts along the road; temporary outhouses are strategically placed. Although the dress, the mise-en-scène, and equipage differ, the atmosphere is pure Renoir.

There are dirtbag mountain bikers bent over their machines, road bikers bent farther over their machines, skaters in skintight Lycra ripping along like the Furies, babies in perambulators, babies in backpacks, babies slung in Nepali shawls, children in strollers, children in wagons, children in Burley's and various other assorted kiddie trailers, children on bicycles, children on bicycles with training wheels, children on tricycles, children on leashes, dogs on leashes, dogs off leashes, dogs pulling people on Rollerblades who hold leashes, runners tugging dogs on leashes, mutts, prize poodles, huskies, Lhasa Apsas, and Irish wolfhounds, cats on leashes, parrots on shoulders, innumerable Frisbees, balls of every kind, shape, and color, kites, Hacky Sacks, buzzing model airplanes, balloons, roller skis, telemark skis, touring skis, skating skis, snowshoes, and old folks just walking along holding hands.

People rest with their backs against snowbanks and drink Gatorade while masticating PowerBars and Clif Bars. Some lounge in Crazy Creek chairs, sip wine, and eat gourmet cheeses on trendy British crackers. Others sprawl on the pavement amid mountain bikes, drinking Teton ale and munching chunks of sourdough bread from the Bunnery or Nature's Kitchen. From a distance, it resembles a child's birthday party, and even up close there remains something incorrigibly childish about it all—grown men on roller skates, grown women on bicycles, all decked out in tights that were once the province of prepubescent dancing classes.

It is such a happy time that no small number of people have suggested the park would be a better place if the road were closed to traffic all year. Perhaps. But then there would be no ceremony or ritual.

And would Americans give up their machines? No. Most people do not want to know the baked metallic heat of summer, the sting of snow in their eyes, the numbing cold. They don't care much about Horse Thief Pass, the spiraled gneiss at Dudley Lake, or that strange animal Lowe and Tackle saw on the summit of the Grand Teton in winter. And that is fine. This is a national park, and as such, it means different things to different people, even different things to those who love it most.

According to one study, 93 percent of the visitors to Grand Teton Natural Park never enter the backcountry—that is, they never walk. This means that each year millions cruise the park, watching the scene unfold through tinted windows, adjusting their climate control, and listening to a taped tour description or a favorite CD. Occasionally they stop in a turnout and take videos of themselves with the Grand Teton in the background. For these visitors, the park is one of many entertainments; soon they will cruise through Yellowstone and Glacier, Rocky Mountain and Zion. Few visitors spend a night in the backcountry—of the more than 4 million visitors in 1998, only 5,600 obtained backcountry permits.

Many backcountry users seem to have permanently conflated the values of recreation and preservation. Recently, a mountain-biking magazine questioned whether mountain bikers should support wilderness designation if they are not allowed to ride their bikes in the wilderness. A piece in our local paper made it clear that bicyclists believe they are entitled to ride their bikes in the park in a safe and pleasant manner—that is, the park is obligated to provide them with special biking paths. Climbing groups are pressuring Congress to prohibit limitations on their sport in national parks and wilderness areas.

What is essential to a national park or of a congressionally designated wilderness area has nothing to do with specialized recreation, equipment, techniques, or fashionable gear—not to mention cars, buses, and motorcycles with electronically controlled environments. Muir did not need equipment to speak to trees and waterfalls. Thoreau did not need technique to climb Katadan. Marshall and Muir wandered the wild in clothes we can now purchase at Kmart. They were content—happy, filled with joy—merely to be in the presence of wild animals, wild places, wild processes. Presence was everything, sport of little consequence, and technique a matter of getting around in the wild, not an end in itself.

Somehow things have been reversed. I myself am culpable.

It has been said that Grand Teton is the most compromised park in the national park system. We have cattle in the park, elk hunting in the park, and a major airport in the park servicing Boeing 737s and private jets galore. We have Jet Skis, motorboats, and snowmobiles—and no speed limits for them. With their free passes and cut-rate camping fees, the elderly threaten to fill the campgrounds with their trailers and campers; a national park is now the cheapest place to live in the United States. All this takes time, energy, and money away from what is essential.

If the parks and wilderness areas must preserve anything, even at the cost of unpopularity, it must be this: the possibility of contact with wild forms of being. This requires two things. First, we must preserve those other beings as freely existing, self-organizing nations in their own right. Second, we must preserve true contact with them, simple, unmediated contact, contact with our bodies, or senses, contact where what we experience is their presence. We evolved together. In many ways we are wired, intellectually and emotionally, for one another's presence, and it would be a tragedy if in the future we were to find this age-old reciprocity had vanished. Increasingly, I find I do not need special equipment or techniques to enjoy the wild. It is enough merely to wander here, not because it is a national park, "but because *truly* being here is so much," as Rilke says.

When I was young, I simply wanted to see the mountains and climb the routes. The range was vast, unknowable. Then, slowly, I realized that what I wanted required me to live here. I have lived here, and it is something precious that cannot be taken from me. Now I want something more, something I cannot describe, something beyond words. At a certain point, language fails and we are left with practice.

For many years, I dreamt of a hermitage in the northern mountains dear to me—somewhere up in Snowshoe Canyon. I would find an well-hidden overhanging glacial boulder in a cul-de-sac with water and a view of the peaks. I would surround the overhang with rock walls just as they have done for millennia in the Hima-

layas. I would leave cushions, a rug, a sleeping bag, some utensils.
Once or twice a year, I would visit and listen to the silence for
weeks on end.

Quite illegal, of course. Illegal in the park, in the wilderness,
and on BLM land too, certainly on private land without permission,
and permission would sabotage the project. Being a hermit has
become illegal; riding the tour buses and viewing the range through
tinted glass the norm. And besides, if I tried to fulfill my dream,
Dan would track me down and give me not a ticket but an order
to appear before the magistrate. And what could I say? I didn't
know? But imagine: mountains without the possibility of hermits!

One walks the open road.

No matter how clear of snow the road is, winter soon returns.
The warm asphalt melts it, but the crowds are gone. Most are fair-
weather lovers. A few dear souls, bundled up like blimps, jog or
walk their dogs. Eventually—always—the cold returns. It can go
down to zero in April. On April 17, when the rest of the country
is blooming and leafing, there is still four feet of snow in Lupine
Meadows and it is 2 degrees. Eventually, though—always—the
warmth returns.

I walk the road in all weathers, enjoying each, and every time
I try to acknowledge my good fortune. I visit my cabin and sit on
the porch on my cushions. I meditate in the sound of Cottonwood
Creek, in the wind in the pines. Sometimes the roaring stream
drowns the wind; sometimes the wind drowns the roaring creek.

Sometimes when the moon is full, I ski across Lupine Meadows
at dusk. Sometimes when I stop to listen to the silence, the crust
on the snow breaks for a hundred feet around me and I sink two
inches. Then silence again. I ski on to the coarse hiss of skis on
hard snow. The great face of Teewinot stands above me in the
dark. I ski on, skirt the lower Moose Pond, and begin my modest
climb up the lower face of Teewinot to a band of cliffs where the

great avalanche gully narrows. In the summer, there is a waterfall here; now it is frozen, covered with snow.

I cut two platforms with my shovel, one above the other. I remove my skis and drive their tails into the snow. From my pack I pull out my Crazy Creek chair and a thermos of mountain tea. I put on my DAS parka and pull the hood over my head. I place the chair on the upper platform, my feet on the lower platform, and loosen the buckles on my ski boots.

I drink some hot tea. The Absaroka and the Gros Ventre ranges line the sky in the east. Timbered Island and Burnt Ridge are black globs within the billion glitters of reflected moon. Moonlight illuminates the meadows beneath me in shades of blue—solid pigment for the trees and forests, diluted washes for ice and snow. The sky is clean. Frost tickles hairs in my nose.

After a while I sing Hakuin's song, "The Song of Zazen." When I finish, I repeat the last four lines:

> *Truly, is anything missing now?*
> *Nirvana is right here, before our eyes;*
> *This very place is the Lotus Land;*
> *This very body, the Buddha.*

I pack, put my skis back on, and then carefully sideslip and kick-turn my way down the face until I can make long traverses along the lower slope. I would not call what I am doing skiing. I return along my tracks to the parking lot beside the cabins. A light is on in a ranger's cabin across the creek—a dot of yellow in a sea of blue, the first ranger of spring. He is early, drawn, no doubt, like me, to the possibility of solitude.

On April 28, I walk up the road to String Lake. The sky is milky, the air warm. At the edges of the road, where the warmth of the asphalt has melted the snow, sagebrush buttercups and an occasional dandelion are poking their way into the world. When I reach String Lake, I put on a small pair of snowshoes and wander down the creek, looking for dippers until I reach Jenny Lake. The creek has melted the ice where it enters the lake. The open surface is luminous. I look at the mountains. It pleases me to look at the Tetons from the northeast. The view on that Union Pacific playing card of long ago is from the northeast. The view from the mounted nickel-a-look binoculars—long gone—was from the northeast. When I imagine the Tetons in my mind's eye, I imagine them from the northeast.

As I walk south along Jenny Lake, clouds drift into the southern range, some small and puffy, like punctuation marks, others spiraled like galaxies. It is late when I reach the Lupine Meadows Junction. I sit on the snowbank and watch the storm wash across the peaks. Then I walk on, happy to be among these mountains and storms.

It is snowing when I cross Cottonwood Creek. The Taggart Lake parking lot is empty. Blowing snow veils the mountains. For a few minutes, they hover above the forest like apparitions. Then they mingle with the clouds and are lost in the immensity and the whiteness of the sky.

# Selected Bibliography

There exists no canonical human history or natural history of the Teton
Range. What information does exist is often in books that are out of print,
obscure, rare, privately published, only partially devoted to the area, or that
describe something that occurs here without describing local information of
its life and ecology, the information that would benefit us most. Almost nothing is known about our insects—the most numerous fauna and the most
important part of the food chain. Leigh Ortenburger wrote a history of the
exploration of the region, but unfortunately, it remains unpublished. This
bibliography is personal and by no means exhaustive.

## GEOLOGY

The complex geology of the Teton Range has been understood only recently.
The following sources are intended for the nonspecialists; more technical information is listed in their bibliographies. *Creation of the Teton Landscape: The
Geologic Story of Grand Teton National Park*, by J. D. Love and John C. Reed
(Moose, WY: Grand Teton Natural History Association, 1984) is the classic
account of the geology of the Teton Range. It is, however, a bit dated and
should be supplemented with recent material relating to discoveries about
roles of volcanic activity and plate tectonics. For this, the best source is *Inter-*

*preting the Landscape: Recent and Ongoing Geology of Grand Teton & Yellowstone National Parks*, by John M. Good and Kenneth L. Pierce (Moose, WY: Grand Teton Natural History Association, 1996). *The Ice-Age History of National Parks in the Rocky Mountains* by Scott A. Elias (Washington, DC: Smithsonian Institution Press, 1996) integrates the most recent geological information with ecology and human history.

Useful maps include Map 1–730 in *Geologic Block Diagram and Tectonic History of the Teton Region, Wyoming-Idaho, Miscellaneous Geologic Investigations*, by J. D. Love, John C. Reed, Jr., Robert L. Christiansen, and John R. Stacy (Washington, DC: Department of the Interior, United States Geological Survey, 1973); and the stunningly beautiful "Geologic Map of Grand Teton National Park, Teton County, Wyoming, Miscellaneous Investigations Series Map I 2031" by J. D. Love, John C. Reed, Jr., and Ann Coe Christiansen (Washington, DC: Department of the Interior, United States Geological Survey, 1992).

## ECOLOGY

Because the altitude varies so much in Grand Teton National Park, there are many different ecosystems. The main ones are covered by the magisterial *Mountains and Plains: The Ecology of Wyoming Landscapes* by Dennis H. Knight (New Haven: Yale University Press, 1994). An excellent introduction to the ecology of Jackson Hole is *The Natural World of Jackson Hole: An Ecological Primer* by Tim W. Clark (Moose, WY: Grand Teton Natural History Association, 1999).

There exists no alpine ecology of the Teton Range, but information of interest to the mountaineer can be found in *Timberline: Mountain and Arctic Frontiers* by Stephen F. Arno and Ramona P. Hammerly (Seattle: Mountaineers Press, 1984) and *Land Above the Trees: A Guide to American Alpine Tundra* by Ann H. Zwinger and Beatrice E. Willard (New York: Harper & Row, 1972).

Most of what I know about winter ecology comes from *Winter: An Ecological Handbook* by James C. Halfpenny and Roy Douglas Ozanne (Boulder: Johnson Books, 1989). On the ecology of air, see David Lukas, "Of Aerial Plankton and the Aeolian Zone," *Orion* 18, no. 2 (Spring 1999).

Although it is a phenology, not a descriptive ecology, I strongly recommend *For Everything There Is a Season: The Sequence of Natural Events in the Grand Teton–Yellowstone Area* by Frank C. Craighead, Jr. (Helena, MT: Falcon

Press, 1994). I consult Craighead's masterpiece more than any other book in my Teton library. Treasure it. There is no one else who could write such a book.

## CLIMBING, SKIING, AND HIKING

Mountaineering literature on the Tetons is dominated by *A Climber's Guide to the Teton Range*, 3rd ed., by Leigh N. Ortenburger and Reynold G. Jackson (Seattle: Mountaineers Press, 1996), which serves not only as a detailed guide to climbing routes in the range but as an introduction to geology, weather, approaches, and history.

Ski mountaineering in the range—routes, equipment, history—is thoroughly covered by *Teton Skiing: A History and Guide to the Teton Range* by Thomas Turiano (Moose, WY: Homestead Publishing, 1995).

Those interested in the first ascent of the Grand Teton should look at *The Grand Controversy: Pioneer Climbing in the Teton Range and the Controversial First Ascent of the Grand Teton* by Orrin H. Bonney and Lorraine G. Bonney (New York: American Alpine Club, 1993). A concise history of early climbing in the range is *Mountaineering in the Tetons, 1898–1940* by Fritiof Fryxell and Phil D. Smith (Jackson, WY: Teton Bookshop, 1978).

Biographies of Exum guides mentioned in this book include *On Belay! The Life of Legendary Mountaineer Paul Petzoldt* by K. Carleson Ringholz (Seattle: Mountaineers Press, 1988); *Glenn Exum: "Never a Bad Word or a Twisted Rope"* by Charlie Craighead (Moose, WY: Grand Teton Natural History Association, 1998); *Ascent: The Spiritual and Physical Quest of Legendary Mountaineer Willi Unsoeld* by Lawrence Leamer (New York: William Morrow, 1999); and *Gary Hemming* by Mirella Tenderinni (Ernest Press, 1995). See also Jeremy Bernstein's essay in *The New Yorker*, "On Vous Cherche," in *Mountain Passages* (Lincoln: University of Nebraska Press, 1978), pp. 87–109. *We Aspired: The Last Innocent Americans* by Peter Sinclair (Logan: Utah State University Press, 1993) provides an insightful account of climbing in the Tetons during the 1960s and 1970s.

There are numerous guides to hiking in the Tetons. The classic is *Teton Trails: A Guide to the Trails of Grand Teton National Park* by Katy Duffy and Darwin Wile (Moose, WY: Grand Teton Natural History Association, 1995). A guide with broader coverage is *Jackson Hole Hikes: Grand Teton Park, Targhee, & Teton Forests* by Rebecca Woods (Jackson, WY: White Willow Publishing, 1996).

## HISTORY

For the prehistory of the park and surrounding region, I suggest *Archeology of Grand Teton National Park* (Midwest Archeological Center, National Park Service) and *Prehistoric Hunters of the High Plains*, 2nd ed., by George F. Frison (New York Academic Press, 1991).

Two early accounts of the Tetons are worth searching for—and good luck: *Camps in the Rockies* by Wm. A. Baillie-Grohman (London: Sampson, Low, Marston, Searle, & Rivington, 1882) and *A Summer on the Rockies* by Major Sir Rose Lambert Price (London: Sampson, Low, Marston & Company, Ltd., 1898). *Camps in the Rockies* is my favorite and I read it whenever I can find a copy. Fortunately, many of the classic early writings about the Tetons, including selections from Baillie-Grohman and Price, have been collected in *A Teton Country Anthology,* edited by Robert W. Richter (Boulder, CO: Roberts Rinehart, 1990).

Richter has also written a fine account of the creation of the park in *Crucible for Conservation: The Struggle for Grand Teton National Park* (Boulder: Colorado Associated University Press, 1982). A standard history of exploration is *The Grand Tetons: The Story of the Men Who Tamed the Western Wilderness* by Margot Sanborn (New York: Putnam, 1978). *Searching for Yellowstone: Ecology and Wonder in the Last Wilderness* by Paul Schullery, (Boston: Houghton Mifflin, 1997) is the best introduction to the Greater Yellowstone ecosystem, of which Grand Teton National Park is one small part.

All my knowledge of John Graul's mine comes from Margaret Kelsey, "John Graul's Mystery Mine," *Teton Magazine* 7 (1974–1975).

*Origins: A Guide to the Place Names of Grand Teton National Park and the Surrounding Area* by Elizabeth Wied Hayden and Cynthia Nielson (Moose, WY: Grand Teton Natural History Association, 1988) is the standard source for names in the range.

For a history of Jackson Hole, my favorite is *Along the Ramparts of the Tetons: The Saga of Jackson Hole, Wyoming* by Robert B. Betts (Niwot: University Press of Colorado, 1978).


## PLANTS

The standard text is *Field Guide to the Vascular Plants of Grand Teton National Park and Teton County, Wyoming* by Richard J. Shaw (Logan: Utah State University Press, 1976), which should be supplemented with Shaw's *Vascular*

*Plants of Grand Teton National Park & Teton County: An Annotated Check List* (Moose, WY: Grand Teton Natural History Association, 1992). He has also published two popular books profusely illustrated with photographs: *Wildflowers of Grand Teton and Yellowstone National Parks* (Salt Lake City: Wheelwright Press, 1991) and *Plants of Yellowstone and Grand Teton National Parks* (Salt Lake City: Wheelwright Press, 1981). Alpine flora is exhaustively treated in *The Alpine Flora of the Rocky Mountains: The Middle Rockies,* vol. 1, by Richard W. Scott (Salt Lake City: University of Utah Press, 1997).

The natural history of many of the plants in the area is presented in two books on the natural history of the Great Basin. Although the Teton Range is only at the edge of the Great Basin, it shares many of the same species. The books are *Trees of the Great Basin: A Natural History* by Ronald M. Lanner (Reno: University of Nevada Press, 1984) and *Shrubs of the Great Basin: A Natural History* by Hugh Mozingo (Reno: University of Nevada Press, 1987).

An interesting historical work covering many plants in the area is *Montana—Native Plants and Early People* by Jeff Hart (Helena: Montana Historical Society, 1976).

My favorite field guide for wildflower remains *A Field Guide of Rocky Mountain Wildflowers* by John J. Craighead, Frank C. Craighead, Jr., and Ray J. Davis (Boston: Houghton Mifflin, 1963) because of the "Interesting Facts" section at the end of each entry. For Rocky Mountain plants in general, the best field guide is *Plants of the Rocky Mountains* by Linda Kershaw, Andy MacKinnon, and Jim Pojar (Edmonton, Canada: Lone Pine Publishing, 1998).

## BIRDS

The most useful book for birds specific to the region is the classic *Birds of Grand Teton National Park and the Surrounding Area* by Bert Baynes (Moose WY: Grand Teton Natural History Association, 1989). My favorite field guide is *A Field Guide to Western Birds* by Roger Tory Peterson (Boston: Houghton Mifflin, 1990). For a natural history of many of the region's birds, see *Birds of the Great Basin: A Natural History* by Fred A. Reyser, Jr. (Reno: University of Nevada Press, 1985).

John Muir's essay "The Water-Ouzel" can be found in *The Mountains of California* (New York: Viking Penguin, 1997). I have also benefited from various labors of ornithological love, including *The Dippers* by Stephanie J. Tyler and Stephen J. Ormerod (London: T & A D Poyser, 1994) and *Crane Music: A Natural History of American Cranes* by Paul A. Johnsgard (Washington,

DC: Smithsonian Institution Press, 1991). The story of the symbiosis of white-back pine and members of the jay family is beautifully told in *Made for Each Other: A Symbiosis of Birds and Pines* by Ronald M. Lanner (New York: Oxford University Press, 1996).


## ANIMALS

Thorough coverage of mammals in the Teton region will be found in *Mammals in Wyoming* by Tim W. Clark and Mark R. Stromberg (Lawrence: University Press of Kansas, 1987) and *Identifying and Finding the Mammals of Jackson Hole* by Darwin Wile (Jackson, WY: 1996).

For grizzly bears, see the fine pamphlet *Field Guide to the Grizzly Bear* by Lance Olsen (Seattle: Sasquatch Books, 1992). For bear attacks, both black bear and grizzly, the classic is *Bear Attacks: Their Causes and Avoidance* by Stephen Herrero (New York: Lyons & Burford, 1985).

For identifying animal tracks, anyone interested enough to make the effort should have both *A Field Guide to Animal Tracks,* 2nd ed., by Olaus Murie (Boston: Houghton Mifflin, 1974) and *A Field Guide to Mammal Tracking in Western America* by James Halfpenny (Boulder: Johnson Books, 1986).


## BUDDHISM

The lines from Jakushitsu Genko and Po-Chü-i are from *The Roaring Stream: A New Zen Reader,* edited by Nelson Foster and Jack Shoemaker (Hopewell, NJ: Ecco Press, 1996). Meal verses and Hakuin's "Song of Zozen" are from Sutra books used at the Ring of Bone Zendo.

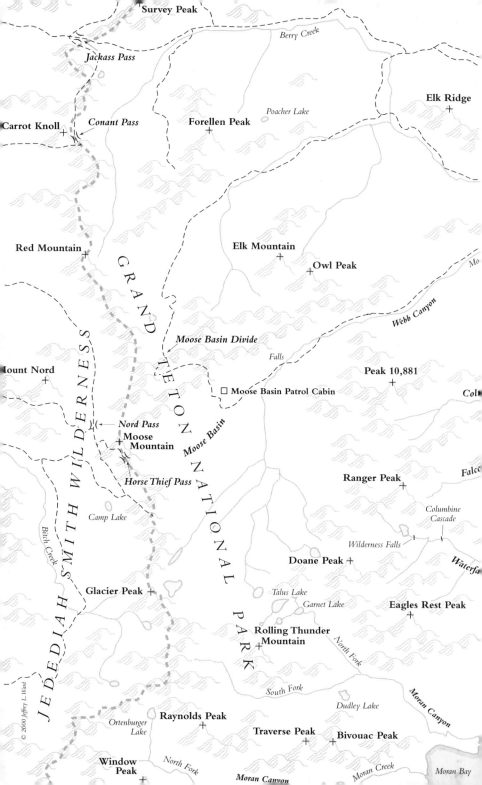